REVIEW AND ASSESSMENT OF THE INDONESIA–MALAYSIA–THAILAND GROWTH TRIANGLE ECONOMIC CORRIDORS

INTEGRATIVE REPORT

Carolina S. Guina

MARCH 2023

ADB

© 2023 Asian Development Bank
6 ADB Avenue, Mandaluyong City, 1550 Metro Manila, Philippines
Tel +63 2 8632 4444; Fax +63 2 8636 2444
www.adb.org

Some rights reserved. Published in 2023.

ISBN 978-92-9269-951-2 (print); 978-92-9269-952-9 (electronic); 978-92-9269-953-6 (ebook)
Publication Stock No. TCS220576-2
DOI: http://dx.doi.org/10.22617/TCS220576-2

Notes:
In this publication, "$" refers to United States dollar, "RM" refers to Malaysian ringgit, and "Rp" refers to Indonesian rupiah.
ADB recognizes "China" as the People's Republic of China.

Cover design by Mike Cortes.

CONTENTS

Tables, Figures, and Maps	iv
Foreword	vii
Acknowledgments	ix
Abbreviations	xi
Executive Summary	xiii

CHAPTER 1 INTRODUCTION — 1
- Overview — 2
- Study Objectives — 3
- Analytical Framework — 3
- Methodology and Study Team — 4
- Structure of the Report — 5

CHAPTER 2: DEVELOPMENT CONTEXT — 6

CHAPTER 3: REVIEW OF THE FIVE IMT-GT ECONOMIC CORRIDORS — 11
- Economic Corridor 1. The Extended Songkhla–Penang–Medan Economic Corridor — 15
- Economic Corridor 2. The Strait of Malacca Economic Corridor — 35
- Economic Corridor 3. The Banda Aceh–Medan–Pekanbaru–Palembang Economic Corridor — 50
- Economic Corridor 4. The Melaka–Dumai Economic Corridor — 64
- Economic Corridor 5. The Ranong–Phuket–Aceh Economic Corridor — 74

CHAPTER 4: PROPOSED ROUTE FOR ECONOMIC CORRIDOR 6 — 86

CHAPTER 5: THE NETWORK OF IMT-GT ECONOMIC CORRIDORS — 118

CHAPTER 6: ECONOMIC CORRIDORS FROM A VALUE CHAIN PERSPECTIVE — 129

CHAPTER 7: ADDRESSING GAPS IN INSTITUTIONAL MECHANISMS FOR ECONOMIC CORRIDOR DEVELOPMENT — 165

CHAPTER 8: SUMMARY OF FINDINGS AND RECOMMENDATIONS — 173

TABLES, FIGURES, AND MAPS

Tables

1 Economic Corridor 1: Maritime Links between North Sumatera Ports and Malaysia Ports — 20
2 Economic Corridor 1: Border Crossing Points: Condition of Infrastructure and Access — 23
3 Economic Corridor 1: Export–Import Value at Thai–Malaysian Border in Songkhla — 25
4 Economic Corridor 1: Export–Import Value at Thai–Malaysian Border in Kedah and Perlis, 2015–2018 — 26
5 Economic Corridor 1: North Sumatera's Trade with Malaysia, 2007, 2011, 2014–2018 — 27
6 Economic Corridor 1: Existing and Additional Provinces and Nodes, by Type — 33
7 Economic Corridor 2: Start and End Points in Thailand — 35
8 Economic Corridor 2: Start and End Points in Malaysia (Wang Kelian–Tanjung Bruas) — 37
9 Economic Corridor 2: Start and End Points in Malaysia (Pengkalan Hulu–Tanjung Bruas) — 37
10 Economic Corridor 2: Maritime Links between Malaysia and Sumatera Ports in the Strait of Malacca — 41
11 Economic Corridor 2: Malaysia's Border Trade with Thailand — 42
12 Economic Corridor 2: Thailand's Border Trade with Malaysia — 43
13 Economic Corridor 2: Existing and Additional Provinces and Nodes, by Type — 47
14 Economic Corridor 3: Trade of Sumatera Provinces with Malaysia and Thailand 2018 ($ million) — 55
15 Economic Corridor 3: Foreign Visitor Arrivals in Economic Corridor 3 Provinces in Sumatera, 2018 — 56
16 Economic Corridor 3: Existing and Additional Provinces and Nodes, by Type — 63
17 Economic Corridor 4: Port Linkages Between Ports in Melaka and Ports in Sumatera — 68
18 Economic Corridor 4: Status of Physical Connectivity — 68
19 Economic Corridor 4: Riau Province's Foreign Trade Volume — 69
20 Economic Corridor 4: Main Trading Ports in Riau Province, 2018 — 70
21 Economic Corridor 4: Existing and Additional Provinces and Nodes, by Type — 73
22 Economic Corridor 5: Maritime Activities of Ports — 78
23 Economic Corridor 5: Aceh's Trade with Thailand through Ports in Aceh, 2014–2018 — 79
24 Economic Corridor 5: Existing and Additional Provinces and Nodes, by Type — 84
25 Provinces, States, and Nodes in the Proposed Economic Corridor 6, by Type — 90
26 Economic Corridor 6: Features of EC6-MR1 and EC6-MR2 — 97
27 Economic Corridor 6: Start and End Points in Thailand — 101
28 Economic Corridor 6: Malaysia Route 1-Connectivity Route from Border Crossing Points in Kelantan to Tanjung Bruas (Melaka) via Terengganu and Pahang — 101
29 Economic Corridor 6: Malaysia Route 2-Connectivity of Border Crossing Points in Kelantan to Tanjung Bruas Port (Melaka) via Ipoh and Lumut Port (Perak) — 102
30 Economic Corridor 6: Maritime Links of Malaysia Ports with Sumatera Ports — 110
31 Economic Corridor 6: Maritime Links of Sumatera Ports with Malaysia Ports — 111
32 Economic Corridor 6: Status of Proposed Connectivity in the Proposed Economic Corridor 6 Routes — 112
33 Economic Corridor 6: Trade Values at Thailand's Malaysian Border Crossing Points, 2014–2018 — 113
34 Economic Corridor 6: Top Five Export and Import Commodities at Thailand's Malaysian Border Crossing Points, 2018 — 113

35 Economic Corridor 6: Trade Values at Malaysia's Thai Border Crossing Points in Kelantan, 2015–2018   114
36 Economic Corridor 6: Trade between Riau Islands and Malaysia, 2014–2018   115
37 Key Provinces and States in the Palm Oil Value Chain   131
38 Palm Oil Plantations and Production in Sumatera, 2018   134
39 Palm Oil Plantations and Production in Malaysia, 2018   137
40 Palm Oil Plantations and Production in Thailand, 2018   138
41 Key Provinces and States in the Rubber Value Chain   142
42 Rubber Plantations and Production in Sumatera, 2018   146
43 Rubber Exports by Port of Loading in Indonesia, 2018   147
44 Rubber Plantations and Production in Malaysia   148
45 Malaysia's Trade with Thailand and Indonesia: Rubber and Rubber Products, 2018   149
46 Rubber Plantations and Production in Thailand, 2018   150
47 Ports of Loading for Exports of Fisheries and Fruits and Vegetables, 2017   158
48 Indonesia's Trade with Malaysia and Thailand on Meat and Fish Preparations and Vegetables and Fruits, 2017   159
49 Halal Establishments in the Manufacturing Sector based on Halal Certification, 2015   160
50 Malaysia Halal Product Exports by Destination, Ranked According to Share of Halal Exports, 2015   161
51 Corridor-Specific Findings and Recommendations   179

Figures

1 Populations in IMT-GT Economic Corridor Provinces and States, 2018   8
2 Indonesia: Gross Regional Domestic Product Growth Rate of Four Provinces in Existing Economic Corridors   9
3 Share of Four Provinces' Gross Regional Domestic Product to Total Gross Domestic Product of Existing Corridors in Indonesia, Average 2014–2018   9
4 Malaysia: Gross Regional Domestic Product Growth Rate of Seven States in Existing Corridors (2014–2018)   9
5 Malaysia: Share of Seven States' Gross Regional Domestic Product to Total Gross Regional Domestic Product of Existing Corridors in Malaysia, Average 2014–2018   9
6 Thailand: Gross Regional Domestic Product Growth Rate of Six Provinces in Existing Corridors (2014–2018)   10
7 Thailand: Share of Six Provinces' Gross Regional Domestic Product to Total Gross Domestic Product of Existing Corridors in Thailand, Average 2014–2018   10
8 Stylized Representation of an Economic Corridor   119
9 Critical Success Factors for Economic Corridor Development   121
10 Economic Corridors as a Focus of the IMT-GT Cooperation   122
11 Palm Oil Value Chain   131
12 Indonesia: Palm Oil Exports by Products, 2015–2019   135
13 Value Chain of Thailand Palm Oil Industry (2018)   139
14 Rubber Value Chain   145
15 Thailand's Rubber Products Value Chain   151
16 Halal Food Supply Chain   156
17 IMT-GT Institutional Coordination Mechanism Structure   169
18 Coordination Mechanisms for Economic Corridor Development   171

Maps

1   Five Indonesia–Malaysia–Thailand Growth Triangle Economic Corridors   13
2   Extended Songkhla–Penang–Medan Economic Corridor (Economic Corridor 1)   16
3   Southern Thailand–Northern Malaysia–North Sumatera Economic Corridor   29
    (Reconfigured Economic Corridor 1)
4   Strait of Malacca Economic Corridor (Economic Corridor 2)   36
5   Andaman Sea–Strait of Malacca Economic Corridor (Reconfigured Economic Corridor 2)   46
6   Banda Aceh–Medan–Pekanbaru–Palembang Economic Corridor (Economic Corridor 3)   51
7   Trans-Sumatera Economic Corridor (Reconfigured Economic Corridor 3)   58
8   Melaka–Dumai Economic Corridor (Economic Corridor 4)   65
9   Central Sumatera–Southern Malaysia Economic Corridor (Reconfigured Economic Corridor 4)   72
10 Ranong–Phuket–Aceh Economic Corridor (Economic Corridor 5)   75
11 Land Bridge between the Gulf of Thailand and the Andaman Sea   81
12 Southwestern Thailand–Northern Sumatera–Northwestern Malaysia Economic Corridor   82
    (Reconfigured Economic Corridor 5)
13 Southeastern Thailand–Eastern Malaysia–Southern Sumatera Economic Corridor   89
    (Proposed Route for Economic Corridor 6)
14 Economic Corridor 6: Proposed Route in Thailand   92
15 Economic Corridor 6: Proposed Malaysia Route 1   94
16 Economic Corridor 6: Proposed Malaysia Route 2   96
17 Economic Corridor 6: Proposed Route in Sumatera   98
18 Rail Routes in Thailand   103
19 Rail Routes in Malaysia   105
20 East Coast Rail Line   106
21 Interlink Corridors in Indonesia   124
22 Interlink Corridors in Malaysia   127
23 Interlink Corridors in Thailand   128
24 Stylized Visualization of the Location of Palm Oil Value Chain Processes   133
    in the Indonesia–Malaysia–Thailand Growth Triangle
25 Stylized Visualization of the Location of Rubber Value Chain Processes   143
    in Indonesia–Malaysia–Thailand Growth Triangle
26 Six Indonesia–Malaysia–Thailand Growth Triangle Economic Corridors   178

FOREWORD

The development of economic corridors has been one of the key focus areas of the Indonesia–Malaysia–Thailand Growth Triangle (IMT-GT) subregional cooperation program since 2007. The three countries were motivated by an area-based cooperation strategy to accelerate the growth of localities especially in Sumatera, Southern Thailand, and northeastern Malaysia. The goal is to facilitate accelerated growth that would also be equitable across the entire IMT-GT subregion, through economic corridors that would serve as "trunk lines" from which development would radiate to neighboring areas through transport and economic linkages.

Although the IMT-GT Road Map (2007–2011) and Implementation Blueprints (2012–2016 and 2017–2021) have included economic corridor development as a focus for the subregion, there has been no definitive framework for economic corridor development at the subregional level. The progress and performance of the IMT-GT economic corridors have not also been assessed. Given the lack of analytical work on IMT-GT economic corridors, at the 24th IMT-GT Ministerial Meeting on 1 October 2018 in Melaka, the IMT-GT signing ministers directed the review of existing IMT-GT economic corridors and a study of the proposed sixth corridor with Asian Development Bank support.

This review and assessment of the IMT-GT economic corridors is the first endeavor that looks at IMT-GT economic corridor development from a holistic perspective and comes in response to a mid-term review of IMT-GT's strategic document—the Implementation Blueprint 2017-2021—to enhance and expand the economic corridors. Hence, it makes a significant contribution as a reference and guide to planning the future direction of IMT-GT economic corridor development and will provide important inputs to the formulation of future Implementation Blueprints toward realizing IMT-GT's Vision 2036.

The coverage of this review is wide-ranging. It includes an assessment of the physical connectivity of the five IMT-GT economic corridors, cross-border trade, the role of economic corridors in three major value chains (palm oil, rubber, and halal foods), and the emerging network of IMT-GT corridors and its implications. This assessment's reconfiguration for each corridor aligns corridors with the countries' development strategies and identifies emerging opportunities in the participating provinces and states. The review also identified the proposed routes for the sixth economic corridor, which has the potential to change the pattern and efficiency of trade in the subregion. The review proposed a package of on-the-ground and practical mechanisms, processes, and activities to move forward on the economic corridor development agenda over the medium term.

The review will be published in four volumes—the integrative report, which highlights the regional perspective, and three separate country reports that present the national perspectives.

We would like to thank the IMT-GT ministers, senior officials, national secretariats, national and local government agencies, the private sector, including the IMT-GT Joint Business Council representatives, and various stakeholders in Indonesia, Malaysia, and Thailand for their substantive inputs and invaluable support in the conduct of this review. We are grateful to the Centre for IMT-GT Subregional Cooperation for facilitating access to information and involving the study team in the IMT-GT meetings.

We hope that this review will contribute to IMT-GT's initiatives to reinvigorate economic corridor development as a vital strategy toward achieving its vision of becoming an integrated, innovative, inclusive, and sustainable subregion by 2036.

Ramesh Subramaniam
Director General
Southeast Asia Department
Asian Development Bank

ACKNOWLEDGMENTS

This technical study was coordinated by a team in the Regional Cooperation and Operations Division (SERC), Southeast Asia Department of the Asian Development Bank (ADB). The technical study forms part of the analytical work produced under the ADB Technical Assistance 9572: Enhancing Effectiveness of Subregional Programs to Advance Regional Cooperation and Integration in Southeast Asia, which has funding support from the People's Republic of China Regional Cooperation and Poverty Reduction Fund, and the Republic of Korea e-Asia and Knowledge Partnership Fund.

The study was conducted by a team of consultants led by Carolina S. Guina, regional cooperation expert and team leader who provided specific guidance in carrying out the study and wrote the integrative report. A team of national consultants conducted the research on economic corridors in Indonesia, Malaysia, and Thailand and wrote the individual country reports. They are Sandy Nur Ikfal Raharjo (Indonesia), Abdul Rahim Anuar (Malaysia), and Pawat Tangtrongjita (Thailand).

Alfredo Perdiguero, director of SERC, and Gary Krishnan, senior country specialist supervised the study team. Maria Theresa Bugayong, senior operations officer (Resource Planning), and Jordana Queddeng-Cosme, consultant, provided technical and logistical support and coordinated the field visits where they also participated.

The Indonesia–Malaysia–Thailand Growth Triangle (IMT-GT) ministers Agus Suparmanto, minister of trade, Republic of Indonesia; Dato' Sri Mustapa Mohamed, minister in Prime Minister's Department (Economy), Malaysia; and Arkhom Termpittayapaisith, minister of finance, the Kingdom of Thailand, at the 26th IMT-GT Ministerial Meeting held in November 2020, provided overall strategic guidance in the course of reviewing the report.

The study benefited from the valuable inputs and insights of the following senior officials: Rizal Affandi Lukman, and Raldi Hendro Koestoer, Coordinating Ministry for Economic Affairs of Indonesia; Saiful Anuar Bin Lebai Hussen, Noor Zari Bin Hamat, Mohd Shafiee B. Mohd Shah, and Sarimah Binti Amran, Economic Planning Unit, Prime Minister's Office of Malaysia; and Danucha Pitchayanan, Pattama Teanravisitsagool, and Wanchat Suwankitti, Office of the National Economic and Social Development Council of Thailand. The national secretariats worked closely with the team, especially the national consultants, in facilitating access to information and data, arranging and participating consultations with various stakeholders and meticulously reviewing the many drafts of the report. They are Netty Muharni, Tri Hidayatno, Sonny Ameriansah Soekoer of the Coordinating Ministry of Economic Affairs in Indonesia; Suhana Binti Md Saleh, Ahmad Zamri Bin Khairuddin, Balamurugan Ratha Krishnan, Nurul Ezzah Binti Md Zin, Mohammad Akhir

Abdul Rahman, and Mattias Murphy Lai of the Economic Planning Unit, Prime Minister's Office in Malaysia; and Thuttai Keeratipongpaiboon, Chiraphat Chotipimai, Orachat Sungkhamanee, Potcharapol Prommatat, and Puntasith Charoenpanichpun of the Office of the National Economic and Social Development Council of Thailand. The Centre for IMT-GT Subregional Cooperation headed by Firdaus Dahlan and relevant IMT-GT working groups also provided insights.

The integrative report and country reports were copyedited by Maria Theresa Mercado and proofread by Maria Guia de Guzman and Jess Alfonso Macasaet. Michael Cortes handled typesetting, graphics generation, and designed the cover artwork. Pamela Asis-Layugan, Alona Mae Agustin, Raquel Tabanao, Nicole Marie Afable, Marian Macabingkil, Cira Rudas, and Camille Genevieve Salvador provided overall assistance in the publications process. Angel Villarez and Rienzi Niccolo Velasco prepared the maps under the supervision of Abraham Villanueva and Carmela Fernando-Villamar. The ADB Department of Communications Team provided invaluable assistance in design and publishing.

ABBREVIATIONS

ADB	Asian Development Bank
AH2	Asian Highway 2
ASEAN	Association of Southeast Asian Nations
BCP	border crossing point
BICT	Belawan International Container Terminal
BIMSTEC	Bay of Bengal Initiative for Multi-Sectoral Technical and Economic Cooperation
BRI	Belt and Road Initiative
CIQ	Customs, Immigration, and Quarantine
CIMT	Centre for IMT-GT Subregional Cooperation
CMGF	Chief Ministers and Governors Forum
CPKO	crude palm kernel oil
CPO	crude palm oil
EC	economic corridor
ECER	East Coast Economic Corridor
ECERDC	East Coast Economic Region Development Council
ECRL	East Coast Rail Link
EU	European Union
FFB	fresh fruit bunches
GDP	gross domestic product
GMS	Greater Mekong Subregion
GRDP	gross regional domestic product
GT	gross tonnage
ha	hectare
HDC	Halal Development Corporation
IB	implementing Blueprint
ICD	inland container depot
ICT	information and communication technology
IMT-GT	Indonesia–Malaysia–Thailand Growth Triangle
JBC	Joint Business Council
km	kilometer
KRC	Kedah Rubber City
KSTP	Kedah Science Technology Park
KTMB	Keretapi Tanah Melayu Berhad (Malayan Railways Limited)
Lao PDR	Lao People's Democratic Republic

LBT	Lekir Bulk Terminal
LCC	low-cost carrier
LSP	logistics service providers
MIFT	Melaka International Ferry Terminal
MOI	Ministry of Interior
MOU	memorandum of understanding
NBCT	North Butterworth Container Terminal
NCER	Northern Corridor Economic Region
NCIA	Northern Corridor Implementing Agency
NESDC	National Economic and Social Development Council
OEM	original equipment manufacturer
PRC	People's Republic of China
RBD	refined, bleached, and deodorized
Ro-Ro	roll on, roll off
RPO	refined palm oil
RTS	rapid transit system
SAPULA	Sabang–Phuket–Langkawi
SEC	Southern Economic Corridor
SEZ	special economic zone
SME	small and medium-sized enterprises
SRT	State Railway of Thailand
TEU	twenty-foot equivalent unit
US	United States

EXECUTIVE SUMMARY

This report provides the first holistic study of economic corridor (EC) development in the Indonesia–Malaysia–Thailand Growth Triangle (IMT-GT), since it became a focus of cooperation in 2007. There has been no comprehensive review of these ECs, even in the IMT-GT's Implementation Blueprints for 2012–2016 and 2017–2021. The only available information on ECs described their broad objectives, main connectivity points, and government projects. Moreover, no benchmarks were set to measure corridor performance. Any progress in EC development has resulted from national initiatives vetted by the IMT-GT platform, rather than evidence-based, subregional, corridor-wide planning. Nonetheless, there has been visible progress in infrastructure connectivity, especially in land-based transport routes, and in the development of border crossing points with facilities. The governments have implemented projects in the ECs, resulting in some degree of economic vibrancy within these zones over the past decade.

Initially, this study noted that apart from land border crossings and main seaports, specific nodes have not been explicitly defined in corridor configurations. Accordingly, this report identifies such places in each EC, to establish economic stakeholders' roles in relation to the major transport backbone and gateways. As reference points for assessing connectivity in ECs and as catalysts in areas influenced by these corridors, such nodes could generate trade connections and economic growth through their infrastructure connectivity in a new configuration.

To reflect the wider region of subnational areas covered by ECs—beyond specific provinces, states, or nodes—this report suggests new names for the reconfigured corridors. This revised nomenclature recognizes ECs are nonlinear, and not merely point-to-point connections; they also cover a wider area of influence affected by the transport backbone, industrial parks, special economic zones (SEZs), ports, inland waterways, and agglomerations. These new labels also allow the flexibility to add nodes in a corridor, based on evolving economic landscapes, opportunities, and challenges.

The review of the five existing economic corridors (Chapter 3) indicated that physical connectivity has made noteworthy progress since 2007 when the IMT-GT decided to adopt the concept of economic corridors as a development strategy. With few exceptions, roads along the transport backbone are in good condition, efficient, and safe. Border crossing points are accessible from the main transport routes, and some could be reached by alternative routes.

Rail connectivity, however, has lagged behind roads given the massive capital outlays required, which affect its economic viability. Nonetheless, rail transport has been increasingly used in recent years to meet the needs of SEZs and industrial parks for a more cost-effective means of transporting goods, especially when sending high volumes of freight to ports. Burning less fuel, trains are also more environmentally friendly. To complement roads, railways are an important emerging priority for medium- to long-term development.

To optimize the subregion's geographic advantage along the Strait of Malacca, **greater focus must be given to enhancing multimodal connectivity with ports along the Strait**. Nationally, this would include:

- Using trains for moving freight to and from seaports, especially containers on high-volume routes. This will reduce port and inland transit costs, and facilitate clearance. Additional rail-linked facilities such as inland container depots (ICDs) and freight wagons will also be needed to meet the demand for intermodal links.

- Effective inland transit systems, including ICDs and bonded logistics facilities, which can improve the efficiency of supply chains by minimizing clearance formalities. Given the increased demand for inland terminals with the establishment of industrial parks and SEZs near ports, the development of inland transit systems can avoid the concentration of dry ports near borders and expedite cargo movements.

Although land routes between major nodes are adequate, there is a need to consider further road links within existing corridors, as industrial parks and new economic centers expand ports' catchment areas and open potential new trade routes. Such additional roads would widen national ECs and increase links to arterial trade and transport routes—as well as secondary borders, which would become more important as local value chains develop.

The IMT-GT's economic activities are mainly oriented toward ports, to capitalize on the subregion's strategic location along the Strait of Malacca. **However, some maritime links intended for the corridors have not materialized:** there is no maritime connectivity between Penang Port and Belawan Port (EC1); the link between Dumai and Melaka is mainly for passenger ferry services (EC4); and there are no commercial shipping routes for cargo from Malahayati Port to Ranong and Phuket (EC5). **However, maritime links have developed between Malaysian and Sumateran ports outside designated corridor nodes, signifying an opportunity to expand such connectivity in the Strait of Malacca**.

Subregional trade facilitation will need to focus on land- and sea-based transport, given the multimodal approach in most of the ECs. The current concentration on land-based facilities will need to be balanced with initiatives fostering port-based facilitation, especially with plans to develop international hub ports in the subregion to handle bulk and container cargoes. Cooperation between countries' ports could be explored, such as removing nontariff barriers to reduce delays; enhancing facilities; increasing compliance with international conventions; and improving operating efficiencies.

Cross-border trade, although active, constitutes a relatively small share of the countries' trade and has not increased significantly through the years. This implies that land connectivity per se may not have had a transformative impact on trade. Most of the trade in IMT-GT, especially in major commodities, goes through the ports, with land routes primarily serving as transit routes for goods to be shipped to international destinations. The trajectory of the IMT-GT countries toward trade outside the subregion, rather than within the region, can be explained by the fact that they produce the same or similar basic commodities, in particular, palm oil, rubber, seafoods, and agricultural food products. This underscores the need to shift from simple border trade to investment-creating trade that promotes processing activities within the value chain.

In addition to reviewing the five existing ECs, this study also explores the recommended route for a sixth—EC6, proposed by Thailand—which aims to open new trade routes between Southern Thailand and northeastern Malaysia through the East Coast Rail Link (ECRL). The ECRL, as part of the Belt and Road Initiative (BRI) of the People's Republic of China (PRC), will connect Peninsular Malaysia's east and west coasts. Proponents believe EC6 will bring significant benefits for the IMT-GT, creating opportunities for expanded trade with the PRC and Europe through ports on the eastern coast.

Covering almost all of the IMT-GT, the recommended route for EC6 involves 17 provinces and states, including:.

(i)   three provinces in Southern Thailand: Pattani, Yala, and Narathiwat;

(ii) eight Malaysian states, in two alternative routes: Kelantan, Terengganu, Pahang, Perak, Selangor, Melaka, Negeri Sembilan, and Johor; and

(iii) six Indonesian provinces: four in mainland Sumatera—South Sumatera, Bengkulu, Jambi, and Lampung; plus two southeastern archipelagic provinces—Riau Islands and Bangka Belitung Islands.

Of the two proposed alternative Malaysian routes, one runs along the eastern coast through Tok Bali, Kuala Terengganu, Kemaman Port, and Kuantan Port, connecting to Port Klang, and up to Tanjung Bruas Port in Melaka; the other has a westward orientation, passing through Perak (Gerik, Ipoh City, Lumut Port), Port Klang, and up to Tanjung Bruas Port in Melaka.

Physical connectivity in the proposed EC6 route indicates that road and rail connections between Malaysia and Thailand are adequate, although gaps in certain segments must be addressed. Sea and air links need to be developed further: while major Malaysian ports have maritime trade connections with ports in Sumatera and Southern Thailand, links with ports in the Riau Islands and Bangka Belitung Islands are limited to ferry services.

The configuration of EC6 and the reconfiguration of the five existing corridors have resulted in a network of transport links throughout the IMT-GT. Chapter 5 discusses the network of IMT-GT corridors that have emerged from the reconfiguration exercise. The additional nodes in the reconfigured corridors link two or more economic corridors and enable them to function as a network, rather than as single corridors. Networked corridors can change the pattern of mobility for goods and people as they bring about access to a larger and more diverse base of inputs (raw materials, parts, energy, or labor) and broader markets for diverse outputs (intermediate and finished goods). Multimodal transport routes in each corridor are connected through nodes that allow corridors, each with their own characteristics, to interact dynamically and create new patterns of regional economic development. This dynamic can contribute to balanced development between lagging areas and growth centers, allowing poorer areas to benefit from economic corridor development spillovers to promote inclusive growth.

Expanding ECs as networks—rather than mere point-to-point connections—makes it imperative to coordinate spatial development across the IMT-GT. To build such networks, piecemeal approaches must be replaced by more comprehensive planning to reduce economic distances between nodes, promote complementary production and trade, and upscale economies for increased competitiveness.

To better understand relationships between value chains and ECs, this study reviewed the journeys of three major products: palm oil, rubber, and halal food. Showing that corridor provinces and states play important roles in production, processing, and distribution within these products' value chains, this report identifies infrastructure improvements to promote the development of those chains.

The IMT-GT has taken steps to map value chains for major products. This exercise involves analyzing the demand and supply of intermediate goods; the countries' capacities to supply such goods for the manufacture of final products; and the logistics services needed, as well as the condition of infrastructure. Value chain mapping should also incorporate the geography of different processes, from production to distribution.

Observing ECs from a value chain perspective, interrelated roles and the continuity of different nodes are vital, underscoring the need to plan the juxtaposition of different nodes in relation to value chains. An underperforming EC can dilute the inherent comparative advantages of certain products. **Thus, mapping value chains must be linked with planning transport networks in particular, for EC development on a broader scale**.

As a truly regional approach to EC development has yet to fully materialize in the IMT-GT, this report proposes practical and incremental measures to elevate coordination of progress across corridors. **District, regency, provincial, and central planning are essential considerations for national schemes and the IMT-GT institutional framework**.

One immediate practical step would be to initiate and institutionalize dialogue among local operations. While policy interventions might still be needed, as most bottlenecks are corridor-specific, they may require customized inputs to enable smoother flows between producers and consumers. Local dialogues or stakeholder meetings could be good initiatives to resolve specific bottlenecks, helping to dismantle administrative and procedural barriers, increasing flows between nodes. Practical measures resulting from such local meetings considering their value chain links could then be reported to the Chief Ministers and Governors Forum (CMGF) and working groups.

INTRODUCTION

Overview

On 1 October 2018 in Melaka, Malaysia, the 24th Indonesia–Malaysia–Thailand Growth Triangle (IMT-GT) Ministerial Meeting directed a review of existing IMT-GT economic corridors (ECs), and a study of the proposed sixth corridor linking Pattani–Yala–Narathiwat in Thailand with Perak and Kelantan in Malaysia, and with southern Sumatera in Indonesia. The countries requested technical assistance from the Asian Development Bank (ADB) in conducting this review.

The economic corridor approach to development was first mentioned in the IMT-GT Road Map 2007–2011 as a spatial anchor for IMT-GT cooperation. The concept was for economic corridors to serve as "trunk lines" from which development would radiate to neighboring areas through transport and economic linkages. The road map identified four economic corridors. Subsequently, a fifth one was added for a total of five economic corridors which are covered in this review.

Following that road map, the Implementation Blueprint (IB) 2012–2016 included EC development programs and projects among flagship transport and energy initiatives. The IB 2017–2021 reaffirmed the importance of ECs in achieving the IMT-GT 2036 Vision: (i) sustainable, inclusive, and innovative agriculture; (ii) competitive, innovative, and advanced industry; and (iii) sustainable, competitive, and inclusive cross-border tourism. To nurture corridor potentials, this latter IB emphasized the needs to (i) build the capacity of industry clusters through innovations; and (ii) develop ECs to benefit wider areas including agglomerations, and other places along corridors' edges.

The IMT-GT strategic framework documents over the past years indicate the absence of a definitive framework for economic corridor development at a subregional level. The diagnostic literature that would have defined the economic rationale for each corridor is scant. The progress achieved so far has resulted from independent national initiatives vetted through the IMT-GT platform, rather than from deliberate, evidence-based, corridor-wide planning at the subregional level. There has been visible progress in infrastructure connectivity, especially in land-based transport routes, as well as in the development of border crossing points and border facilities, notwithstanding.

This is the first comprehensive review of ECs from a wider perspective, since they became a focus of IMT-GT cooperation in 2007. The corridors' progress was not reviewed, even during the creation of IBs for 2012–2016 and 2017–2021. Previous work on ECs has mainly described their broad objectives, key connections, and national government initiatives. No benchmarks were set to assess levels of physical connectivity or performance. Nonetheless, the governments have implemented several programs and projects in corridors, creating some economic vibrancy in these zones over the past decade.

Study Objectives

In assessing the IMT-GT economic corridors, this review aims to:
(i)   analyze the corridors' connections by road, rail, sea, and air;
(ii) identify gaps in such connections, and recommend new routes for expansion of economic opportunities;
(iii) review the proposed sixth EC, and recommend its configuration;
(iv) review links between ECs and the emerging subregional corridor network;

(v)   review ECs from a value chain perspective;

(vi) recommend ways to improve EC development.

The study's primary purpose is to assess transport connectivity as the backbone of ECs. Examining corridor provinces, states, and nodes—as well as internodal activities—this report provides details in the context of national development strategies. Analyzing development in the ECs, we also identify emerging opportunities for their expansion.

Analytical Framework

A corridor approach to development typically involves connecting nodes or economic centers, through a transport backbone (a transport corridor). For an economic corridor to be viable, it must connect nodes or centers with actual or potential economic growth.[1] Although an economic corridor is defined by a transport backbone, it can influence a much wider space that includes production centers (manufacturing hubs, industrial clusters, special economic zones [SEZs]) and demand centers (cities and major urban centers). Transnational or regional ECs include border crossings and seaports that provide access to international markets. Economic centers in the vicinity of transport corridors can be deliberately planned as part of corridor development, or they may be in the nature of market responses resulting from the spillovers of physical connectivity.

Large economic centers such as cities are defined as major nodes, given their important functions in corridors. Commercial nodes may serve as intermediaries in the supply chain, or as end nodes for the arrival and departure of goods. Border nodes are near national boundaries, facilitating the movement of goods and people. Gateway nodes are generally end points providing access to international markets, and tourist nodes are centers of tourism activity.

Several factors determine the extent to which an economic corridor can realize its growth potential:

(i)   the extent to which economic centers, serving as nodes in each country, are connected;

(ii) the location of economic centers relative to all other centers within a country, and to other countries;

(iii) the "thickness" of overland borders, as manifested by the time and cost it takes to cross national borders;

(iv) the extent to which concentration or convergence occurs between villages and cities, or between lagging and leading areas in a country; and

(v)   the strengthening of weak links along a corridor that are important to the transmission and facilitation of flows along the corridor.

Factors (i) and (ii) are concerned with infrastructure connectivity, which affects a location's access to markets for increasing its economic opportunity: this covers roads, railways, maritime links, and air transport. The extent of such connectivity can determine the size of potential markets—both inside and outside a corridor—and the ease of reaching them. This can be manifested in value chain linkages and cross-border trade.

While the first two are concerned with physical distance, the third factor is concerned with economic distance manifested by the time and cost it takes to cross a national border within a corridor. The "thickness" of the border can sometimes reduce the advantage of physical proximity and can affect trade flows. The fourth factor

---

[1]   P. Srivastava. 2011. Regional Corridors Development in Regional Cooperation. *ADB Economics Working Paper Series*. No. 258. Manila: ADB.

involves the concentration of people (consumer markets) and production units as part of the geographic location of an economic corridor.

Methodology and Study Team

As an initial activity, the study identified specific nodes in each corridor to establish the role of different economic units in relation to the major transport backbone and gateways. The nodes provided the reference points for assessing connectivity in the corridor. It also provided the basis for identifying linkages with potential nodes by way of expanding the corridor configuration based on emerging national strategies and economic opportunities. The nodes were classified according to the roles they perform: capital cities and urban areas, commercial nodes, border crossing points, maritime gateway ports, and tourism nodes.

The study identified possibilities for expanding existing corridors to other provinces and states. The motivation was to loop in strategically positioned areas in the government's spatial strategy into the regional economic corridors to derive additional benefits from continuity and scale effects. The reconfigured corridor would optimize regional spatial use by taking advantage of new production, growth and logistics centers located in a wider area; enhance supply chain opportunities and contribute to a more equitable distribution of benefits. The additional provinces and states can upgrade to the main logistic routes that connect to other corridor networks, thus diversifying economic and social outcomes. The interlink corridors emerging from the proposed reconfiguration of the existing corridors were also identified.

The study also looked at the value chains[2] of three major products in IMT-GT—palm oil, rubber, and halal foods—to get a broad perspective on the geography of their production, processing, and distribution components in the economic corridors. Knowing the geography of value chain components is useful for planning appropriate interventions to make economic corridors more responsive to value chain development.

The study is qualitative and draws its observations and findings from inferences and interpretation of data collected from official and other sources. Desk research was conducted on IMT-GT documents, reports of meetings, and references and research materials. Country consultations were conducted intermittently from 21 October to 7 December 2019.[3] The consultations covered many of the corridor provinces and states and involved the national secretariats, relevant line ministries, bodies responsible for spatial development programs or national corridors, provincial and state planning units, ports authorities, and Customs houses at border crossing points (BCPs). The study team consulted closely with the national secretariats in the course of its work.

The study was conducted by a team of consultants headed by a team leader based at ADB Headquarters in Manila, and three national consultants (one for each country) selected by the national secretariats, based in their respective country duty stations. The team was supervised at the operational level by the Southeast Asia Cooperation and Operations Coordination Division, Southeast Asia Department. The national secretariats provided overall guidance.

---

[2]   In this study, the distinction between the terms "value chain" and "supply chain" is not strictly applied. It is noted that a value chain is the process by which a company adds value to its raw materials to produce products eventually sold to consumers, while the supply chain represents all the steps required to get the product to the customer.

[3]   The country consultations took place on the following dates: Indonesia Part 1, 21–26 October 2019; Malaysia, 3–8 November 2019; Thailand, 11–15 November 2019; and Indonesia Part 2, 3–7 December 2019.

Data collection was facilitated by the national consultants with the support of the national secretariats and the Centre for IMT-GT Cooperation (CIMT). National consultants conferred regularly with the national secretariats in the course of the study.

Structure of the Report

The integrative report consists of eight chapters:

(i)   Introduction (Chapter 1),

(ii)   Development Context (Chapter 2),

(iii)   Review of the Five Existing Economic Corridors (Chapter 3),

(iv)   Proposed Route for Economic Corridor 6 (Chapter 4),

(v)   The Network of IMT-GT Economic Corridors (Chapter 5),

(vi)   Economic Corridors from a Value Chain Perspective (Chapter 6),

(vii) Addressing Gaps in Institutional Mechanisms for Economic Corridor Development (Chapter 7), and

(viii) Summary of Findings and Recommendations (Chapter 8).

This integrative report is supplemented by three separate publications for Indonesia, Malaysia, and Thailand—with each of these containing a country report presenting reviews of ECs from their national perspectives.

CHAPTER

2

DEVELOPMENT CONTEXT

The IMT-GT subregional economic cooperation program was established in 1993 with the goal of accelerating the economic transformation of the member states and provinces in the three countries by exploiting their underlying complementarities and strategies. Since its establishment in 1993, IMT-GT has expanded to its present geographic scope of 32 provinces and states—10 provinces in Sumatera, Indonesia; eight states in Malaysia; and 14 provinces in Thailand. Some of these provinces and states are the least developed in the countries and in the subregion. Of these 32 provinces and states, 20 are part of the existing economic corridors—four in Indonesia, seven in Malaysia, and nine in Thailand.

The 32 IMT-GT provinces and states have a combined population of 82.2 million or 22% of the total combined population of 368 million of the three countries. The population in the 20 economic corridor provinces and states is 56.7 million (2018) or 68.9% of the population of the IMT-GT provinces and states (Figure 1). The combined gross regional domestic product (GRDP) of these 20 economic corridor provinces and states amounted to $272 billion in 2018 or 17.6% of the combined gross domestic product (GDP) of the three countries.

Indonesia is the largest economy with a nominal GDP of more than $1.0 trillion. It is the world's largest archipelagic nation with a high degree of bio- and cultural diversity. The provinces participating in IMT-GT are all located in Sumatera Island, one of the Sunda Islands in western Indonesia and sixth largest island in the world.

Of the 10 provinces in Indonesia participating in IMT-GT, four are part of existing economic corridors (ECs)—North Sumatera (EC1, EC3); Riau (EC3, EC4); South Sumatera (EC1, EC3, EC6); and Aceh (EC3, EC5). These four provinces are among the most dynamic economies in Sumatera. North Sumatera, South Sumatera, and Riau are major producers of palm oil and rubber. They are part of Sumatera's growth corridor along the eastern coast, which are being developed to catalyze growth through accelerated development of toll roads, ports, industrial parks, and SEZs. These four provinces have a combined population of 34.9 million representing 60.4% of Sumatera's population or 13% of Indonesia's total population.

The four provinces contributed 14% to Indonesia's GDP on average during 2014–2018 and registered positive growth during the period. North Sumatera and South Sumatera grew by about 5% on average, higher than the 4.28% average growth rate for Sumatera (Figure 2). Among the four provinces, North Sumatera had the highest GRDP share of 4.9% (Figure 3), while Riau had the highest GDP per capita of $5,261.

Seven of the eight IMT-GT participating states in Malaysia are part of existing corridors: Kedah (EC1, EC2); Penang (EC1, EC2); Perlis (EC1, EC2); Selangor (EC2); Perak (EC2); Negeri Sembilan (EC2); and Melaka (EC2, EC4). Kelantan, although a participating state in IMT-GT, is not part of any existing corridor. The seven states had a combined population of 15.2 million which is 47% of Malaysia's total population (Figure 1-Malaysia). All the states maintained positive GRDP growth rates for 2014–2018, ranging from an average of 3% (Perlis) to 7% (Selangor), although Melaka experienced a steep decline in 2018 (Figure 4). The seven EC states combined contributed an average of about 45% to Malaysia's GDP during 2014–2018, with Selangor accounting for about half (23.7%) of this contribution, followed by Penang (6.7%) (Figure 5). In 2018, Penang had the highest per capita GDP of $12,818 followed closely by Selangor at $12,347.

Figure 1: Populations in IMT-GT Economic Corridor Provinces and States, 2018
('000)

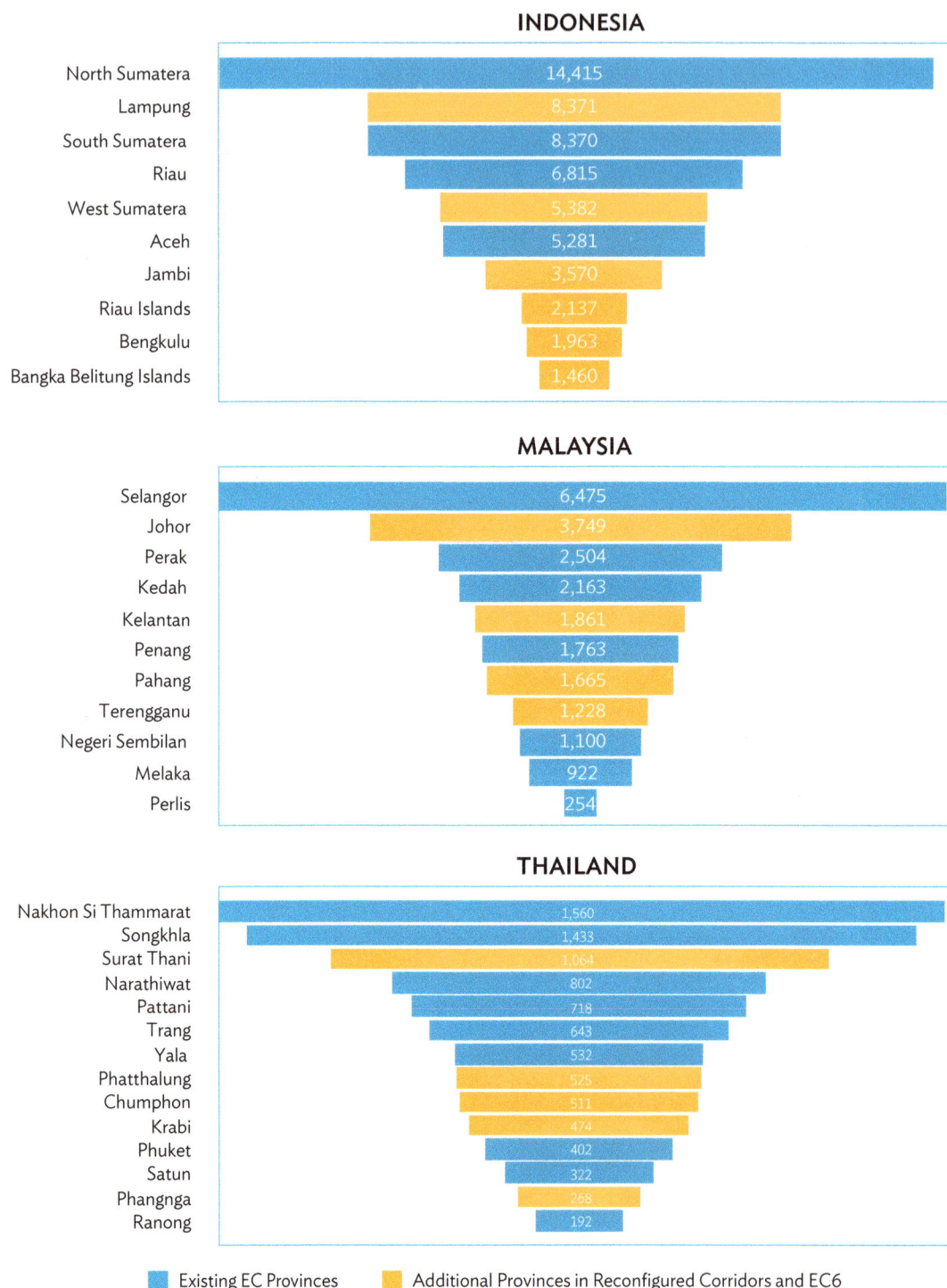

INDONESIA

Province	Population
North Sumatera	14,415
Lampung	8,371
South Sumatera	8,370
Riau	6,815
West Sumatera	5,382
Aceh	5,281
Jambi	3,570
Riau Islands	2,137
Bengkulu	1,963
Bangka Belitung Islands	1,460

MALAYSIA

State	Population
Selangor	6,475
Johor	3,749
Perak	2,504
Kedah	2,163
Kelantan	1,861
Penang	1,763
Pahang	1,665
Terengganu	1,228
Negeri Sembilan	1,100
Melaka	922
Perlis	254

THAILAND

Nakhon Si Thammarat	1,560
Songkhla	1,433
Surat Thani	1,064
Narathiwat	802
Pattani	718
Trang	643
Yala	532
Phatthalung	525
Chumphon	511
Krabi	474
Phuket	402
Satun	322
Phangnga	268
Ranong	192

■ Existing EC Provinces   ■ Additional Provinces in Reconfigured Corridors and EC6

EC = economic corridor, IMT-GT = Indonesia–Malaysia–Thailand Growth Triangle.
Note: Johor, Terengganu, and Pahang are not participating IMT-GT states but are proposed for inclusion in the economic corridors.
Source: Study team.

Figure 2: Indonesia: Gross Regional Domestic Product Growth Rate of Four Provinces in Existing Economic Corridors

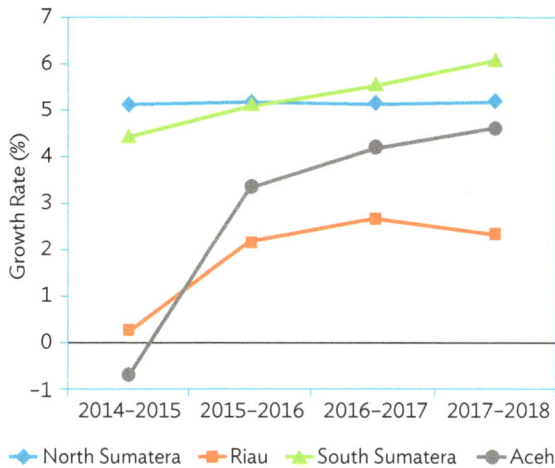

Source: Author.

Figure 3: Share of Four Provinces' Gross Regional Domestic Product to Total Gross Domestic Product of Existing Corridors in Indonesia, Average 2014–2018

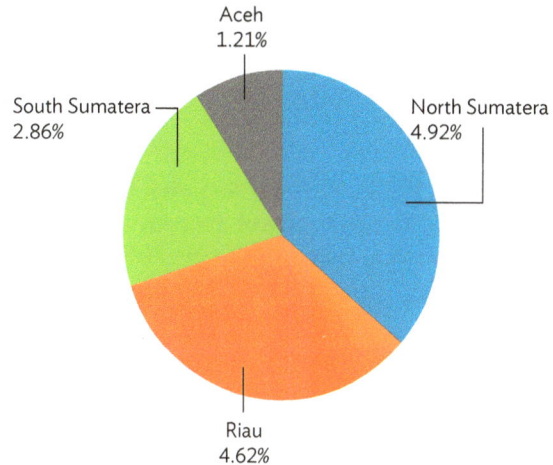

Aceh 1.21%
South Sumatera 2.86%
North Sumatera 4.92%
Riau 4.62%

Source: Author.

Figure 4: Malaysia: Gross Regional Domestic Product Growth Rate of Seven States in Existing Corridors (2014–2018)

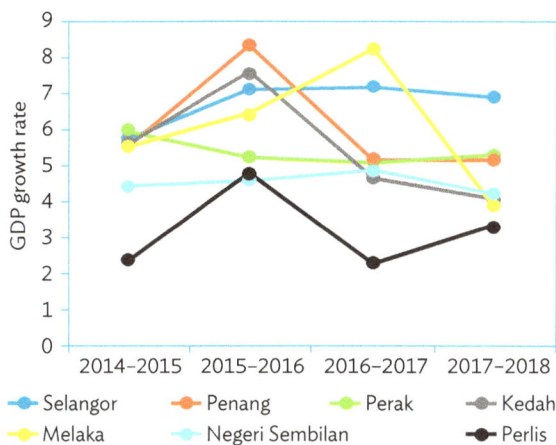

GDP = gross domestic product.
Source: Author.

Figure 5: Malaysia: Share of Seven States' Gross Regional Domestic Product to Total Gross Regional Domestic Product of Existing Corridors in Malaysia, Average 2014–2018

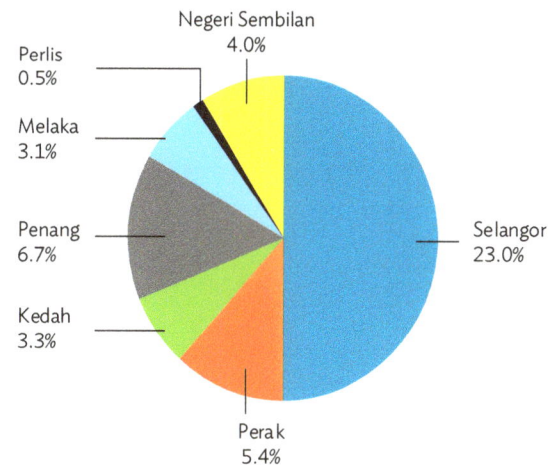

Negeri Sembilan 4.0%
Perlis 0.5%
Melaka 3.1%
Penang 6.7%
Kedah 3.3%
Selangor 23.0%
Perak 5.4%

Source: Author.

In Thailand, 9 out of 14 participating provinces are part of economic corridors: Songkhla, Narathiwat, Pattani, Yala, and Nakhon Si Thammarat (EC1); Trang and Satun (EC2); Ranong and Phuket (EC5). Most of these provinces are in the southern part of Thailand bordering Malaysia. They have a combined population of 6.6 million or 9.5% of Thailand's total population (Figure 1 - Thailand). A number of provinces suffered a slump in their economic performance in 2017, although they were able to recover in 2018 (Figure 6). In 2018, the combined GRDP of these provinces amounted to $18.0 billion, with Songkhla and Phuket contributing the largest share of about 28% each (Figure 7). Phuket had the highest per capita GDP of $12,489 in 2018, way above Songkhla with the second highest at $4,701.

Figure 6: Thailand: Gross Regional Domestic Product Growth Rate of Six Provinces in Existing Corridors (2014–2018)

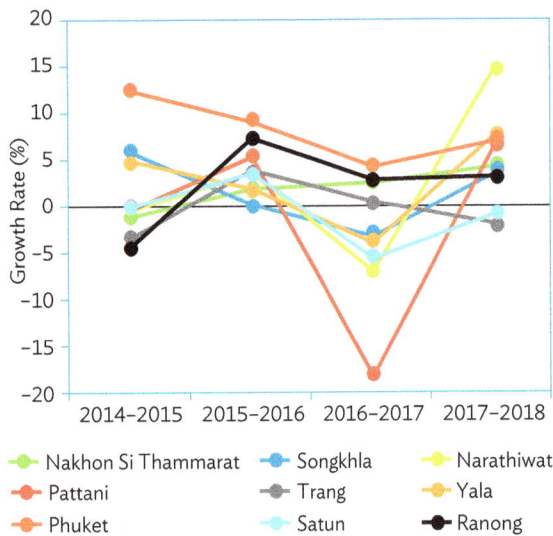

Source: Author.

Figure 7: Thailand: Share of Six Provinces' Gross Regional Domestic Product to Total Gross Domestic Product of Existing Corridors in Thailand, Average 2014–2018

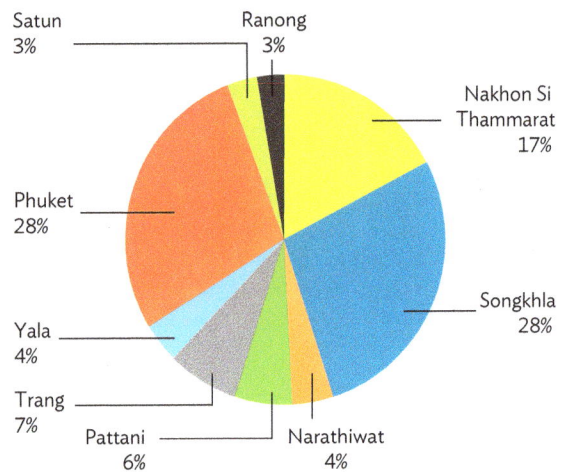

Source: Author.

CHAPTER

3

REVIEW OF THE FIVE IMT-GT ECONOMIC CORRIDORS

The five IMT-GT economic corridors each have unique characteristics. Four are subregional corridors; one is a national corridor in Sumatera. Two corridors have overland links between economic centers in Malaysia and Thailand, complemented by maritime links to Sumatera ports in Medan (EC1) and Dumai (EC4). One is a maritime corridor connecting the northern part of Sumatera with Southern Thailand (EC5). One is a coastal corridor along the western coast of Malaysia and Thailand. The land and maritime links are supplemented by air connectivity (Map 1).

The five economic corridors are as follows:

- **The Extended Songkhla–Penang–Medan Economic Corridor (EC1)** is primarily an overland corridor connecting Thailand's southern provinces of Nakhon Si Thammarat, Phatthalung, and Pattani with the international gateway port in Songkhla, Yala, and Narathiwat; an overland route from Songkhla to Penang, and a maritime connection to the port of Medan in Sumatera.

- **The Strait of Malacca Economic Corridor (EC2)** is a coastal corridor connecting the provinces of Trang and Satun in Thailand with Perlis, Port Klang, Penang, and Melaka along the western coast of the Strait of Malacca.

- **The Banda Aceh–Medan–Pekanbaru–Palembang Economic Corridor (EC3)** is a national corridor in Sumatera. Connectivity among the provinces is envisaged to build traffic volume leading to Sumatera's international ports along its eastern coast—Banda Aceh, Medan, Pekanbaru, Dumai, and Jambi—complementing coastal connectivity with ports in Penang and Melaka.

- **The Melaka–Dumai Economic Corridor (EC4)** is mainly a maritime corridor that builds on the strategic location of the ports of Dumai and Melaka located opposite each other in one of the narrowest stretches of the Strait of Malacca. The corridor includes the development of land connectivity to Dumai Port, as well as the development of Tanjung Bruas Port.

- **The Ranong–Phuket–Aceh Economic Corridor (EC5)** is mainly a maritime corridor linking ports in the northern part of Sumatera (mainly Ulee Lheue and Malahayati) with Phuket Port in Southern Thailand, with the aim of exploiting tourism potential.

The sixth economic corridor (EC6) is a new corridor proposed by Thailand during the 24th IMT-GT Ministerial Meeting held on 1 October 2018 in Melaka, Malaysia. The proposed EC6 is envisaged to open new trade routes between Southern Thailand and Malaysia through the East Coast Rail Link (ECRL). The link between Sumatera and Malaysia will be through maritime mode across the Strait of Malacca, while the link with Thailand will be through multimodal links via the Malaysian Peninsula.

Designation of Corridor Nodes

At the onset, the study observed that specific nodes have not been explicitly defined in the existing corridor configuration except for land border crossings and main gateway ports. As an initial activity, the study identified the nodes in each corridor to establish the role of different economic units in relation to the major transport backbone and gateways. The nodes identified in the study are the points or areas that perform catalytic roles in the corridor influence areas and have the potential to contribute to trade and economic growth by leveraging on infrastructure connectivity. The nodes provided the reference points for assessing connectivity in the corridor. It also served as reference points for identifying potential nodes that could enhance corridor linkages under a new configuration.

Map 1: Five Indonesia–Malaysia–Thailand Growth Triangle Economic Corridors

INDONESIA-MALAYSIA-THAILAND GROWTH TRIANGLE

Ranong–Phuket–Aceh Economic Corridor (EC5)

Extended Songkhla–Penang–Medan Economic Corridor (EC1)

Strait of Malacca Economic Corridor (EC2)

Melaka–Dumai Economic Corridor (EC4)

Banda Aceh–Medan–Pekanbaru–Palembang Economic Corridor (EC3)

Andaman Sea

THAILAND

Chumphon, Ranong, Surat Thani, Phangnga, Krabi, Phuket, Phuket Port, Nakhon Si Thammarat, Trang, Phatthalung, Songkhla, Satun, Padang Besar, Pattani, Yala, Kangar, Narathiwat, Kota Bharu, Buketa, Pengkalan Hulu, Kuah, Alor Setar, Langkawi Island, Perlis, Kedah, Gerik, Kelantan, Kuala Terengganu, Marang, Terengganu, Gua Musang, Kemasik, Penang Port, Butterworth, George Town, Penang, Kulim, Ipoh, Perak, Kuala Lipis, Pahang, Kuala Sepetang, Bagan Datuk, Kuantan, Selangor, Shah Alam, Temerloh, Peninsular Malaysia, Kuala Lumpur, Port Klang, Negeri Sembilan, Seremban, Port Dickson, Tanjung Bruas Port, Melaka, Mersing, Muar, Johor, Kota Tinggi, Johor Bahru, Singapore

Sabang Port, Balohan Port, Malahayati Port, Banda Aceh, Ulee Lheue Port, Sigli, Lhokseumawe, Langsa, Rimba Raya, Aceh, Belawan Port, Belawan, Medan, Kuala Tanjung Port, Binjai, Tebingtinggi, Kisaran, Pematangsiantar, Lake Toba, Rantau Prapat, North Sumatera, Sibolga, Dumai Port, Dumai, Aek Kanopan, Pekanbaru, Riau, Rengat, Sumatera, Teluk Kuantan, Pariaman, Padang, West Sumatera, Jambi, Indonesia, Lahat, Bengkulu, Baturaja, South Sumatera, Palembang, Tanjung Api-Api Port, Pangkalpinang, Bangka Belitung Islands, Belitung, Lampung, Bandar Lampung, Java Sea, Indian Ocean, Enggano, Siberut, Pagai, Batu, Nias, Simeulue, Riau Islands, Tanjungpinang, Lingga, Strait of Malacca

Legend:
- National Capital
- Provincial/State Capital
- City/Town
- Airport
- National Road
- Other Road
- Provincial Boundary
- International Boundary
- EC = economic corridor
Boundaries are not necessarily authoritative.

Kilometers 0 50 100 150 200 250

This map was produced by the cartography unit of the Asian Development Bank. The boundaries, colors, denominations, and any other information shown on this map do not imply, on the part of the Asian Development Bank, any judgment on the legal status of any territory, or any endorsement or acceptance of such boundaries, colors, denominations, or information.

Source: Asian Development Bank.

Nodes, broadly defined, are the points that connect different economic units. In the economic corridor context, nodes are

- strategic points within a corridor where people, production areas, and transport routes converge or cluster; and

- generally compact, transit-oriented areas along or adjacent to a transport corridor with at least medium concentration of economic activity (commercial nodes).

The nodes were classified as follows:

- **Capital city**: the main urban and administrative center in a province or state; the area is compact, transit-oriented, and densely populated, and where high concentrations of residential, employment, retail, and key services are located;

- **Border crossing point** (BCP): the point where border areas between two countries in the corridor converge and where customs, immigration, and quarantine (CIQ) facilities are provided to enable the entry and exit of goods across the borders;

- **Commercial node**: an area where there is a high concentration of economic activity such industrial parks, SEZs, and distribution centers; usually accompanied by redevelopment around the area that includes residential, retail, and services facilities;

- **Maritime gateway port**: an area for the transport of cargo and/or passengers to external markets and/ or destinations comprising a land domain (the port's region and its locality) and the maritime domain which services ships for global trade;

- **Tourism node**: an area with a medium-to-high density of tourists having the full range of facilities, services, and amenities, usually part of a cluster of destinations where tourists can engage in a variety of activities beyond visiting a single attraction or tourist site.

The review of the five existing economic corridors covered: (i) the status of transport connectivity by land, rail, sea, and air; (ii) the condition of infrastructure at border crossing points (BCPs); and (iii) cross-border trade. To determine possible enhancements in the corridor, the roles of the different economic units (nodes) were analyzed in relation to other economic units emerging or being developed as part of the governments' development plans. These new set of nodes were proposed to form the reconfiguration of the economic corridors.

Economic Corridor 1. The Extended Songkhla–Penang–Medan Economic Corridor

Overview

The Extended Songkhla–Penang–Medan Economic Corridor (EC1) consists of three main sections: two overland routes and a maritime route. The two overland routes connect (i) the Southern Thailand provinces of Nakhon Si Thammarat, Phatthalung, and Pattani with the international gateway ports in Songkhla, Yala, and Narathiwat; (ii) an overland route from Songkhla to Penang; and (iii) the maritime route links Penang to Medan, the capital of North Sumatera, across the Strait of Malacca. Within North Sumatera, the important land connectivity is between Medan City and Belawan Port. Belawan Port in Medan is currently the main international port which supports this maritime connectivity segment (Map 2).

At present, there are five provinces or states mentioned in EC1's descriptive name (Songkhla, Kedah, Perlis, Penang, and North Sumatera), but the main transport backbone of EC1 actually traverses eight provinces or states that includes Chumphon, Surat Thani, Nakhon Si Thammarat, and Phatthalung in Thailand. Originally, the route for EC 1 covered these three provinces to the north of Songkhla and extended southwards to Pattani, Yala, and Narathiwat. The southern branch is now proposed to form part of the new EC6 connecting Kelantan and southern Sumatera.

EC1 was envisaged to provide maritime links between North Sumatera in the eastern coast of Sumatera Island with Penang Port in Malaysia's west coast. Belawan Port in Medan is currently the main international port that supports this maritime connectivity segment. It provides container, bulk and break-bulk cargo, Ro-Ro (roll on, roll off), and domestic terminal services. The Belawan International Container Terminal (BICT), under Pelindo I, provides container loading and unloading services from/to ships and other container services. However, due to inadequate depth and lack of vessel channels, BICT functions only as a feeder port to Singapore and Malaysia (Port Klang in Selangor and Tanjung Pelepas in Johor).

Existing Provinces and Nodes

Indonesia

North Sumatera. North Sumatera is among the 10 provinces in Sumatera identified as belonging to the "growth corridor" under the National Medium-Term Development Plan (RPJMN) 2020–2024. Within North Sumatera, the specific growth areas include Medan (the capital city), Sei Mangkei (SEZ), Kuala Tanjung (industrial zone), and Lake Toba (tourism zone).

Medan. Medan is the capital city and principal economic anchor in North Sumatera for EC1. It is the biggest city in Sumatera with a population of 2.26 million (2018), which could reach up to 4.2 million if the surrounding regencies are included. Medan is a node in the Eastern Sumatera National Highway and Trans-Sumatera toll road. It is the home base for several rubber downstream companies with plantations all over North Sumatera. Medan is also known as Sumatera's "coffee axis" since coffee from various regencies are processed there and exported to domestic and international markets. North Sumatera contributes close to 20% of Sumatera's foreign trade. Under the RPJMN 2020–2024, Medan will be developed as Metropolitan Medan, together with Palembang.

**Map 2: Extended Songkhla–Penang–Medan Economic Corridor
(Economic Corridor 1)**

Source: Asian Development Bank.

Belawan Port. Belawan Port is currently the main international feeder port that supports connectivity in EC1. Located along the Deli River, about 12 kilometers (km) from Medan, Belawan Port is Indonesia's busiest port outside of Java. It can support all container types, Ro-Ro, bulk, and break-bulk cargo. Belawan Port has four major berths that consist of many smaller berths or jetties used for specific activities such as general cargo, bulk cargo, crude palm oil, containers, and passengers. Pelindo 1 operates BICT and the Domestic Container Terminal Belawan (TPKDB) to provide container loading and unloading services in the ports. Because of its low water depth, Belawan Port's container terminal serves only the transshipment routes to bigger and deeper ports along the Strait of Malacca such as Singapore Port, Port Klang (Selangor), and Tanjung Pelepas (Johor). To enhance maritime connectivity with its neighboring countries, the Government of Indonesia is developing Kuala Tanjung Port as a new international hub port to handle liquid bulk cargo (crude palm oil [CPO]), dry bulk cargo, general cargo, and container for the provinces of North Sumatera and Aceh.

Products transported through Belawan Port are mainly CPO and crude palm kernel oil (CPKO) (upstream products), but there are also downstream products such as cooking oil, margarine, shortening, and oleochemicals. North Sumatera has the second largest area planted to rubber in Indonesia (12.7%), after South Sumatera. Rubber being exported through Belawan are in the form of rubber crumb, gloves, inner tubes, outside tires, etc. It also presently serves as a gateway for the cement industry based in West Sumatera, and the fertilizer industry based in South Sumatera.

Malaysia

The state capitals involved in EC1 are Kangar (Perlis), Alor Setar (Kedah), and George Town (Penang). These major cities are important economic nodes, and serve as commercial and administrative centers that provide services to the public, business communities, and industry players to facilitate economic activities in the states.

Penang Port. Malaysia's role in EC1 centers on Penang Port as the country's second premier port and key maritime gateway for Thailand and North Sumatera exports to international markets.

Penang Port, located in the state of Penang in the northwest part of Peninsula Malaysia is the oldest and longest established port in Malaysia.[4] It is a deep-water seaport consisting of seven terminals along the Penang Strait—six of which are in mainland Seberang Perai, specifically in the towns of Butterworth and Perai, and one in George Town in Penang Island as the Swettenham Pier Cruise Terminal.

Within the existing port at Butterworth is the North Butterworth Container Terminal (NBCT) which is the main location for container handling. NBCT's expansion is being planned to revitalize Penang Port. There are also plans to redevelop the old Perai wharf into a fully dedicated modern bulk terminal to handle lime stones, iron ore, and cement clinkers.

Swettenham Pier in George Town has evolved into becoming Malaysia's busiest harbor for cruise ships, overtaking Port Klang in 2017. In recent years, growth in the global cruise market has shown increasing interest in Malaysia, with Penang Port's Swettenham Pier right next to George Town's United Nations Educational, Scientific and Cultural Organization (UNESCO) world heritage site. It is the second most important port of call for cruise ships in Malaysia, accounting for 36% of all passenger arrivals at ports of call in the country. Penang is one of the ports that will benefit most from the rise in cruise tourism with expansion being planned to accommodate larger cruise ships.

---

4   The information for Penang Port were compiled from Penang Port found at https://www.penangport.com.my/.

Thailand

Nakhon Si Thammarat. Nakhon Si Thammarat Province in Southern Thailand is a regional hub for commercial activity, tourism, education, and culture. Located on the western shore of the Gulf of Thailand, its neighboring provinces include Songkhla, Phatthalung, Trang, Krabi, and Surat Thani. It has become a first-tier tourist province, receiving around four million tourists in 2018—80% of them domestic—largely attracted by religious heritage sites.

Songkhla. Songkhla Province has the largest population and gross provincial product and hosts most commercial and industrial activities in Southern Thailand. Most of the processing activities are in seafood, rubber, and rubber wood for domestic or export markets. Processed products are distributed to the domestic market or exported via Thai–Malaysian border checkpoints at Sadao, Padang Besa, and Ban Prakop; or via Songkhla Port to Laem Chabang Port and then to the People's Republic of China (PRC) and other trading partners. Songkhla is also a popular tourist destination among Thais and Malaysians.

Songkhla Port. In Thailand, the transport system in EC1 primarily serves the transport of agricultural produce from plantation to factories and to the domestic and export markets. A key node in the transport system is Songkhla Port, which transports goods between the south and the central plains of Thailand. Songkhla Port also serves as an important maritime gateway in the transport of goods to the Thai–Malaysian border checkpoint headed to Penang Port in Malaysia, or to Laem Chabang Port in Chonburi Province headed to the Greater Mekong Subregion (GMS).

To further expand capacity and increase the efficiency of the port, the Songkhla 2 Port Project is being planned, proposed to be located at the Chana District, Songkhla Province, about 40 km south of the existing port. The plan includes developing the route providing maritime transport services from Laem Chabang or Sriracha Port to Songkhla Port to reduce congestion in transporting goods from the south to the Bangkok Metropolitan Region. The routes would also be an alternative for transporting and distributing goods from the south to other regions in the country and to the GMS countries.

Physical Connectivity

Road Connectivity

EC1 starts in Nakhon Si Thammarat and goes through Songkhla until the Thai–Malaysian border checkpoints. The route in Thailand is divided into nine sections.[5] The states in Malaysia in EC 1 are the northern states of Perlis, Kedah, and Penang. The Asian Highway 2 (AH2) route connects Songkhla Province to Kedah through the Bukit Kayu Hitam–Sadao border checkpoint. EC1 links with Sumatera in Medan City through maritime links.

---

[5]   The nine sections of EC1 in Thailand are: (i) Nakhon Si Thammarat Mueang District–Phatthalung Mueang District; (ii) Phatthalung Mueang District–Hat Yai District; (iii) Songkhla Mueang District–Hat Yai District; (iv) Songkhla–Padang Besa Border Checkpoint (v) Songkhla–Sadao Border Checkpoint (vi) Songkhla–Ban Prakop Border Checkpoint; (vii) Hat Yai–Padang Besa Border Checkpoint (viii) Hat Yai–Sadao Border Checkpoint; and (ix) Hat Yai–Ban Prakop Border Checkpoint.

The route of EC1 in Thailand covers the distance between 30.6 km and 140 km depending on the start and end points. All routes are safe, equipped with traffic signs, traffic lines, and complete and undamaged safety equipment, curved guideposts, and complete guard rails in good condition. The road surface is smooth in the entire route.

From the Thai border at Hat Yai, there are three alternative routes to Malaysia through three BCPs:

- Sadao (Songkhla)–Bukit Kayu Hitam (Kedah)
- Padang Besa (Songkhla)–Padang Besar (Perlis) and
- Ban Prakop (Songkhla)–Durian Burung (Kedah)

From Sadao, the North–South Expressway (E1), which is also the route for AH2 connects Bukit Kayu Hitam (Kedah) to Penang Port in Butterworth and George Town. The distance between Bukit Kayu Hitam border and the Penang Port (George Town, Seberang Perai) is 166 km. The Penang Bridge (E36), which is 17.5 km, connects the Penang Port in George Town and Butterworth (Penang Island).

The second alternative route is from Hat Yai (Songkhla) to Padang Besar (Perlis) and continues to Penang Port in George Town and Butterworth. There is no expressway in Perlis but only federal and state roads. The federal, state, and expressway (E1/AH2) route connects Padang Besar to Penang Port in George Town and Butterworth. The distance between the main entrance of the Padang Besar border to Penang Port George Town is 204 km.

The third alternative connectivity route is from Hat Yai (Songkhla) to Durian Burung (Kedah) and continues to the Penang Port in George Town and Butterworth through the federal, state, and expressway routes. The distance between the main entrance of the Durian Burung (Kedah) border to the Penang Port (Butterworth) is 184 km.

In Sumatera, land connectivity between Belawan Port and Medan City is via the Belawan–Medan–Tanjung Morowa Toll Road along 12 km (34 km for total toll road length with 2x2 lanes) operating since 1986. Through Medan, Belawan Port can connect to the Eastern Trans-Sumatera National Highway (Jalan Lintas Timur Sumatera), as well as the Trans-Sumatera Toll Road, which is being developed to connect all provinces in Sumatera Island. The route to Medan from Penang Port (Butterworth and George Town) is via ship through the Strait of Malacca. The distance between Butterworth Penang Port and Belawan Port is 228 km (123 nautical miles).

Overall, road connectivity in all segments of the EC1 are adequate. Roads connecting the states in Malaysia with the provinces in Thailand are in good condition, efficient, and safe since they are parts of national or federal or state road systems and expressways. Land connectivity between Belawan Port and Medan City is via a toll road that has been operating since 1986.

Rail Connectivity

Railway links complement road connectivity. From Bangkok, the State Railway of Thailand (SRT) southern line at Hat Yai splits into two routes. The main route goes southeast to Su-ngai Kolok at the Thailand–Malaysian border in Narathiwat Province. The other route goes southwest to Padang Besa in Songhkla. The rail route from Hat Yai and Padang Besa Border checkpoint covers 45 kms. The main rail connection ends in Su-ngai Kolok because the railway service between Pasir Mas/Tumpat (Kelantan) and Su-ngai Kolok stations, which have been operating since 1954, was terminated in 1999 due to smuggling and human trafficking activities.

The missing rail link between Su-ngai Kolok in Narathiwat and Pasir Mas in Kelantan should be revived as part of the proposed route in EC6. The revival of this railway link is presently being considered by the governments of Thailand and Malaysia to increase connectivity between Narathiwat and Kelantan.[6] In Malaysia, the railway from Padang Besar in Perlis continues to Johor Bharu and Singapore. At present, there are no cross-border trains going across the Malaysia–Thailand border.

Malaysia's rail link with Southern Thailand is via the SRT southern line, which runs from Bangkok to Hat Yai, connects to the Padang Besar Station in Perlis and continues to Johor Bharu and Singapore (Woodlands CIQ). The Hat Yai train station is the interchange node to Padang Besar Station and Su-ngai Kolok. From Su-ngai Kolok Station, passengers can travel by car over the Friendship Bridge to Rantau Panjang (Kelantan) and continue to other states in the peninsula. There is a proposal to construct a second bridge at the Kolok River to Rantau Panjang interchange. The railway track to the north from Penang begins at Butterworth and ends at Padang Besar, Perlis. The length of the railway line between Butterworth and Padang Besar is 157 km through the railway station and cargo terminal.

Maritime Connectivity

Penang Port serves as the main gateway for shippers in the northern states of Malaysia and the southern provinces of Thailand. The port is strategically located along the Strait of Malacca, one of the busiest shipping routes in the world. Penang Port is fully equipped to handle all types of cargo such as containers, liquid, dry bulk, break-bulk among others. It also caters to ferry services between Penang and places like Langsa, Aceh in Indonesia and the islands of Langkawi and Pulau Payar in the northern state of Kedah. Penang Port is accessible by land from the southern provinces of Thailand.

Belawan Port is the main international feeder port in North Sumatera that would link to Penang in EC1. A Belawan–Penang ferry route had previously existed but was terminated in 2010 due to its low occupancy rates. Currently, there is no direct maritime connection between Belawan International Container Port and Penang Port—the designated maritime nodes in EC1. Although Belawan Port has specific berths equipped with modern facilities and equipment for domestic and international container movements, its inadequate depth and lack of vessel channels allows it to function only as a feeder port to Singapore and Malaysia (Port Klang and Tanjung Pelepas). To enhance maritime connectivity, the Government of Indonesia is developing Kuala Tanjung Port as a new international hub port for North Sumatera and Aceh (Table 1).

Table 1: Economic Corridor 1: Maritime Links between North Sumatera Ports and Malaysia Ports

North Sumatera Port	Malaysia Port	Type of Maritime Activity
Belawan	Port Klang (Selangor)	Container cargo
	Tanjung Pelepas (Johor)	Container cargo
Kuala Tanjung	Port Klang (transshipment for imports from Sumatera)	Container cargo
Tanjung Balai Asahan	Port Klang	Passenger ferry
	Hutan Melintang Port (Perak)	Passenger ferry

Source: Study team.

---

[6]   Thai-Malaysian Rail Line Revival Proposal. 2019. *Bangkok Post.* 3 May.

Connectivity between Malaysia and Thailand, is serviced by a ferry between the Kuah Jetty Ferry Terminal in Langkawi and Tammalang Port and Ko Lipe Marine Port in Satun—thus, connecting economic activity between Satun with Langkawi in Kedah.

Smaller ports. In addition to Belawan and Kuala Tanjung, two smaller ports serve international trade: Tanjung Balai Asahan and Sibolga/Gunung Sitoli. Tanjung Balai Asahan Port can only serve vessels under 150 gross tonnage (GT). Recently, it has become the only port in North Sumatera and Aceh provinces that operates an international ferry service to Malaysia. Meanwhile, Sibolga Port is in the west coast of North Sumatera. It can accommodate four large ships with a maximum size of 6,000 GT. Sibolga Port is now serving containers and passengers and will serve liquid bulk cargo in the future.

Land Bridge Services

Keretapi Tanah Melayu Berhad (KTMB), in collaboration with SRT has provided a rail land bridge to transport cargo from Perai (Penang Port, Butterworth) to Surat Thani, Thung Song, and Hat Yai in Thailand, thus complementing the route via road and further enhancing cross-border trade between the Northern Corridor Economic Region (NCER) in Malaysia and provinces in Southern Thailand. Land bridges, as an intermodal option, have operated since 1999. The land bridge service permits cross-border movement of containers between Malaysia and Thailand ports by rail and as such, serves as an intermodal service involving land–sea transport as an alternative to transport service entirely by sea. The land bridge also involves partnerships with road transport operators, freight forwarders, and vessel operators that provide 28 weekly services to various points between Thailand and Malaysia. The services cover the routes between Penang Port at Butterworth with Surat Thani, Thung Song (Nakhon Si Thammarat), and Hat Yai (Songkhla).

The land bridge provides a third alternative to road and sea transports between Malaysia and Thailand, as well as an overland transit link from the Malaysian ports to GMS countries such as Cambodia, the Lao People's Democratic Republic (Lao PDR), and Viet Nam. Cargoes normally transported using this service include steel, chemical, gypsum boards, machinery, electronic products, and consumer goods.[7] The advantages include shorter travel time: 2.5 days (60 hours) by land bridge versus 5–7 days by sea from Port Klang to Bangkok, or 3–4 days by truck from Port Klang to Bangkok. The seamless border, cheaper freight rates, and guaranteed security is making Malaysia's land bridge an attractive option. In this service, the containers are sealed once for the entire trip and cargo clears both Malaysian and Thai Customs at the point of origin.

Air Linkages

Direct flights within provinces and states within EC1 are limited. There are several flights between Penang and Medan; but there are no direct flights from Penang to Songkhla. Air connectivity is mostly indirect and goes through the capitals—Bangkok, Kuala Lumpur, and Jakarta, as well as other domestic destinations. Several low-cost carriers (LCCs) operate in major international airports.

Air connectivity from North Sumatera. North Sumatera has eight airports—two of which serve international routes. These are Kualanamu International Airport (37.7 km from Medan) from which there are direct flights to Malaysia (Kuala Lumpur, Penang) and Thailand (Bangkok, Phuket), and Sisingamangaraja XII International

---

[7]   Information adapted from KTMB land bridge. Retrieved at https://www.ktmb.com.my/Kargo.html.

Airport (formerly Silangit International Airport) located near Lake Toba as the prominent tourism center in North Sumatera. This airport has direct flights to Kuala Lumpur, operated by AirAsia.

Air connectivity from Malaysia. Within the IMT-GT economic corridors, air connectivity of Malaysia with Sumatera is from Kuala Lumpur International Airport to airports in Medan, Banda Aceh, Padang, Pekanbaru, and Palembang. Connectivity with Southern Thailand is from Kuala Lumpur International Airport to airports in Krabi, Phuket, Hat Yai, and Surat Thani.

From Kedah (Sultan Abdul Halim Airport in Alor Setar and Langkawi International Airport) and Penang (Penang International Airport, Bayan Lepas), LCCs Firefly and Malindo service limited routes to Sumatera, focused on Banda Aceh and Medan. There are international airlines operating at domestic airports, including aircrafts from Indonesia, namely Sriwijaya Air, and Lion Air. Sriwijaya Air and Lion Air utilize Penang International Airport for their flights to Medan.

Air connectivity from Thailand. There are no direct flights from Hat Yai to EC1 provinces and states in Sumatera and Malaysia; airlines connect principally through Bangkok and Kuala Lumpur. Hat Yai International Airport is an important gateway for Moslems' pilgrimage to Mecca, Saudi Arabia. Hat Yai International Airport in Songkhla is ranked fifth among Thailand's major airports with five airlines operating domestic routes and three airlines operating international routes.

Cross-Border Infrastructure

There are three land BCPs between Malaysia and Southern Thailand:
* Padang Besar (Perlis)–Padang Besa (Songkhla)
* Bukit Kayu Hitam (Kedah)–Sadao (Songkhla)
* Durian Burong (Kedah)–Ban Prakop (Na Thawi, Songkhla)

The road from Penang to Songkhla goes through the Bukit Kayu Hitam–Sadao (Danok) checkpoint. An alternative route from Songkhla to Penang is via Durian Burung–Ban Prakop border checkpoint.

The BCPs are connected by good roads from the capital and with each other. Road infrastructure leading to the BCPs are in good condition, alternating between two to four lanes and are part of the national or federal or state roads systems (Table 2).

CIQ facilities at BCPs are in good condition and compliant with Customs standards. Service efficiency has been improving as CIQ facilities continue to adopt modern Customs practices, including automation, aligned with international standards. Malaysia reports a reduction of between 40%–50% in transaction errors, and a reduction in turnaround time from 4 to 2 days with the application of automation in Customs. Thailand reports that processing time at CIQ takes between 5–34 minutes depending on the procedure involved. Thailand and Malaysia have lined up several initiatives to further improve and expand the facilities at the BCPs to accommodate increasing trade volume and visitor flows. The operating hours at the border points are generally synchronized.

Table 2: Economic Corridor 1: Border Crossing Points: Condition of Infrastructure and Access

Malaysia		Thailand	
Distance/Access/Condition	Border Crossing Point	Border Crossing Point	Distance/Access/Condition
• 81 kilometers (km) to Padang Besa via R4054, R4, and 407 • 35 km from Kangar • Road infrastructure (two-way in Federal 79 and 7 and State R132 and 122) is in good condition	Padang Besar (Perlis)	Padang Besa (Songkhla)	• 1.7 km to Padang Besa (rail) • 67.4 km from Songkhla • Road infrastructure is in good condition via 414 and Route 1027
• 14.8 km to Sadao • 49 km from Alor Setar • Road infrastructure is in good condition with the E1 expressway route.	Bukit Kayu Hitam (Kedah)	Sadao (Songkhla)	• 18.9 km to Bukit Kayu Hitam via Route 4 and AH 2 • 69.1 km from Songkhla • Road infrastructure is in good condition via AH2 and Route 4
• 73 km to Ban Prakop • 65 km from Alor Setar • Road infrastructure to Durian Burung Customs, Immigration, and Quarantine is in good condition with two federal and state roadways	Durian Burung	Ban Prakop (Songkhla)	• 5.8 km to Durian Burung via Jl Durian Burung • 91.2 km to Songkhla • Road infrastructure is in good condition via Route 4113

Source: Study team.

In Thailand, the new Sadao Customs House will help facilitate the increasing volume of goods traded with Malaysia as well as the flow of visitors and tourists. The new facility at Sadao will include a new small- and medium-sized enterprises (SMEs) SEZ factory outlet and an inland container depot (ICD) near the border. The new Ban Prakop BCP is being developed as an alternative import–export channel and equipped with modern CIQ facilities. Other initiatives include: (i) upgrading of Padang Besa Customs house in Songkhla; (ii) expansion of Wang Prachan CIQ in Satun; (iii) upgrading of Betong Customs house in Yala; (iv) upgrading of Buketa Customs house and construction of the new Tak Bai CIQ in Narathiwat; (v) construction of the second bridge in Narathiwat (near the new bridge over the Kolok River); (vi) construction of the bridge over the Kolok River in Tak Bai, Narathiwat–Tumpat, Kelantan; (vii) construction of the second bridge over the Kolok River in Su-ngai Kolok, Narathiwat–Rantau Panjang, Kelantan; and (viii) the green cities initiatives in Songkhla (Hat Yai and Songkhla municipalities).

In Malaysia, Bukit Kayu Hitam in Kedah is an important growth node and catalyst in the border regions because its industrial parks have the status of SEZ and Special Border Economic Zone. There is efficient road connectivity from Bukit Kayu Hitam to Butterworth (Penang Port), Selangor (Port Klang), Kuala Lumpur, Johor Bahru, and Singapore. The bordering towns serve as strategic transit points with Southern Thailand through the North–South Expressway 1 and 2 (E1 and E2) in the peninsula linking with AH2 in Songkhla. Bukit Kayu Hitam is also an important tourist transit route accounting for 42% of Thai inbound tourists, and 40% of Malaysian outbound tourists. Bukit Kayu Hitam is being developed as a key logistic hub in the Northern Peninsula with a truck and ICD that can service containers from Southern Thailand. This truck depot is essential since Bukit Kayu Hitam BCP accounts for 73% ($5.0 billion) of Malaysia–Thailand's total trade worth an average of $7 billion a year for 2015–2018. The proposed truck depot will make Bukit Kayu Hitam the main transport backbone for manufacturers in Southern Thailand.

The Kedah Science Technology Park (KSTP)[8] Project under NCER Blueprint 2.0 (2016–2025) will be implemented in Bukit Kayu Hitam and has been accorded an SEZ status. Investment flows and the resulting business and employment opportunities created by KSTP will make Bukit Kayu Hitam as a growth node and catalyst center toward creating a conurbation in the Bukit Kayu Hitam–Kubang Pasu development.

Durian Burung is an alternative entry point to Kedah from Songkhla Province. It serves as a catalyst for its border regions and the Padang Terap district. The Kedah Rubber City (KRC) Project under the NCER Blueprint 2.0 (2018–2025) has the status of an SEZ. A priority initiative of the IMT-GT, the KRC Project establishes a rubber industry supply chain between Kedah and Songkhla (Southern Thailand), Tanjung Api-Api (South Sumatera), and Sei Mangkei SEZ (North Sumatera). Efficient road transport from Durian Burung to Penang Port via Federal Road and E1, has enabled manufacturers in the rubber cities to export their products to international markets via Penang Port. Although trade through Durian Burung accounts for less than 1% (average of $58 million a year) of Malaysia–Thailand total trade (average of $7 billion a year from 2015–2018), border trade at the Durian Burung–Ban Prakop border is expected to increase significantly on account of the KRC Project.

Penang Port will be an important trade gateway for manufacturers in the KRC Project to export their products to the international market due to the efficient connectivity from Durian Burung to Penang Port (Butterworth) via Federal Road and E1. Durian Burung provides an important alternative transport route to Alor Setar and Butterworth for which Penang Port is an important trade gateway for the rubber products manufacturers in the KRC.

Padang Besar is the main gateway to Perlis from Padang Besa in Songkhla. There is a rail link from Padang Besar to the Southern Line Track in Hat Yai and which continues to Bangkok, complementing connectivity by road. The Padang Besar Terminal on the rail land bridge is for containers shipped from Port Klang to Thailand. The rail route continues to Butterworth Container Depot and the NBCT in Penang. The Perlis Inland Port Project planned under the NCER Blueprint 2.0 (2016-2025) will further reinforce the importance of Padang Besar in the development of the Perlis–Satun/Songkhla cross-border trade. Thailand is planning to construct a new bridge connecting Satun and Perlis along the coasts of with the distance of appropriately 14 km. Padang Besar is also the second most important transport route for visitors accounting for 19% of inbound visitors from Thailand and 18% of outbound visitors from Malaysia.

The CIQ at Padang Besa/Padang Besar are co-located in the station at Padang Besar. It is Malaysia's only juxtaposed BCP where CIQ for both Malaysia and Thailand are located inside the station in the Malaysian territory. Passengers disembarking at Padang Besar can therefore go through the CIQ processes in one location. The facilities for each country operate from separate counters inside the station at the platform level. Padang Besar also has a freight yard that serves as a dry port for the northern part of Malaysia and other parts of the IMT-GT.

---

[8]   KSTP consists of seven clusters, namely: agro-science, advanced materials, information and communication technology (ICT), halal science, research and development and manufacturing, green technology, and biotechnology.

Cross-Border Trade

Cross-border trade in Thailand. Cross-border trade at Thailand's BCP with Malaysia increased moderately at an average of 3% from 2015–2018. In 2018, the trade flows at the Thai–Malaysian border in Songkhla amounted to $17.6 million or about 40.8% of total Thailand's total border trade. Total trade is split almost evenly between exports and imports and has remained in this stable pattern since 2014 (Table 3). Overall, Thailand enjoys has enjoyed a border trade surplus over Malaysia during 2015–2018 although this has been diminishing. In 2018 the surplus was valued at over $ 480 million at the border in Songkhla.

Table 3: Economic Corridor 1: Export–Import Value at Thai–Malaysian Border in Songkhla

Province	Trade value ($ million)					Compounded Annual Growth Rate (%)
	2014	2015	2016	2017	2018	
Songkhla	15.7	15.0	15.3	17.3	17.6	3.0
Export	8.5	7.7	7.9	9.6	9.0	1.6
Import	7.2	73	7.5	7.7	8.6	4.5

Source: Compiled by the study team from Department of Foreign Trade, Bank of Thailand, 2019. Retrieved from https://www.bot.or.th/App/BTWS_STAT/statistics/ReportPage.aspx?reportID=123&language=th.

About two-thirds of total trade at the border in Songkhla goes through Sadao Customs House, followed by Padang Besa with a share of one-third. The adjacent borders in Malaysia at Bukit Kayu Hitam and Padar Besar (Perlis) traces this pattern with equally significant shares in the country's total border trade. The share of Ban Prakop BCP is relatively small.

Thailand's exports to Malaysia at Sadao and Padang Besa Customs Houses consist mainly of rubber and rubber products and machine and machine parts; while imports consist of data storage devices, television, and machine parts. Trade going through Ban Prakop consists mainly of food products.

Cross-border trade in Malaysia. Cross-border trade at Malaysia's BCP with Thailand increased minimally at an average of 0.6% during 2015–2018 due to the overall regional economic slowdown that negatively impacted Malaysia's trade volume with Thailand. During this period the total cross-border trade through all Malaysia-Thailand BCPs averaged $6.5 billion a year. Total cross-border exports to Thailand were around$2.8 billion a year and imports from Thailand were around $3.7 billion a year for 2015–2018. Malaysia recorded a trade deficit with Thailand during this period (Table 4).

Table 4: Economic Corridor 1: Export–Import Value at Thai–Malaysian Border in Kedah and Perlis, 2015–2018 ($ million)

Border Crossing Point/Customs, Immigration, Quarantine	2015	2016	2017	2018	Average (2015–2018)	Average Share to All Malaysia–Thai Border Crossing Points Trade (2015–2018), %	Compounded Annual Growth Rate (2015–2018) %
KEDAH	**4,890**	**4,744**	**4,779**	**4,882**	**4,824**	**74**	**(0.1)**
Export	1,904	1,895	1,986	2,101	1,971	68	3.3
Import	2,986	2,849	2,793	2,781	2,852	78	(2.4)
Bukit Kayu Hitam	4,824	4,669	4,729	4,840	4,765	73	0.1
Export	1,898	1,891	1,974	2,095	1,964	68	3.3
Import	2,926	2,778	2,755	2,745	2,801	77	(2.1)
Durian Burung	66	75	51	42	58	1	(14.0)
Export	6	5	12	6	7	0	2.4
Import	60	71	39	36	51	1	(15.9)
PERLIS [1]	**1,400**	**1,445**	**1,549**	**1,507**	**1,475**	**23**	**2.5**
Export (road and rail mode)	797	850	816	790	813	28	(0.3)
Import	603	594	733	716	662	18	5.9
Padang Besar (road mode)	1,338	1,309	1,408	1,418	1,368	21	1.9
Export	739	724	684	703	712	25	(1.7)
Import	599	586	724	714	656	18	6.1
Padang Besar (rail mode)	6	12	14	7	10	0	3.1
Export	3	4	5	5	4	0	25.0
Import	4	8	9	2	6	0	(23.0)
Total KEDAH and PERLIS	**6,290**	**6,189**	**6,328**	**6,388**	**6,299**	**96**	**–**
All Malaysian–Thai Border Crossing Points	**6,515**	**6,420**	**6,574**	**6,620**	**6,532**	**–**	**0.5**
Export	2,792	2,848	2,904	2,985	2,882	–	2.3
Import	3,723	3,572	3,670	3,634	3,650	–	(0.8)

– = not available, ( ) = negative.
Note: [1] Perlis trade, including Wang Kelian border crossing point trade.
Source: Compiled by the study team from the trade data of Royal Malaysia Customs Department, 2019.

Among the BCPs, Bukit Kayu Hitam (Kedah) is the main trade gateway to Thailand. Bukit Kayu Hitam BCP accounted for 73% of the BCP's total trade with Thailand, followed by Padang Besar (Perlis) BCP accounting for 21%. The share of Durian Burung (Kedah) adjacent to Ban Prakop is relatively small.

Malaysia's exports to Thailand at BCPs in Bukit Kayu Hitam, Durian Burung, and Padang Besar consist mainly of animal and animal products, chemical and allied industrial products, foodstuffs, machinery and electrical products, metals, rubber and plastics, textiles, transportation products, and vegetable products.

Major imports from Thailand comprise mainly of animal and animal products, chemical and allied industrial products, foodstuffs, machinery and electrical products, metals, mineral products, rubber and plastics, stone and glass products, transportation products, vegetable products, and wood and wood products

North Sumatera's trade with Malaysia. Malaysia is among North Sumatera's top 10 export markets, ranking sixth after the PRC, the United States, India, Japan, and the Netherlands. For imports, Malaysia is the third highest country of origin for North Sumatera's imports after the PRC and Singapore.

The share of North Sumatera's total trade with Malaysia has been relatively small—around 6.8% in 2014, sliding down to 4.5% in 2018 (Table 5).

Table 5: Economic Corridor 1: North Sumatera's Trade with Malaysia, 2007, 2011, 2014–2018
('000 ton)

Item	2014	2015	2016	2017	2018	Average 2014–2018	Compounded Annual Growth Rate 2014–2018 (%)
Foreign Trade	16,479	15,862	15,207	16,021	16,861	16,086	0.6
Exports	9,088	9,009	8,387	8,982	9,646	9,022	1.5
Imports	7,391	6,854	6,819	7,038	7,215	7,064	(0.6)
Trade w/ Malaysia	1,124	842	766	721	755	842	(9.5)
Exports	363	227	235	162	221	242	(11.6)
Imports	761	615	531	559	534	600	(8.5)
Share of Malaysia (%)	6.8	5.3	5.0	4.5	4.5	5.2	
Exports	4.0	2.5	2.8	1.8	2.3	2.7	
Imports	10.3	9.0	7.8	7.9	7.4	8.5	

( ) = negative.
Source: Processed by the study team from various publications of BPS-Statistics Indonesia.

An average 88% of North Sumatera's exports, consisting mostly of rubber and palm oil, were shipped through Belawan Port during 2014–2018, compared to Kuala Tanjung's share of 9.2%. Kuala Tanjung is currently being developed as the main international hub port to complement Belawan. Kuala Tanjung Port's expanded capacity of 60 million twenty-foot equivalent units (TEUs) will provide North Sumatera with more opportunities to diversify its exports and transshipments to Malaysia to include mineral fuels, oil products, chemicals, and fertilizers among others.

North Sumatera's trade with Thailand. Exports from North Sumatera to Thailand has been relatively small, contributing less than 1% to North Sumatera's trade volume in 2014–2018; the share of imports was bigger at 3.2% during the same period. The top three exports to Thailand in 2018 consisted of fruits and nuts; alcohols, phenols, phenol-alcohols; and soap. Despite the small volume, there is an opportunity to explore further trade with Southern Thailand in halal products.

Reconfiguration of Economic Corridor 1

The reconfiguration of EC1 takes into account the countries' current development plans, the role of existing nodes, and the proposed addition of new provinces and nodes to generate greater synergy within the corridor. The proposed corridor extensions for EC1 were influenced by the anticipation of added benefits, including supply chain diversity, logistics efficiency, trade and market expansion, investment attraction, tourism promotion, and increased economic activities with neighboring countries, both within and outside the IMT-GT.

Based on the additional provinces and nodes described below, the reconfigured **EC1 has been renamed Southern Thailand–Northern Malaysia–North Sumatera Economic Corridor** (Map 3).

Indonesia

Indonesia's strategy for EC1 aligns with the development of Sumatera Island that focuses on the development of downstream products for agriculture, fisheries, and mining-based industries and catalyzing export-oriented growth centers to create increased value-added. This strategy leverages on the ongoing construction of the Trans-Sumatera Toll Road, the planned expansion of ports and airports, and the establishment of industrial parks and SEZs. Targeted commodities (cacao, coconut, palm oil, rubber, coffee, pepper, nutmeg, sugarcane, gold, tin, petroleum, natural gas, coal, capture fisheries, and aquaculture) will be processed in industrial zones strategically located near the ports.

To complement the roles of Belawan Port and Medan under the existing configuration, three additional nodes in North Sumatera were added in the new configuration:

- Kuala Tanjung Port and industrial zone
- Sibolga Port and Sibolga City
- Lake Toba

Kuala Tanjung Port is being developed as the new international hub port that will provide the additional capacity to trade in more diversified products and markets. With its capacity of 600,000 TEUs per year, and facilities for handing liquid bulk (CPO), dry bulk, container, and general cargo, the port can strengthen Sumatera's position as a global maritime gateway, thus boosting the economy not only of North Sumatera but also of surrounding provinces. The port will strengthen Sumatera's position as a global maritime gateway and boost the economy of North Sumatera and surrounding provinces. The port will benefit from its proximity to the Sei Mangkei SEZ with its vast hinterland of palm oil plantations.

Sibolga Port is emerging as an important port in the western part of North Sumatera for the shipment of liquid bulk (CPO). Sibolga Port can accommodate four large ships with a maximum size of 6,000 GT and has become one of the important unloading ports for North Sumatera's imports. In 2017, it became the third biggest unloading port after Belawan and Kuala Tanjung. Sibolga port is now serving container cargo and passengers and will also serve liquid bulk to accommodate the distribution of CPO.

Sibolga City is an important node in the Trans-Sumatera Toll Road under the Prapat–Taruntung–Sibolga segment. Covering about 101 km, the route will connect Sibolga with Medan and Kuala Tanjung through Tebingtinggi. Under the Concept and Direction of Provincial Regional Policy in Infrastructure Development for Sumatera Island 2015, there is a plan to develop the Sibolga–Padang–Bengkulu Strategic Development Area

**Map 3: Southern Thailand–Northern Malaysia–North Sumatera Economic Corridor
(Reconfigured Economic Corridor 1)**

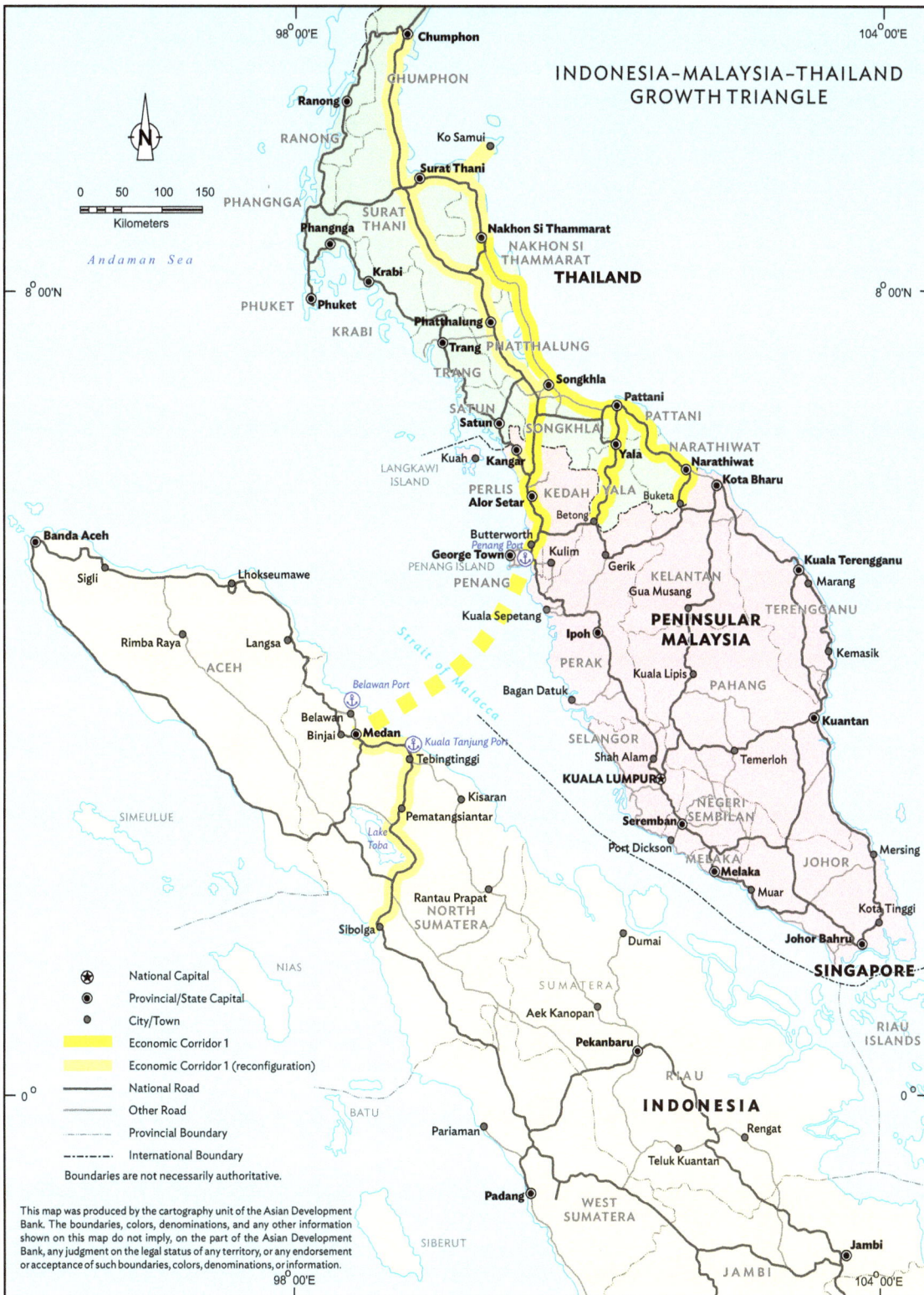

INDONESIA–MALAYSIA–THAILAND
GROWTH TRIANGLE

THAILAND

PENINSULAR
MALAYSIA

KUALA LUMPUR

SINGAPORE

INDONESIA

NORTH
SUMATERA

WEST
SUMATERA

Andaman Sea

Strait of Malacca

	National Capital
	Provincial/State Capital
	City/Town
	Economic Corridor 1
	Economic Corridor 1 (reconfiguration)
	National Road
	Other Road
	Provincial Boundary
	International Boundary

Boundaries are not necessarily authoritative.

This map was produced by the cartography unit of the Asian Development
Bank. The boundaries, colors, denominations, and any other information
shown on this map do not imply, on the part of the Asian Development
Bank, any judgment on the legal status of any territory, or any endorsement
or acceptance of such boundaries, colors, denominations, or information.

Source: Asian Development Bank.

as a center for fishery and tourism that will connect to other development areas: Sibolga-Tebingtinggi (on the east coast near Kuala Tanjung Port), Padang–Pekanbaru, and Bengkulu–Palembang. The plan intends to connect Sibolga–Padang–Bengkulu to growth and commercial areas on the east coast of Sumatera. The document states that subregional economic cooperation under IMT-GT would support Sumatera as an Indonesian gateway for international trade.

Lake Toba has one of the most comprehensive tourism potentials in Indonesia. Its natural environment is pristine and has a distinctive and unique culture, which has made it one of the main tourist attractions in Indonesia. Located in North Sumatera, about 176 km from Medan City, Lake Toba has contributed around 65% of the total tourist visitors to the province. The Government of Indonesia has designated Lake Toba as one of the 10 "New Bali" sites in the country. Lake Toba will be developed as part of the National Strategic Tourism Zone under the RPJMN 2020–2024.

Malaysia

Malaysia's strategy in EC1 centers on Penang Port as the country's second premier port and key maritime gateway for Thailand and North Sumatera exports to international markets. No additional nodes are proposed in EC1, but major developments in the border areas in Bukit Kayu Hitam, Durian Burung, and Padang Besar will likely have significant impact on the economic activities in the corridor in the near to medium term.

Malaysia's focus on the role of Kedah and Perlis at the border with Southern Thailand is linked to planned developments for these two states under the NCER Blueprint 2.0 (2016–2025). Growth nodes have been added in EC2 to support development in these two states: (i) the Chuping Valley Industrial Area (Perlis), (ii) Perlis Inland Port (Perlis), (iii) Batu Kawan Development Project (Penang), (iv) Greater Kamunting Conurbation (Perak), and (iv) Baling–Pengkalan Hulu–Betong Border Zone (Kedah/Perak).

These important developments at the Malaysia–Thailand border will further enhance the role of border nodes in EC1.

- Bukit Kayu Hitam is being developed as a key logistic hub in the northern peninsula with a truck and ICD that can service containers from Southern Thailand. A railway spur line from Bukit Kayu Hitam to Arau Railway Station linking to Penang is being planned to provide a direct rail cargo route that will significantly benefit exporters from Southern Thailand in terms of improved efficiency and lower transportation cost.

- Durian Burung will play an increasingly important role in supporting rubber supply chains between Malaysia and Thailand under the Rubber Cities initiative. Durian Burung's road connectivity with Penang Port can facilitate the transport of rubber products exports which are projected to increase as rubber value chains between the two countries develop and mature under the IMT-GT Rubber Cities initiative.

- Padang Besar is anticipated to take on more traffic with several developments being planned by Thailand to improve connectivity between Satun, Surat Thani, and Songkhla. These developments will take advantage of Padang Besar's good road connectivity with Port Klang and Penang Port, as well as efficient rail connectivity with Hat Yai–Bangkok.

- The Malaysia–Thailand land bridge that will link the Port of Songkhla and Penang Port will catalyze rapid growth in Kedah and facilitate faster, easier, and more efficient movement of cargoes between Asia, Europe, and the Middle East. The railway spur line from the Port of Songkhla to Hat Yai will create a land bridge for east–west trade, cutting across the peninsula. The land bridge which spans 226 km, will take about 4 hours by rail or road compared to that by ship of about 2 days via the Strait of Malacca.

Thailand

Thailand's approach to EC1 is based on the Southern Economic Corridor (SEC) development strategy. The SEC aims to integrate production networks for rubber and rubber products (rubber latex, rubber wood, seafood, and halal food) with supply chains along EC1 and the proposed EC6, through multimodal connectivity and industrial clusters (industrial parks, SEZs). The SEC also focuses on creating an inland tourism network that will connect tourist destinations along the Gulf of Thailand (EC1) with destinations along the Andaman Sea (EC5). A land bridge linking provinces in the two coastal areas will support the development of new inland tourist destinations, and other high-potential community attractions to create an inland tourism network. This would involve linking the provinces of Phuket, Phangnga, Krabi in EC5, with the provinces of Surat Thani (Ko Samui, Ko Pha-ngan, Ko Toa), Chumphon, and Nakhon Si Thammarat (Sichon and Khanom beaches) in EC1. Linking EC1 with EC5 will position EC1 as a world-class tourist destination. Tourists in EC1 provinces can also travel from Songkhla to the EC6 provinces of Pattani, Yala, Narathiwat, and onwards to Malaysia. Phangnga's (EC1) location will serve as a link to tourism routes in EC5 to EC2 (Krabi, Trang, and Satun). EC1 and EC5 focus on ecotourism, i.e., promoting tourism in parallel with environmental and natural resources conservation to preserve and enhance the quality of tourist destinations. Tourism along the Andaman Sea will promote health-related tourism and cruise tourism.

The five sectors of interest to Thailand in EC1 are: (i) agriculture and agro-based industry, (ii) tourism, (iii) transport, (iv) trade and investment, and (v) halal products and services. Thailand's development approach to EC1 consists of the following strategies:

(i)   linking tourist destinations in the south of Thailand by connecting the tourism routes along the Gulf of Thailand (EC1) with Andaman Sea (EC5) (e.g., beaches, islands, and hinterland tourism between Chumphon, Ranong, Surat Thani, Phangnga, Phuket, and Krabi; connecting tourism activities at Phangnga with the EC2;

(ii) integrating provincial with regional production networks for rubber latex, rubber wood, seafood, and halal food supply chains along the EC1 and EC6; and

(iii) upgrading transportation infrastructure and utilizing multimodal connectivity (roads, rails, seaports, and airports) to link CIQs, SEZs, ICDs, and relevant facilities to accommodate investment, trade, and tourism along the EC 1 and between the EC1, EC2, EC5, and EC6.

Three provinces in Thailand were added in the reconfigured EC1:

*   Chumphon
*   Surat Thani
*   Phatthalung

These three provinces, together with the two existing provinces Songkhla and Nakhon Si Thammarat, will form a collective base for agriculture production and agro-processing centers in Southern Thailand. Ko Samui (Surat Thani) and Songkhla Port (Songkhla) were also included as tourism and maritime gateway nodes, respectively, in EC1. The capitals of the provinces, as commercial and growth centers, were included as additional nodes.

Chumphon and Surat Thani, together with Songkhla are the collective areas of agricultural production for processing and distribution to the domestic market as well as for exports through the Thailand–Malaysia borders, or through Songklha Port and Laem Chabang Ports headed for the PRC and other international destinations. Most processing industries in Chumphon, Surat Thani, and Songkhla are for seafood, rubber, and rubber wood. Chumphon and Surat Thani were included in EC1 to enhance the agriculture production-distribution chain in the corridor with its link to Songkhla.

Apart from being major agricultural producers, Chumphon and Surat Thani are also popular tourist destinations. Ko Samui in Surat Thani is one of the most outstanding tourist destinations in EC1 with a wide range of attractions and is being developed to become a world destination for yacht and cruise tourism. The attractions include Rajjaprabha Dam (Surat Thani), Khao Luang Natural Park, (Nakhon Si Thammarat), as well as other high-potential community attractions in Phuket, Phangnga, and Krabi. Ko Samui accommodates and channels tourists to destinations in the south of Thailand.

Chumphon city is the gateway to Thailand's southern provinces. It is home to processing plants of major agricultural products in the south such as palm oil, rubber, and fruits. It connects marine tourism with Surat Thani both by land and by sea. Ferries transporting tourists from Chumphon to Ko Samui (Surat Thani) operate daily. Tourist destinations can be connected via land from Chumphon to Surat Thani, Ranong, Phangnga, Phuket, and Krabi.

Surat Thani is both a tourism and commercial center and offers world-class destinations in its pristine islands of Ko Samui, Ko Pha-ngan, and Ko Toa. Nakhon Si Thammarat connects Surat Thani and Songkhla and will support the inland tourism network in EC1. Ko Samui, an island off the coast of Surat Thani, is an area with a heavy concentration of tourists and has a role in attracting and channeling tourists to other tourist destinations in Southern Thailand. This role is key to supporting the development of an inland tourism network that will eventually connect tourist destinations in EC1 (Surat Thani and Nakhon Si Thammarat along the Gulf of Thailand) with destinations in EC5 (Phangnga, Phuket, and Krabi, along the Andaman Sea).

Phatthalung's main economic activities are rice and rubber cultivation, livestock, fishery. Narathiwat has been the focus of halal, rubber, and rubber wood industry activities and linked to SBEZ cluster development in the province.

Songkha Port was added as a node in the province of Songkhla. The route of EC1 in Thailand serves primarily the transport of agricultural products from plantation to factories and to the domestic and export markets. Songkhla Port is an important node for transporting goods between the south and the central plains of Thailand. Songkhla Port also serves as an important maritime gateway to the Thai–Malaysian border checkpoint headed to Penang Port in Malaysia, or to Laem Chabang Port in Chonburi Province headed to the GMS.

To further expand capacity and increase the efficiency of the port, the Songkhla 2 Port Project is being planned to be located at the Chana District, Songkhla Province, about 40 km south of the existing port. The plan includes developing the route providing maritime transport services from Laem Chabang/Sriracha Port to Songkhla Port to reduce congestion in transporting goods from the south to the Bangkok Metropolitan Region. The route would also be an alternative for transporting and distributing goods from the south to other regions in the country and to the GMS countries. The existing and additional provinces/states and nodes in the reconfigured EC1 are summarized in Table 6.

Table 6: Economic Corridor 1: Existing and Additional Provinces and Nodes, by Type

Province/State	Node	CAP	COM	BCP	MGP	TOUR
INDONESIA						
North Sumatera	Belawan Port				✓	
	Medan	✓				
	Kuala Tanjung Port*		✓		✓	
	Sibolga*		✓		✓	
	Lake Toba*					✓
MALAYSIA						
Penang	Penang Port					
	• Butterworth		✓		✓	✓
	• George Town					
Kedah	Bukit Kayu Hitam		✓	✓		✓
	Durian Burung		✓	✓		
	Alor Setar	✓				
Perlis	Padang Besar		✓	✓		✓
	Kangar*	✓				
THAILAND						
Songkhla	Songkhla	✓				
	Songkhla Port*				✓	
	Hat Yai		✓			
	Sadao			✓		
	Padang Besa			✓		
	Ban Prakop			✓		
Nakhon Si Thammarat	Nakhon Si Thammarat	✓				
Chumphon*	Chumphon*	✓				
Surat Thani*	Surat Thani *	✓	✓			
	Ko Samui*					✓
Phatthalung*	Phatthalung City*	✓				
Pattani**	Pattani City	✓				
Yala**	Yala City	✓				
Narathiwat**	Narathiwat City	✓	✓			

BCP = border crossing point, CAP = capital, COM = commercial, MGP = maritime gateway port, TOUR = tourism.
Notes:
* denotes additional provinces and nodes.
** Pattani, Yala, and Narathiwat were part of the extended EC1 but these provinces have been integrated with the proposed route for EC6 to link with the eastern part of Malaysia.
Source: Study team.

Findings and Recommendations

Roads connecting existing corridor nodes are in good condition. Roads connecting the provinces and states of Malaysia and Thailand in EC1 are in good condition, efficient, and safe. Most roads are part of national, federal, or state road systems or expressways. In general, overland border links by road are adequate.

Rail services between Su-ngai Kolok and Pasir Mas need to be revived. Roads are complemented by rail links between Hat Yai and Padang Besa Terminal in Songkhla. However, there is a critical missing rail link that must be reestablished between Su-ngai Kolok (2 km) in Narathiwat and Pasir Mas (18 km) in Kelantan as part of the proposed route for EC6.

There are no cross-border trains between Malaysia and Thailand although there is a juxtaposed CIQ at Padang Besar that facilitates movement of people and cargo. SRT's international express is no longer serving the route up to Butterworth. Malaysia's KTM trains are also no longer servicing the route to Hat Yai. All passengers have to disembark at Padang Besar for customs and immigration before boarding the train to Hat Yai. The same is true for passengers coming from Hat Yai bound for Malaysia. The juxtaposed CIQ at Padang Besar facilitates the movement of people and cargo. The CIQ at Padang Besa and Padang Besar are co-located in the station at Padang Besar. It is Malaysia's only juxtaposed BCP where CIQ for both Malaysia and Thailand are located inside the station located in the Malaysian territory.

There is no maritime connectivity between Penang and Belawan at present. However, the development of Kuala Tanjung Port as an alternative hub port with increased capacity to handle bigger cargo volumes is envisaged to boost trade with Penang. Kuala Tanjung will eventually replace the role of Belawan Port, which will become an interisland domestic port by 2027. At the same time, Penang Port as the main gateway for shippers in the northern states of Malaysia and the southern provinces of Thailand, would need to be revitalized to handle the increasing volume of container traffic especially with planned developments of industrial parks and conurbation areas under NCER's Blueprint 2.0. Plans are underway to expand the NBCT to increase its capacity for container handling. Shipping services will have to eventually evolve between Penang and Kuala Tanjung.

North Sumatera's declining trade with Malaysia suggests the need for diversification of traded products aligned with the planned development of new ports. Although Malaysia is an important trading partner of Sumatera, its share to North Sumatera's total trade is relatively small. This trend could be explained by the similarity in the major commodities produced by North Sumatera and Malaysia, namely rubber and palm oil. These commodities are among North Sumatera's major exports to Malaysia shipped at Belawan Port which is a feeder port. The development of Kuala Tanjung Port as the main international hub will provide an opportunity to diversify North Sumatera's export products to Malaysia to include mineral fuel, oil products, chemicals, and fertilizers.

Economic Corridor 2. The Strait of Malacca Economic Corridor

Overview

The Strait of Malacca Economic Corridor (EC2) is a coastal corridor connecting Thailand's southern provinces of Trang and Satun with the Malaysia's states of Perlis, and on to Port Klang, Penang, and Melaka along the western coast. The maritime gateways in EC2 under the existing configuration are Tammalang Port (Satun), Port Klang (Selangor), Penang Port (Penang), and Tanjung Bruas Port (Melaka) (Map 4). The approach to corridor connectivity is multimodal, with land and coastal linkages.

Due to the proximity of this corridor to Sumatera along its eastern coast, there is considerable potential for linking it to Indonesia. This will offer opportunities for value chain linkages with the economic and industrial zones located near Sumatera's eastern coasts along the Strait of Malacca. The expanded corridor can also serve as a halal food hub, since several food terminals and centers are being planned along the corridor.

Status of Physical Connectivity

The main transport route for EC2 starts in Trang Province (Route 404/416) going to the border at Wang Prachan in Satun. From Wang Prachan, one route goes to Tammalang Port, which connects by land to Penang Port, and another goes to Padang Besa in Sadao across the border at Padang Besar in Perlis. An alternative route from Wang Prachan goes to Wang Kelian, also in Perlis. A third entry point from Thailand is at Betong, Yala at the border of Pengkalan Hulu in Perak. The BCPs in EC2 are

- Wang Prachan (Satun)–Wang Kelian (Perlis)
- Padang Besa (Songkhla)–Padang Besar (Perlis)
- Betong (Yala)–Pengkalan Hulu (Perak)

Road Connectivity

In Thailand, the land route for this corridor traverses three districts: (i) Trang Mueang District–Satun Mueang District, (ii) Satun Mueang District–Wangprachan Customs Checkpoint, and (iii) Satun Mueang District–Tammalang Port. The roads linking the three districts are in good condition. The road surface is smooth in the entire section. The route is safe, equipped with traffic signs, traffic lines, complete and undamaged safety equipment, curved guide posts, and complete guard rail in good condition (Table 7).

Table 7: Economic Corridor 2: Start and End Points in Thailand

Start Point	End Point	Route	Distance (kilometer)	Traffic Lanes	Road Classification
Trang	Satun	404/416	139	2/4	I
Satun	Wang Prachan Border	406/4184	39	2/4	I
Satun	Tammalang Port	406	14	2/4	I

Source: Study team.

Map 4: Strait of Malacca Economic Corridor
(Economic Corridor 2)

INDONESIA–MALAYSIA–THAILAND GROWTH TRIANGLE

98°00'E

104°00'E

Chumphon

CHUMPHON

Ranong

RANONG

Andaman Sea

Surat Thani

SURAT THANI

PHANGNGA

Phangnga

Nakhon Si Thammarat

NAKHON SI THAMMARAT

Krabi

THAILAND

Phuket

8°00'N

PHUKET

KRABI

Phatthalung

Trang

PHATTHALUNG

Kantang Port

TRANG

8°00'N

Songkhla

SATUN

Pattani

Satun

Wang Prachan

SONGKHLA

TARUTAO ISLAND

Padang Besar

PATTANI

Wang Kelian

Yala

NARATHIWAT

Kuah

Kangar

YALA

Narathiwat

LANGKAWI ISLAND

PERLIS

KEDAH

YALA

Kota Bharu

Alor Setar

Pengkalan Hulu

Butterworth

Penang Port

George Town

Kulim

Kuala Terengganu

Banda Aceh

PENANG ISLAND

Gerik

KELANTAN

Marang

Sigli

PENANG

Gua Musang

TERENGGANU

Lhokseumawe

Kuala Sepetang

Kemasik

Rimba Raya

Langsa

Ipoh

PENINSULAR MALAYSIA

ACEH

PERAK

PAHANG

Belawan

Kuala Lipis

Bagan Datuk

Binjai

Medan

Kuantan

Tebingtinggi

SELANGOR

Shah Alam

Temerloh

Kisaran

Strait of Malacca

Pematangsiantar

KUALA LUMPUR

Lake Toba

Port Klang

NEGERI SEMBILAN

SIMEULUE

Seremban

JOHOR

Mersing

Port Dickson

MELAKA

Rantau Prapat

NORTH SUMATERA

Melaka

Muar

Sibolga

Kota Tinggi

NIAS

Dumai

Johor Bahru

SINGAPORE

RIAU ISLANDS

SUMATERA

Aek Kanopan

BATU

Pekanbaru

RIAU

0°

INDONESIA

0°

Pariaman

Rengat

Teluk Kuantan

Padang

WEST SUMATERA

SIBERUT

Jambi

JAMBI

98°00'E

104°00'E

Legend:

⊛ National Capital
◉ Provincial/State Capital
● City/Town
— Economic Corridor 2
— National Road
— Other Road
— Provincial Boundary
- - - International Boundary
Boundaries are not necessarily authoritative.

0   50   100   150
Kilometers

N

This map was produced by the cartography unit of the Asian Development Bank. The boundaries, colors, denominations, and any other information shown on this map do not imply, on the part of the Asian Development Bank, any judgment on the legal status of any territory, or any endorsement or acceptance of such boundaries, colors, denominations, or information.

Source: Asian Development Bank.

From Satun, EC2 continues in Malaysia through the CIQ at Wang Kelian in Perlis (bordering Wang Prachan in Satun). Wang Kelian (Perlis) is the main border entrance from the Satun Province to Perlis and other states in the peninsula. The distance from Wang Kelian (Perlis) to Tanjung Bruas Port is 717 km via Kangar, Penang Port (Butterworth) and Port Klang (Selangor). Access to Wang Kelian is through State Road R15. Both federal and state roads have two traffic lanes (one in each direction). Wang Kelian CIQ has good road connectivity to Butterworth and George Town (Penang) through Federal Road and Expressway E1. Penang Port in Butterworth and George Town are international gateways and links to Medan under EC1. The land routes in Malaysia connecting Perlis to Melaka along the coastal stretch of the Strait of Malacca are in good condition as they are part of national or federal/state roads systems (Table 8).

Table 8: Economic Corridor 2: Start and End Points in Malaysia
(Wang Kelian–Tanjung Bruas)

Start Point	End Point	Route	Distance (kilometer)	Traffic Lanes	Road Class
Wang Kelian Checkpoint (Perlis)	Kangar, Perlis	R15, R121, 7	38	2	Federal and state road
Kangar, Perlis	Penang Port, Butterworth	7, E1/AH2	143	2–4	Federal road and expressway
Penang Port, Butterworth	Port Klang, Selangor	E15, P191, E1/AH2, 2	366	4	Expressway
Port Klang, Selangor	Tanjung Bruas Port	181, E5, E1 and E2/ AH2, 19, M9, 5	170	2–4	Federal, state road, and expressway

Source: Study team.

From Yala province, EC2 continues in Malaysia through the CIQ at Pengkalan Hulu in Perak (bordering Betong in Yala). Access to Pengkalan Hulu is through Federal Road 77 (from Penang) and 1157 (from Ipoh). Pengkalan Hulu CIQS has good road connectivity to Penang Port (Butterworth) and Port Klang through Federal Road and Expressway E1. The distance from Pengkalan Hulu to Tanjung Bruas Port is 631 km via Penang Port (Butterworth), Ipoh and Port Klang (Selangor) (Table 9).

Table 9: Economic Corridor 2: Start and End Points in Malaysia
(Pengkalan Hulu–Tanjung Bruas)

Start Point	End Point	Route	Distance (kilometer)	Traffic Lanes	Road Class
Pengkalan Hulu Border Checkpoint, Perak	Penang Port, Butterworth	77, 76, 67,4,E15,1	95	2–4	Federal and state road; expressway
Penang Port, Butterworth	Port Klang, Selangor	E15, P191, E1/AH2, 2	366	4	Federal and state road; expressway
Port Klang, Selangor	Tanjung Bruas Port, Melaka	181, E5, E1 and E2/AH2, 19, M9, 5	170	2–4	Federal, state road, and expressway

Source: Compiled by authors.

Rail Connectivity

Road connectivity is complemented by rail links between Port Klang, Perak, and Songkhla as well as a land bridge from Port Klang extending all the way to Hat Yai. The construction of a new bridge connecting Satun and Perlis will further enhance land connectivity along the Andaman Sea coast from Tammalang in Satun to Perlis in Malaysia by shortening the trip from Bangkok to Padang Besar/Bukit Kayu Hitam and Kedah and will stimulate economic activities in the local community.

Within Thailand, rail connectivity along EC2 is limited. There is rail connectivity between Chumphon and Satun but long-distance rail service to/from Trang Station is not frequent.

In Malaysia, the KTMB railway track in EC2 to the south begins at Kamunting (Perak) and ends at Pulau Sebang (Melaka). The distance of the railway line between Kamunting and Pulau Sebang is 421 km. For secondary ports in EC2, there is no railway spur line connecting Lumut Port and Tanjung Bruas Port with the KTMB trunk railway line. There is a proposal to create a spur line from Ipoh Cargo Terminal to Lumut Port and Pulau Sebang Railway Station to Tanjung Bruas Port. Both ports are only accessible by federal roads and the expressway. This is a constraint faced by the rail connectivity between urban and hinterland areas—the problem of the last mile connectivity. Port Klang has a rail link to KL Sentral through Port Klang Terminal depots. The connection between the EC2's rail link with Port Klang makes the country's premier port the main trade gateway for manufacturers in the southern Perak, Selangor, and Melaka.

Port-to-Port Connectivity

The key maritime gateway ports in EC2 are: Tammalang Port (Satun), Kantang Port (Trang), Port Klang (Selangor), Penang Port (Penang), Tanjung Bruas Port (Melaka), and Lumut Port. These ports are accessible by good roads from urban and commercial centers in the corridor.

Thailand

Tammalang Port (Satun). The main port in Thailand is Tammalang Port, which is currently a pier for cruises to Malaysia. It provides ferry service to Langkawi Island in Kedah, generally for a one-day tour. Other tourism routes include Tammlang–Lipe, and Tammalang–Tarutao Islands. There is high-potential to initiate new tourist routes between Tammalang and Belawan. Presently, no containerized goods go through this port. The route from Tammalang Port to Penang Port covers 301 km, using Highways 406 and 4184 in Thailand (49.2 km) and AH2 in Malaysia (covering 251.8 km). The route has two traffic lanes with alternating four traffic lanes. The road surface is in good condition.

Kantang Port (Trang). Goods transported via Kantang Port (Trang) include rubber, rib smoked sheet, and processed rubber wood, which are shipped to Penang Port headed to farther destinations. The port however can accommodate only small vessels with its limited depth of 4–6 meters. Connectivity of Kantang Port by rail to the Thung Song Cargo Distribution Center—the logistic hub of Nakhon Si Thammarat (EC1) and Southern Thailand—will enhance the transport route for goods in Southern Thailand. In Nakhon Si Thammarat, Thung Song Station is the junction for the southern main line (Bangkok–Padang Besa–Su-ngai Kolok) and the southern branch line to Trang Province and Kantang Port. Thung Song is also a link to Surat Thani, Krabi, Trang, and Phatthalung Province.

Malaysia

Port Klang (Selangor). Port Klang is Malaysia's premier port and the world's 12th busiest port. The port's Northport Terminal is positioned as an intra-Asian transshipment and regional trading hub, serving domestic and coastal trade routes to ports in Sabah, Sarawak, and Brunei Darussalam as well as short-seaport destinations in Indonesia, Thailand, and Viet Nam. The Asa Niaga Harbor City Terminal is a regional passenger ferry terminal that serves high-speed passenger ferries plying between Port Klang and the ports of Dumai and Tanjung Balai in Sumatera. The Boustead Cruise Centre is a dedicated cruise terminal and has emerged as an important port of call for international cruise liners, recording 364,511 passenger arrivals in 2018, or about 40% of all passenger arrivals at Malaysia's ports of call.

Port Klang accounted for a yearly average of 46% of total cargo volume exported (226 million tons) and 58% of cargo volume imported (205 million tons) during the period 2014–2018. The government plans to develop Port Klang as a regional maritime center and a cargo logistic hub by improving Port Klang's transportation ecosystem and network with other commercial nodes in the country. All commercial nodes in Selangor have good road and rail connectivity with Port Klang. There is also a land bridge from the port extending all the way to Hat Yai. Port Klang serves as a major link between EC1, EC2, and EC6 through road and railway connectivity with Hat Yai and Perak, as well as with EC3 through maritime connectivity with Sumatera via Dumai.

Port Klang has maritime links with 10 large and small ports in Sumatera. Its trading is concentrated in the North Sumatera, Riau, West Sumatera, Jambi, South Sumatera, and Lampung regions. Like Penang Port, Port Klang exports and imports cargo and container to/from the port in Sumatera.

Penang Port (Penang). Penang Port a strategic gateway node for both EC1 and EC2. The port serves as the main gateway for shippers in the northern states of Malaysia and southern provinces of Thailand. The oldest and longest established port in Malaysia, Penang Port is a deep-water seaport consisting of seven terminals along the Penang Strait—six of them in mainland Seberang Perai, particularly the towns of Butterworth and Perai, and one in George Town in Penang Island as the Swettenham Pier Cruise Terminal. Swettenham Pier Cruise Terminal also caters to ferry services between Penang and places like Langsa, Aceh in Indonesia, and the islands of Langkawi and Pulau Payar in the northern state of Kedah.

Lumut Port (Perak). Lumut Port is s secondary port and strategically located off the Strait of Malacca, on the west coast of Peninsular Malaysia, in Perak.[9] The port was established as a state port and a catalyst for economic growth, development, and industrialization of the state. The state government owns and operates the port at Kampung Acheh (Lumut), which was officiated on 24 July 1995 and have been in operation for more than 20 years. In 2002, Lumut Port began to operate and manage Lekir Bulk Terminal (LBT). LBT is a deep-water seaport, and with a natural depth of 20 meters, LBT is currently Southeast Asia's largest dry bulk unloading facility. The terminal can berth an entire range of vessels in Panamax and Capemax ships up to 165,000 deep-water terminal. LBT is designed to handle dry bulk cargoes. It currently is a dedicated terminal to handle coal for Sultan Azlan Shah Power Station in Seri Manjung (Perak).

---

[9]   The information for Lumut Port was compiled from http://lumutport.com/about/.

Tanjung Bruas Port (Melaka). Tanjung Bruas Port is the main trade gateway to Melaka and to other states in the Peninsula from Riau Province in Sumatera. The implementation of the Melaka–Dumai Ro-Ro Project (EC4) will further boost exports and imports of cargo freights between Melaka and the Riau Province. In addition, the Melaka International Ferry Terminal (MIFT) is affiliated with the Port of Bandar Sri Laksamana, Bengkalis, which provides ferry services for passengers from Melaka to the Riau Province.

Tanjung Bruas Port is one of the world's busiest trade routes at the center and narrowest point of the Strait of Malacca. Situated within a large, developed hinterland drawn from Melaka, Negeri Sembilan, and northern Johor, Tanjung Bruas Port is surrounded by more than 500 manufacturing companies that ship both conventional and container cargoes through the port. Comprehensive improvements are being planned to develop the port as a hub for sea–air cargoes. In Melaka, Tanjung Bruas Port has trade links with the port in Dumai (Riau). Tanjung Bruas Port is an interchange node linking EC1–EC2 in Peninsular Malaysia with EC3 in Sumatera via Dumai.

Tanjung Bruas Port has maritime links with ports in Sumatera, particularly Palembang and Lhokseumawe (Aceh). Commodities imported from Palembang are gypsum and coal and from Aceh, ammonia gas. Tanjung Bruas Port also has maritime links with the port in Bangkok (Thailand); Kaohsiung (Taipei,China); Jurong (Singapore); Saiki (Japan); and Humen (PRC).

The Strait of Malacca separates Langkawi Island (Kedah) from Kuala Perlis (Perlis). There are ferry services that connect the Kuah Jetty (Langkawi) to the Kuala Perlis Jetty (Perlis). The distance between the two jetties is 33 km or 18 nautical miles. Langkawi is an important tourism node for Kedah and has been a tourist destination for local and international tourists.[10] The Kuah Perlis Jetty also has maritime links with the Penang Port (George Town) and Kuala Kedah Jetty (Kedah) via ferry service. There are also maritime links between Kuah Jetty and Ko Lipe and Tammalang Port in Satun. The Strait of Malacca also separates Tanjung Bruas Port (Melaka) with Dumai (Port of Bandar Sri Junjungan). A ferry service connects the two ports. The distance between Tanjung Bruas Port and Port of Bandar Sri Junjungan (Dumai) is 177 km (96 nautical miles).

There is scope for expanding connectivity of EC2 to Sumatera Island which can further increase trade along the Strait of Malacca. The growth centers in Sumatera's eastern coast can benefit from connectivity with Malaysian ports. As shown in Table 10, Port Klang, Lumut Port, and Tanjung Bruas Port have existing links with several ports in Sumatera. Alternatively, maritime connectivity can also be enhanced between EC2 and EC3 ports with the proposed expansion of EC3 to include other provinces in Sumatera.

---

[10]   Langkawi has the status as a tax-free island since 1987 and has been designated by UNESCO as a Global Geopark in June 2007.

**Table 10: Economic Corridor 2: Maritime Links between Malaysia and Sumatera Ports
in the Strait of Malacca**

Port	Sumatera Province	Links to Ports in Sumatera	Type of Maritime Activities
Port Klang, Selangor	North Sumatera	Belawan, Medan	Cargo and container
		Tanjung Balai	Cargo
	Riau	Buatan	Container
		Dumai	Cargo and container
		Pekanbaru	Cargo and container
		Perawang	Container
	West Sumatera	Padang, Teluk Bayur	Cargo and container
	Jambi	Jambi	Cargo
	South Sumatera	Palembang	Cargo and container
	Lampung	Panjang	Container
Lumut Port, Perak	Riau	Pelintung	Barge
	Riau Islands	Batam, Batu Ampar	Barge
	Jambi Province	Jambi	Barge
		Kuala Tunggal	Barge
	Bengkulu Province	Bengkulu	Barge
	South Sumatera Province	Muara Lematang	Barge
		Palembang	Barge
Tanjung Bruas Port, Melaka	Riau Province	Dumai Port	Ferry Ro-Ro (cargo)
	South Sumatera Province	Palembang	Cargo
	Aceh	Lhokseumawe	Cargo

Ro-Ro = roll on, roll, off.
Sources: (i) Port Klang Statistical Bulletin 2018; (ii) Penang Port Authority (2019); and (iii) Tanjung Bruas Port Authority (2020); Lumut Port (2019) Sumatera.

Air Linkages

In Malaysia, air connectivity with Sumatera and Southern Thailand is through airports in Perak, Selangor, and Melaka. From these airports, there are flights to Surat Thani, Krabi, Phuket, and Hat Yai. Thani, although there are no direct flights to the EC2 provinces in Southern Thailand. There are also flights to Banda Aceh, Medan, Pekanbaru, and Padang originating from these airports.

In Thailand, air connectivity from Satun, Trang, and Yala is limited. The airport in Trang has direct flights to Bangkok but not to other destinations in EC2. Airports in nearby provinces to Satun are used to access the province. The new international airport in Betong (Yala) is expected to give a boost to tourism on account of the good road connectivity between the airport and states in Malaysia through Pengkalan Hulu.

Cross-Border Infrastructure

Access to the BCPs by road and rail is adequate. Roads leading to Thailand BCPs at Wang Prachan and Padang Besa are in good condition. Most of the two-lane roads to Betong BCP (except for a four-lane road to Mueang District) runs through Yala's mountainous terrain and take a longer time to travel, but otherwise the road condition is good and safe. The border infrastructure in Malaysia BCPs—Wang Kelian, Padang Besar, and Pengkalan Hulu are also adequate and in good condition.

The building and facilities at BCPs are well-maintained and adequate space is available for inspection and other formalities. Operating hours are generally the same for the BCPs. Current initiatives to further upgrade the BCP facilities and infrastructure at Wang Prachan and Wang Kelian anticipates an increase in border trade from major industrial initiatives in Perlis, as well as the increasing importance of Satun under the SEC. Two important projects are

- the joint initiative for the development of Customs checkpoint at Wang Kelian and Wang Prachan involving the upgrading of the Customs House, and establishment of low-rise commercial zones linked to nearby ecotourism tourism areas and commodities trade; and

- the construction of a new bridge connecting Satun and Perlis along the Andaman Sea coast to accommodate the increase in transport demand resulting from economic growth.

Cross-Border Trade

Border trade between Malaysia and Thailand is concentrated in Padang Besar and Padang Besa BCPs. Trade at the BCPs in Wang Prachan–Wang Kelian and Betong–Pengkalan Hulu are relatively small.

Malaysia's exports via road in Padang Besar contributed 21% to Malaysia's total border exports (Table 11). Over 2015–2018, exports slipped by an average of 0.3% annually. The major products exported to Thailand include machinery and electrical products, agricultural products, food, and chemicals. Imports at Padang Besar increased by an average of 6% during the same period. Rubber and plastics are the leading imports from Thailand accounting for 27% of total border imports. Imports coursed through Wang Kelian and Pengkalan Hulu are very small. There has been an increasing use of rail transport for exports to Thailand.

Table 11: Economic Corridor 2: Malaysia's Border Trade with Thailand

Item	Padang Besar	Wang Kelian	Pengkalan Hulu
Average Total Trade 2015–2018 ($ million)	1,378	97	86
Share to Malaysia's Total Border Trade, 2018 (%)	21	1.5	1.3
Average Growth Rate of Exports (2015–2018 (%)	(0.3)	14.3	12.6
Average Growth Rate of Imports (2015–2018) (%) (Ringgit)	5.9	1.8	2.4

( ) = negative.
Source: Compiled by the study team from the trade data of Royal Malaysia Customs Department (2019).

Thailand's border trade with Malaysia is driven mostly by imports that have grown faster than exports on average over 2015–2018. Thailand's trade with Malaysia at the border of Padang Besa contributed 12.5% to Thailand's total border trade in 2018 (Table 12). Border trade at Wang Prachan and Betong is very small at less than 1%. Imports grew at an average of 16.84% at Padang Besa, and 62% for Wang Prachan over 2015–2018, overtaking exports, which grew much slower. Major imports at Padang Besa consisted mostly of consumer durables, while major exports were natural rubber, synthetic rubber, and sawn wood.

Table 12: Economic Corridor 2: Thailand's Border Trade with Malaysia

Item	Padang Besa	Wang Prachan	Betong
Average total trade 2015–2018 ($ '000)	5,339,250	7,750	99,740
Share to Thailand's Total Border Trade, 2018 (%)	12.50	0.02	0.2
Average Growth Rate of Exports (%)	0.12	(15.70)	0.9
Average Growth Rate of Imports (%)	16.80	62.20	(7.9)

( ) = negative.
Source: Padang Besa, Wang Prachan, Betong Customs Houses (2019).

Presently, the Wang Prachan–Wang Kelian joint development project will establish a Customs checkpoint that provides one-stop service. Similar arrangements should be initiated in other BCPs, including for intermodal nodes. There is a juxtaposed CIQ at Padang Besar where CIQ for both Malaysia and Thailand are located inside the station located in the Malaysian territory. Passengers disembarking at Padang Besar can therefore go through the CIQ processes in one location.

Development Strategies

Malaysia's NCER Blueprint 2.0 (2016–2025) has identified major initiatives that could benefit from regional trading networks and physical connectivity along the Strait of Malacca to spur and catalyze growth. Malaysia's strategy for EC2 aligns with the development strategy for the NCER to leverage good physical connectivity and regional trade networks with the development of core industry clusters for the region to achieve a world-class economic status by 2025. The logistics cost advantage to the industries resulting from their proximity to the ports would enhance their competitiveness. The industry clusters are also part of planned conurbation areas that can spawn innovation and talent needed to bring emerging industries to the cutting edge. The long-term development objective is to achieve intra- and interregional imbalances in the northern region toward a more inclusive economic growth. Penang Port and Port Klang are the two major maritime gateway ports in Malaysia under EC2. The economic linkages among states in EC2 can be further enhanced with the designation of additional nodes to build synergies among industrial clusters and conurbation areas in NCER.

Thailand's strategy for EC2 involves the development of trade gateways in EC2 and EC5 by connecting networks in the west coast via Ranong Port, Tammalang Port, and Wang Prachan BCP that would link the East Coast Economic Corridor (ECER) to the Bay of Bengal Initiative for Multi-Sectoral Technical and Economic Cooperation (BIMSTEC) and IMT-GT countries. More specifically, the strategy involves (i) connecting tourist destinations along the coasts of the Andaman Sea both by land and by sea; (ii) connecting the route for transport of goods both via land and rail to Kantang Port (rail from Thung Song Cargo Distribution Center in Nakhon Si Thammarat in EC1); and (iii) connecting routes for tourism and the transport of goods via sea between Tammalang Port to islands in Indonesia, Malaysia, and Thailand.

The reconfiguration of EC2 involving additional nodes in Malaysia, and additional provinces and nodes in Thailand will support the development strategies of the two countries.

Reconfiguration of EC2

Malaysia

The additional nodes in Malaysia are (i) Kamunting and Lumut (Perak), (ii) Chuping Valley and Kuala Perlis (Perlis), (iii) Batu Kawan (Penang), (iv) Kuah and Langkawi (Kedah), (v) Seremban and Port Dickson (Negeri Sembilan), and (vi) Tanjung Bruas Port (Melaka).

- Kamunting and Lumut are catalyst centers with the potential to generate a high impact on the local regions. The Kamunting Industrial Park and Lumut Port Industrial Park are being developed to attract investments into industries that will have an impact on the local supply chain. Kamunting and Pengkalan Hulu are connected by good roads to Penang Port and Lumut Port as well as by rail to Ipoh, the state capital.

- The Chuping Valley Industrial Area is being developed by the state government. Under the area, it was recommended that the Perlis Industrial Park be established as a logistics hub to increase the efficiency of cargo movement between Malaysia and Thailand. The Kuala Perlis Jetty, which is the tourist gateway to Langkawi and Satun, has been expanded to accommodate the increasing number of domestic and international tourists. This will have a large impact on the development of Kuala Perlis. The Kuala Perlis–Langkawi–Satun connectivity has greatly promoted the tourism industry in Perlis and Langkawi.

- Batu Kawan (Seberang Perai, Penang) is being positioned as the next satellite township in the northern region. It is now undergoing rapid development sparked by the completion in 2014 of the second Penang Bridge. The Batu Kawan Industrial Park hosts several multinational companies in high-technology and skills-intensive industries.

- Kuah town, together with Langkawi (Kedah) are tourism nodes in Malaysia that link with Thailand's tourism corridor through Thammalang Port (Satun). Kuah town and Langkawi are major destinations for domestic and international tourists. The Kuah Jetty is one of the ports of call for cruise tourism in the Strait of Malacca, in addition to the MIFT, Port Klang, and Penang Port.

- Tanjung Bruas Port (Melaka) is an important maritime link between southern part of the peninsula to Riau Province (Sumatera). The port has a vast hinterland of industrial parks. The Ro-Ro ferry service between Tanjung Bruas Port and Dumai (under EC4) will expedite the delivery of goods by trucks between Malaysia and Sumatera, thus providing a more cost-efficient route for micro, small, and medium-sized enterprises compared to transporting goods by ship.

- Port Dickson and Seremban are under the Malaysia Valley Vision 2.0, which was launched in 2018 to generate economic growth for the state toward a high-income economy. Seremban, which is the capital city of Negeri Sembilan, is the center of administration and business that facilitates state economic activities by providing services to the public, business communities, and industry players. Port Dickson is the trade gateway for Negeri Sembilan. This port serves as a major oil terminal as well as a minor port for general cargo.

Thailand

To support the SEC tourism strategy, EC2 was extended northward to include Phangnga and Krabi to develop land and sea connectivity along the Andaman Sea coast for tourism and pave the way to connect EC2 with Ranong and Phuket in EC5.

- Krabi's inclusion in EC2 will expand the tourism routes along the Andaman Sea coast to cover Ranong, Phangnga, Phuket Trang, and Satun and onwards to Perlis, Selangor, and Penang. The route can eventually link to Sumatera through the maritime mode.

- Expansion to Phangnga and Krabi will also enhance value chains in agriculture and agro-based industries between EC2 and EC1 (Chumphon, Surat Thani, and Songkhla). Phangnga, Krabi, Trang, and Satun are primary producers of palm oil, rubber, and fruits that are sent to processing factories in Chumphon, Surat Thani, and Songkhla.

- Expanding the economic potential of EC2 will involve the inclusion of additional nodes in Thammalang Port and Tarutao Islands in Satun, with its potential to expand cruise tourism in Langkawi, as well as in Sumatera through a potential link with Belawan. It can leverage on its existing maritime connectivity with Port Klang and Penang Port to exploit more tourism opportunities in Indonesia and Malaysia.

Because of the inclusion of Thailand provinces along the Andaman Sea, **EC2 has been renamed Andaman Sea–Strait of Malacca Economic Corridor** (Map 5). The existing and additional provinces and nodes in the reconfigured EC2 is summarized in Table 13.

Map 5: Andaman Sea–Strait of Malacca Economic Corridor (Reconfigured Economic Corridor 2)

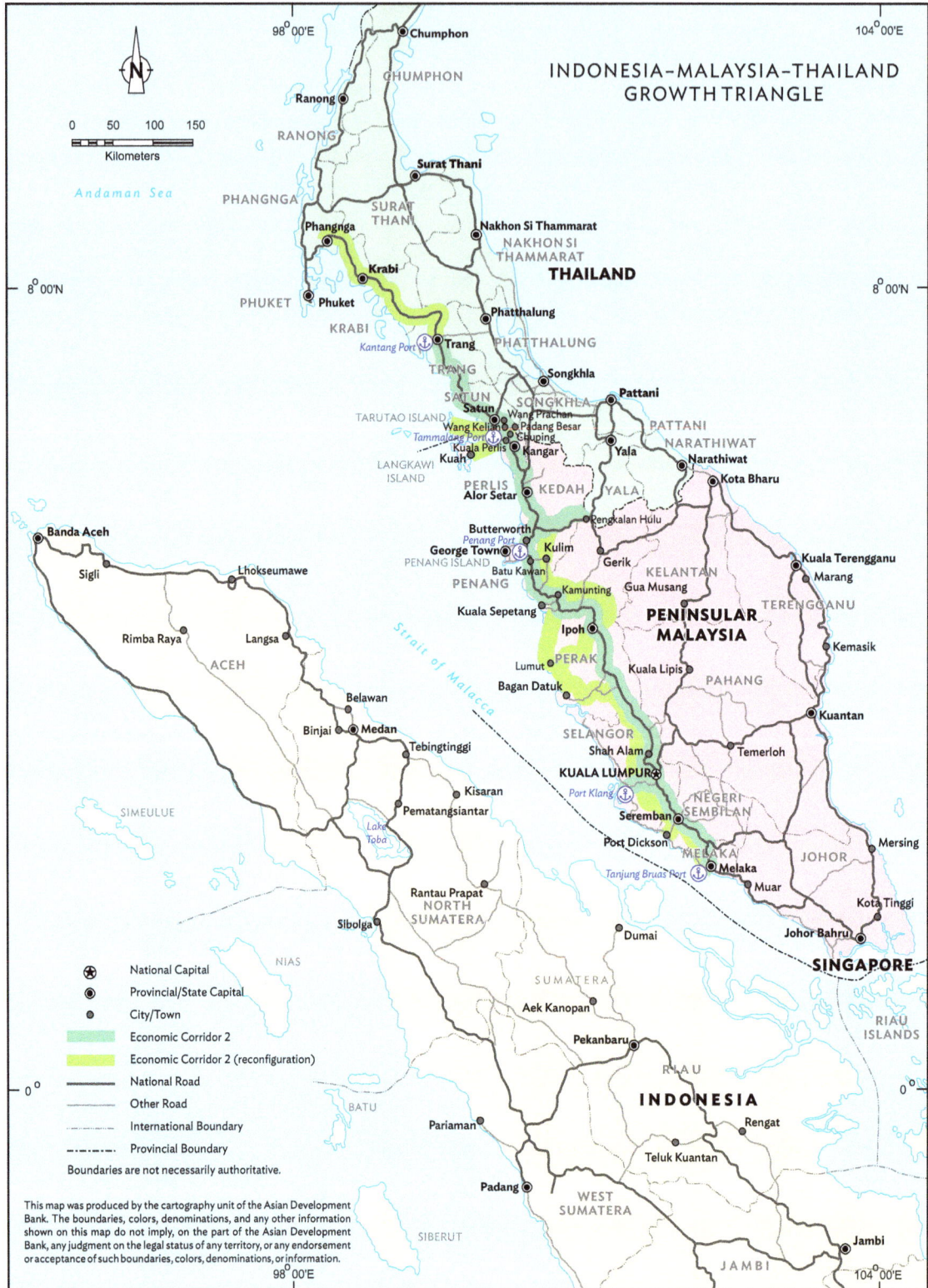

Source: Asian Development Bank.

Table 13: Economic Corridor 2: Existing and Additional Provinces and Nodes, by Type

Province/State	Node	CAP	COM	BCP	MGP	TOUR
MALAYSIA						
Perlis	Wang Kelian			✓		✓
	Padang Besar			✓		✓
	Chuping Valley*		✓			
	Kuala Perlis*		✓			
Perak	Pengkalan Hulu			✓		✓
	Kamunting*		✓			
	Lumut*		✓			
Penang	Penang Port • Butterworth • George Town				✓	✓
	Batu Kawan*		✓			
Selangor	Port Klang				✓	✓
Kedah	Kuah*				✓	✓
	Langkawi					✓
Melaka	Melaka City	✓				✓
	Tanjung Bruas Port (Port of Melaka)*				✓	
Negeri Sembilan	Port Dickson*		✓		✓	✓
	Seremban*	✓	✓			
THAILAND						
Krabi*	Krabi City*	✓	✓			✓
Phangnga*	Phangnga City*	✓	✓			
Trang	Trang City	✓	✓			
	Kantang Port				✓	
Satun	Satun City	✓	✓			
	Wang Prachan			✓		
	Tammalang Port*				✓	✓
	Tarutao Island*					✓

BCP = border crossing point, CAP = capital, COM = commercial, MGP = maritime gateway port, TOUR = tourism.
Note: * denotes additional provinces and nodes.
Source: Study team.

Findings and Recommendations

Roads connecting Thailand and Malaysia ports along the Strait of Malacca are adequate and in good condition as they are part of national or federal or state roads systems. The distance between Trang and Satun can be traveled in good, safe, and efficient roads up to the border at Wang Prachan. In Malaysia, the BCPs at Wang Kelian and Padang Besar are connected by good roads to Butterworth and George Town (Penang Port), which are international gateways linked to Medan (in EC1). Road connectivity is complemented by rail links between Port Klang, Perak, and Songkhla as well as a land bridge from Port Klang extending all the way to Hat Yai.

Access to the BCPs by road and rail is adequate. Roads leading to Thailand BCPs at Wang Prachan and Padang Besa are in good condition. Most of the two-lane roads to Betong border checkpoint (except for a four-lane road to Mueang District) runs through Yala's mountainous terrain and takes a longer time to travel, but otherwise the road condition is good and safe. The border infrastructure in Malaysia BCPs—Wang Kelian, Padang Besar, and Pengkalan Hulu are also adequate and in good condition.

The building and facilities at BCPs are well-maintained and adequate space is available for inspection and other formalities. Operating hours are generally the same for the BCPs. Current initiatives to further upgrade the BCP facilities and infrastructure at Wang Prachan and Wang Kelian anticipates an increase in border trade from major industrial initiatives in Perlis, as well as the increasing importance of Satun under the SEC. Two important projects are

- joint initiative for the development of Customs checkpoint at Wang Kelian and Wang Prachan involving the upgrading of the Customs building, and establishment of low-rise commercial zones linked to nearby ecotourism tourism areas and commodities trade; and

- construction of a new bridge connecting Satun and Perlis along the coasts of the Andaman Sea to accommodate the increase in transport demand resulting from economic growth.

One-stop services should be made a regular feature of BCP operations, and the required facilities should be made part of CIQs expansion and improvements. Presently, the Wang Prachan–Wang Kelian joint development project will establish a Customs checkpoint that provides a one-stop service. Similar arrangements should be explored and initiated in other BCPs, including for intermodal nodes. Coordinated development of border facilities is needed to enable the development of complementary facilities, in addition to ensuring quality infrastructure.

Although the land routes between major nodes are adequate, there is a need to look into a second generation of road links within the corridor as industrial parks and new economic centers expand the catchment areas of the ports and open potential new trade routes. Expanding existing last mile road connectivity and new trade routes can extend to the hinterlands and spur economic growth over a much wider geographic area where poverty resides and where balanced and inclusive growth are needed. The expansion to the hinterlands has the effect of widening the corridor, implying the need to also develop links to arterial trade and transport routes and secondary borders that would become more important as local supply chains develop.

The construction of a new bridge at Satun and Perlis is an important project that will support land connectivity along the Andaman seacoast along the coasts of Tammalang in Satun to Ko Puyu and then to Perlis in Malaysia. The bridge will also have a positive impact on the local economies. The state government of Perlis supports the plan of the Government of Thailand to build a 13 km bridge connecting Tammalang in Satun to Bukit Putih (Kuala Perlis) in Perlis. The bridge will shorten the 187-km trip to carry cargo from Bangkok to Padang Besar or Bukit Kayu Hitam in Kedah. Currently container trucks take the Satun–Songkhla–Hat Yai–Sadao–Padang Besar or Bukit Kayu Hitam route.[11] This bridge will be the third border checkpoint in Perlis, in addition to Padang Besar and Wang Kelian. The national security concern and funding will be an important agenda in the planning of the bridge.

---

[11]   Perlis Hails Thai proposal to building Tamelang–Bukit Putih Bridge. 2017. *The Sun Daily*. 4 October.

There is scope for enhancing multimodal connectivity along the Strait of Malacca. Except for Port Klang and Penang Port (which are supported by land bridges), other ports in Malaysia (e.g., Lumut Port and Tanjung Bruas Port) lack connectivity with other modes of transport (e.g., rail and aviation). The use of rail transport to move train load-like traffic to and from seaports, especially for the transit of containers on high-volume routes, should be developed further. This will reduce the overall cost of the modal interface at the port, lower inland transit cost, and facilitate clearance. Additional rail-connected facilities like ICDs and freight wagons would also be needed to cater to the demand for intermodal links.

Multimodal transport systems will require developing effective inland transit systems. This would involve among others, the use of ICDs and bonded logistics facilities, which can enhance the efficiency of the supply chain without undergoing clearance formalities and duty payment at the borders. Given the potential increase in the demand for inland terminals with the establishment of industrial parks and SEZs near the ports, the development of inland transit systems can avoid the concentration of dry ports near the border and further expedite border movement of goods.

Given the multimodal approach to EC2, transport and trade facilitation will need to focus on both land and sea-based transport. The current focus on land-based trade facilitation will need to be balanced with initiatives for port-based trade facilitation, especially with the expansion in port capacities to handle bulk and container cargoes. This could include resolving nontariff barriers within the port environment to reduce port dwell times and enhance port facilitation.

Since several Malaysia ports are already part of existing IMT-GT corridors, expanding connectivity of EC2 to Sumatera Island can further increase trade along the Strait of Malacca. Most of the growth centers in Indonesia's National Medium-Term Development Plan 2020–2024 are in Sumatera's eastern coast along the Strait of Malacca and can benefit from enhanced connectivity with Malaysian ports. Indonesia may consider including cargo and container ports, currently linked with Port Klang and Penang Port, and those near economic and industrial zones along the eastern coast, as part of EC2. Alternatively, connectivity can also be enhanced through maritime links between EC2 ports and EC3 ports, which are envisaged to be included under the proposed expansion of EC3 to include other provinces in Sumatera Island. To support Indonesia's balanced development strategy for Sumatera, connectivity can be extended to the western coast of Sumatera at a later stage depending on the pace of development in that area.

Economic Corridor 3. The Banda Aceh–Medan–Pekanbaru–Palembang Economic Corridor

Overview

The Banda Aceh–Medan–Pekanbaru–Palembang Economic Corridor (EC3) is a national corridor passing through four provinces in Sumatera Island: Aceh, North Sumatera, Riau, and South Sumatera. It is a land-based corridor (Map 6).

Establishing connectivity within Sumatera is a critical building block for further enhancing Indonesia's connectivity with other IMT-GT economic corridors. EC3 is important to EC1 (extended Songkhla–Medan–Penang Corridor) as it improves the flow of goods to major trading centers and staging posts in Sumatera that can connect to northern Malaysia and Southern Thailand. Improved connectivity within Sumatera will enable provinces to access ports in the eastern coast that can link with Malaysia's ports along the Strait of Malacca, complementing EC2 (Strait of Malacca Economic Corridor) and EC4 (Melaka–Dumai Economic Corridor). The ongoing Trans-Sumatera Toll Road Project of the government that connects Aceh in the north across 2,704 km of road to Lampung in the south, is a massive effort to accelerate economic and inclusive growth in Sumatera by strengthening internal connectivity. The toll road will traverse the four EC3 provinces in three segments: Banda Aceh–Medan, Medan–Pekanbaru, and Pekanbaru–Palembang.

Existing Provinces and Nodes

Aceh is located at the northern tip of Sumatera and belongs to the island's "growth corridor." Banda Aceh, the capital of the province, is a base for processing companies of yellow fin tuna coming from Meulaboh, Pulau Aceh, Laweng, and Ulee Lheue. The frozen tuna and tuna loin are sold mainly in the domestic market, and some are exported to Japan, the Republic of Korea, and Thailand. Around 90% of captured tuna are sent to Medan unprocessed, suggesting a huge untapped potential to further develop the tuna processing industry. Coffee bean processing is also a thriving industry in Banda Aceh, especially for Robusta coffee produced in Ulee Kareng (Banda Aceh) and Arabica coffee from Gayo Highland (Aceh Tengah and Bener Meriah Regencies). The coffee products are marketed to other places in North Sumatera along with other products such as betel nut and CPO. Aceh exports coal to Thailand and India. Banda Aceh is 23 km away from Malahayati Port in Aceh Besar Regency, which is a logistics distribution center for exports and imports. It is also a popular destination for halal tourism among Indonesians and Malaysians.

North Sumatera is among the 10 provinces in Sumatera identified as belonging to the "growth corridor" under the RPJMN 2020–2024. North Sumatera contributes close to 20% of Sumatera's foreign trade. Within North Sumatera, the specific growth areas include Medan (the capital city), Sei Mangkei (SEZ), Kuala Tanjung (industrial zone), and Lake Toba (tourism zone). Medan is a node in the Eastern Sumatera National Highway and Trans-Sumatera toll road. It is the home base for several rubber downstream companies with plantations all over North Sumatera. Medan is also known as Sumatera's "coffee axis" since coffee from various regencies are processed there and exported to domestic and international markets. Under the RPJMN 2020–2024, Medan will be developed as Metropolitan Medan, together with Palembang.

Map 6: Banda Aceh-Medan-Pekanbaru-Palembang Economic Corridor (Economic Corridor 3)

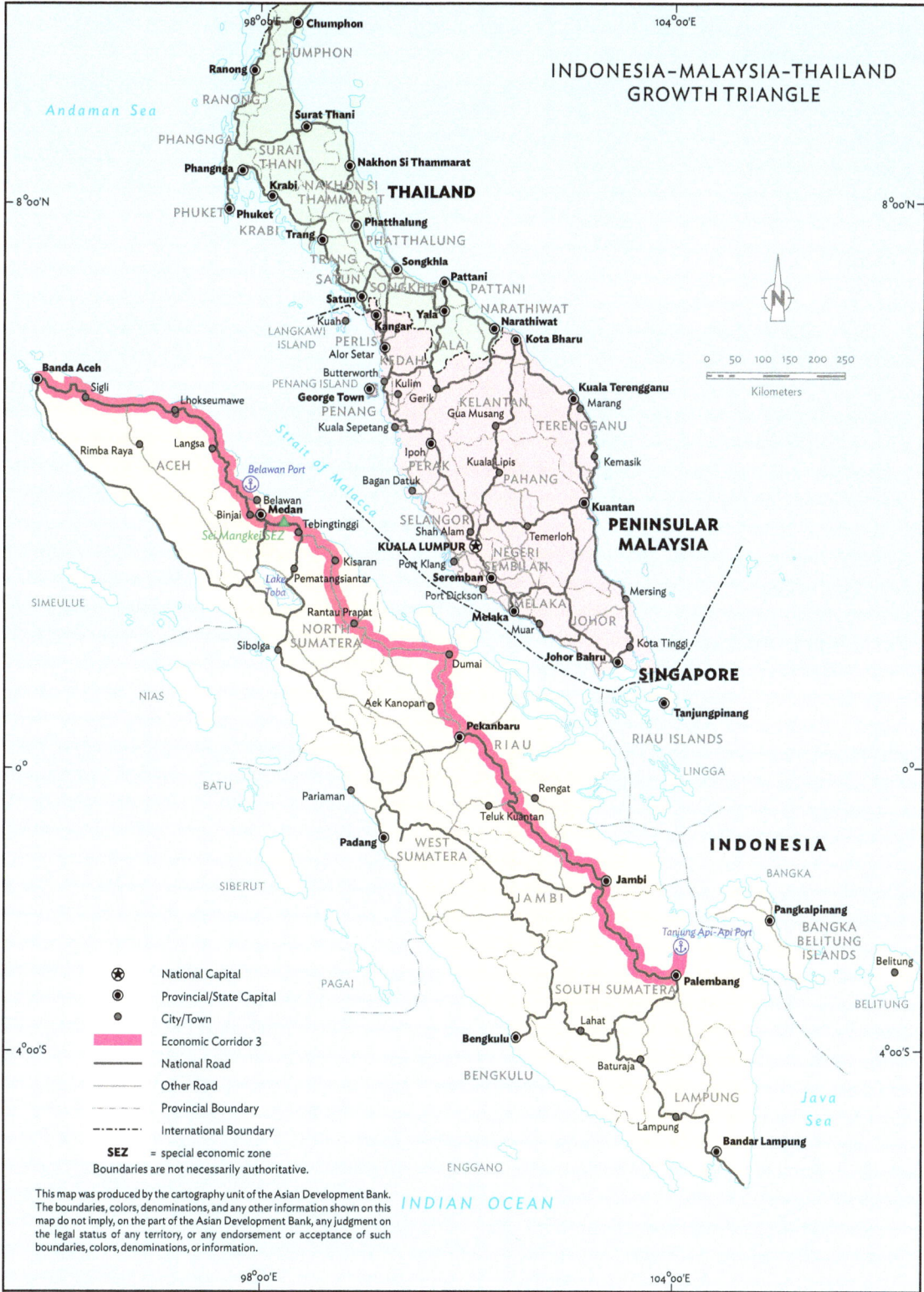

Source: Asian Development Bank.

Expansive plantations in North Sumatera, Aceh, and Riau Province transport their produce to Belawan Port, making it an important gateway for palm oil exports. CPO and CPKO are the main upstream products transported to Belawan Port but there are also downstream products such as cooking oil, margarine and shortening, and oleochemical (fatty acid, fatty alcohol, and glycerol). North Sumatera is also a major rubber producer, having the second largest rubber plantation in Indonesia (12.7%) after South Sumatera. Belawan Port handled 88% of North Sumatera's exports in 2018, as well as exports of Aceh (44.5%) and West Sumatera (approximately 20.5%).[12] Among Indonesia's ports, Belawan Port is the third biggest in terms of export volume handled (2014–2018) after Tanjung Priok in Jakarta and Tanjung Perak in Surabaya (the latter two are in Java Island).

Riau Province is located at the central eastern coast of Sumatera. Energy, mining, and agriculture are the dominant sectors of the economy. Riau Province had the highest GDP per capita of $4,861 in Sumatera in 2018. The province's population was estimated at 6.8 million in 2018 or 11.8% of Sumatera's population. Pekanbaru, the capital, is in the middle of Sumatera Island, connecting the northern region (Aceh and North Sumatera) with the southern region (South Sumatera, Jambi, Lampung). Dumai Port, located 157.6 km from Pekanbaru, is the biggest gateway for CPO exports in Sumatera handling 6 million tons per year, compared to Belawan Port in Medan which only handles 3.5 million tons of CPO exports per year.[13] Almost 80% of Riau's exports and 42% of its imports are shipped through Dumai Port. Dumai Port has the advantage of having a shorter distance to Peninsular Malaysia (approximately 107.8 km) compared to other major ports in Sumatera. Its strategic location has made it the center for at least five feeder ports, namely Bagansiapiapi, Tanjung Lumba-Lumba, Tanjung Medang, Sinaboi, and Panipahan.

South Sumatera, located in the southeast section of Sumatera Island, has a GRDP per capita of $2,463. South Sumatera has the largest area for rubber plantations in Indonesia—837,000 hectares (ha) or 23.6% of the national total land area planted to rubber. South Sumatera also has large plantations (1.19 million ha) for CPO, which is sold to North Sumatera for processing. CPO, urea fertilizer, and coal are among the major products sold to other provinces such as North Sumatera, Lampung, and Bengkulu. Palembang, the provincial capital, has strong economic ties with Bengkulu and Bangka Belitung Islands dating back centuries ago during the Sriwijaya empire. Under the RPJMN 2020–2024, the plan is to develop Metropolitan Palembang, together with Medan.

Status of Physical Connectivity

Road Connectivity

Connectivity among the four provinces (Aceh, North Sumatera, Riau, and South Sumatera) under the existing EC3 is adequate, but the quality of roads is uneven, with most of the segments having two lanes and classified as Class II. EC3 starts from Banda Aceh and traverses Medan, Pekanbaru, and Palembang via Asian Highway (AH) 25. The road surface is smooth but travel in some segments can be slow (average of 40–60 kilometers per hour) due to congestion and occasional potholes resulting from poor maintenance.

---

[12]   Based on the total sale of West Sumatera to North Sumatera in 2018.

[13]   Pelindo I Akan Tingkatkan Kapasitas Pelabuhan Dumai. 2018. *Pelindo 1 Cabang Dumai*. 31 October.

Roads in EC3 are part of the Trans-Sumatera Toll Road—a comprehensive government infrastructure project to connect all provincial capitals in Sumatera Island, from Aceh to Bakauheni (Lampung). The estimated 2,704-km road project is designed to improve connectivity, reduce logistic costs, and stimulate industrial growth in Sumatera Island.[14] Based on the Presidential Regulation No. 117/2015, there are eight priority sections that were supposed to be operational by the end of 2019.[15] As of the end of August 2020, the total length of completed sections is about 21.8% of the entire toll road. The other sections are expected to be operational by 2024.

Cargo terminals along the corridor route in Banda Aceh, Meulaboh, and Langsa serve as transit points for trucks coming from Medan and other locations. From the cargo terminals, the goods are transferred into smaller trucks before entering the cities to prevent damage to roads and reduce congestion in the cities. The Transport Department operates the cargo terminals in their respective locations.

Rail Connectivity

No single railway line connects the provinces in Sumatera Islands although there is a plan by the Ministry of Transport to construct a Trans-Sumatera Railway. At present, there are only partial railway links that facilitate transport of goods from production centers to the ports. There are also minor rail links (light rail) that facilitate the movement of people to, and from, the airports. As value chains develop in Sumatera, and external trade expands, railways as an alternative and more efficient mode of transport will become increasingly important.

Rail transport in Aceh and North Sumatera provinces is under the management of PT Kereta Api Indonesia (Persero) Regional Division I North Sumatera, a state-owned company operating in Java and Sumatera Island. To connect Aceh with North Sumatera, the government planned in 2016 to reactivate the 80-km railway from Besitang (Aceh) to Binjai (North Sumatera) and build a new railway along 428 km that will pass through Malahayati, Lhokseumawe, and Kuala Langsa, which are prominent ports in Aceh Province. By the end of 2019, Besitang (Langkat)–Langsa segment for about 35 km has been completed, while the other segments are still being developed. There is also a 28-km railway line from Medan to Kualanamu International Airport.

To support the railway connection between Riau and neighboring cities, the government of Indonesia initiated the development of the Rantau Prapat–Duri–Pekanbaru railway in 2017. The railway will connect Rantau Prapat and Kota Pinang in North Sumatera, as well as Dumai and Pekanbaru in Riau. As of end 2019, the Rantau Prapat–Kota Pinang (North Sumatera) route (33 km) has been completed. The missing rail link from Pekanbaru to Jambi (402 km) should have been started in 2018 as these railways are included in the list of national strategic projects. As of August 2020, the projects are still undergoing design preparation and environmental impact assessment. There is also a 232.6 km missing rail link from Jambi to Palembang, which the government plans to construct in 2024. There is a light rail transit in South Sumatera covering a 23.4-km stretch from Sultan Mahmud Badaruddin II Airport (Palembang City), to Jakabaring Sports Center and Ogan Permata Indah areas passing over the Musi River. There are 13 stations along the track.

---

[14]   Data on the total length of Trans-Sumatera toll road differ. Hutama Karya, the appointed contractor, places it at 2,704 km, while the Ministry of General Works and Housing places it at 2,974 km. The variance may be due to the fact that some sections are still undergoing feasibility studies.

[15]   These sections are (i) Medan–Binjai, (ii) Palembang–Indralaya, (iii) Pekanbaru–Dumai, (iv) Bakauheni–Terbanggi Besar, (v) Terbanggi Besar–Pematang Panggang, (vi) Pematang Panggang–Kayu Agung, (vii) Palembang–Tanjung Api-Api, and (viii) Kisaran–Tebingtinggi. As of the end of August 2020, the sections that have been completed are: (i) Medan–Binjai (17 km) including the Medan–Kualanamu–Tebingtinggi (62 km) in North Sumatera; (ii) Bakauheni–Terbanggi Besar (140 km) in Lampung; and (iii) Terbanggi Besar–Pematang Panggang–Kayu Agung (185 km), extended to Palembang (33 km); (iv) Palembang–Indralaya (22 km); (v) part of Aceh–Sigli section (14 km), and Pekanbaru–Dumai (131 km).

International Gateway Ports

Although EC3 is basically a land-based corridor, the competitive position of Sumatera ports will strongly underpin the benefits to be derived from the corridor because of its strategic location along the Strait of Malacca and Sumatera Island's proximity to mainland Asia. The government has prioritized developing its ports, including those in Sumatera, to improve port performance, increase connectivity, and expand the port network. The development strategy for EC3 therefore should go beyond land connectivity and focus on the entire transport corridor chain that connects land to ports and ports to their destination markets.

Each of the four EC3 provinces has its own international port located in the vicinity of the capital city and SEZs or industrial zones. Three major ports in EC3—Belawan, Malahayati, and Dumai—serve as international gateways for major exports of Sumatera. These ports are also gateway nodes in EC1 (Belawan), EC4 (Dumai), and EC5 (Malahayati). The role of these ports continues to evolve, driven by such factors as containerization, trade patterns, market integration, and business penetration of global shipping lines.

Malahayati Port (Krueng Raya Malahayati Port) in Banda Aceh is an international gateway port for container freight serving domestic containers in the shipping routes from Tanjung Priok–Belawan–Malahayati and Tanjung Priok–Belawan–Lhokseumawe–Malahayati. Commodities transported in these routes are consumer goods. Plans for Malahayati Port to serve as a feeder to Belawan is part of Indonesia's agenda to develop sea highways (*tol laut*). Malahayati Port is used to export pozzolan (a mixture of cement) to India and Dubai and to import liquid asphalt from Singapore. Malahayati Port has the potential to become a loading port for coffee, processed tuna, halal foods, and export to Thailand because of its proximity to Arun Lhokseumaawe SEZ.

Belawan Port in Medan (North Sumatera) is an international feeder port handling containers, Ro-Ro, bulk, and break-bulk cargo. Belawan Port plays an important role as a feeder port linking with smaller ports in other provinces. To support Belawan Port, the government is developing Kuala Tanjung Port to become a regional hub port for liquid bulk (CPO), dry bulk, container and general cargo for North Sumatera Province and Nanggroe Aceh Darussalam Province. Belawan will eventually become a domestic feeder port once the facilities of Kuala Tanjung Port are completed and operational. In March 2020, Kuala Tanjung made its first container shipment to Port Klang. Kuala Tanjung has been designed to also serve as an outlet/inlet for the Sei Mangkei SEZ.

Dumai Port is the main international gateway for goods and passengers and is a transit point for goods from other parts of Riau and other provinces in Sumatera. It is the main gateway for exports of CPO of Riau Province bound for India, the PRC, and Saudi Arabia. CPO exports at Dumai Port is about 6 million tons per year, compared to 3.5 million tons per year exported in Belawan Port, Medan.[16] It is also a gateway for exports to Malaysia and Thailand of CPO derivatives (stearin, palm kernel expeller, and palm kernel shell) from processing plants in various parts of the province. Dumai Port is the center for at least 5 feeder ports, namely Bagansiapiapi, Tanjung Lumba-Lumba, Tanjung Medang, Sinaboi, and Panipahan.[17]

In addition to these three international gateway ports, South Sumatera has two main ferry ports: Tanjung Api-Api Port and Boom Baru Port located in Palembang City. Tanjung Api-Api is an international seaport located

---

[16]   Pelindo I Akan Tingkatkan Kapasitas Pelabuhan Dumai. 2017. *Pelindo 1 Cabang Dumai.* 31 October.

[17]   Pelabuhan Pusat dan Pelabuhan Feedernya di Riau. 2019. *Pelindo 1 Cabang Dumai.* 5 October.

onshore in the Banyuasin district 80 km from Palembang. It is one of the major ports in Indonesia strategically located near Indonesia's sea lane of communications[18] and the Strait of Malacca.

Air Linkages

Domestic flights are well-served by airports in the four provinces. These airports are: (i) Sultan Iskandar Muda International Airport (Banda Aceh, Aceh); (ii) Kualanamu International Airport (Medan, North Sumatera); (iii) Sultan Syarif Kasim II International Airport (Pekanbaru, Riau); and (iv) Sultan Mahmud Badaruddin II International Airport (Palembang, South Sumatera). International routes in Asia served by these airports include Kuala Lumpur, Penang, Singapore, and Phuket. Several carriers fly directly to Kuala Lumpur and Singapore, with a few flying to Penang and Phuket. Phuket is the only destination in Thailand flown by carriers in these airports. Good air connectivity with Malaysia has resulted in Malaysians dominating foreign visitor composition in all four provinces. The low number of Thai visitors to the EC3 provinces in Sumatera is due to the limited number of carriers flying to Southern Thailand, except a few flying to Phuket and a Lion Air direct flight from Medan to Bangkok.

Foreign and Domestic Trade

The four EC3 provinces in Sumatera trade actively with Malaysia and Thailand. Malaysia is a prominent trading partner of North Sumatera, Riau, and South Sumatera, while Aceh has stronger trade ties with Thailand. In 2018, North Sumatera had the highest value of imports from Malaysia ($476.2 million) while Riau had the highest value of exports to Malaysia, consisting mainly of palm oil (Table 14).

Table 14: Economic Corridor 3: Trade of Sumatera Provinces with Malaysia and Thailand 2018
($ million)

Item	Total Trade	Malaysia	Share (%)	Thailand	Share (%)
Aceh	**168.3**	**7.5**	**4.5**	**27.4**	**16.3**
Export	138.6	4.4	3.2	18.3	13.2
Import	29.7	3.1	10.6	9.1	30.7
North Sumatera	**14,439.6**	**746.4**	**5.2**	**390.4**	**2.7**
Export	8,787.2	270.2	3.1	173.7	1.9
Import	5,652.4	476.2	8.4	216.7	3.8
Riau	**17,499.1**	**1,341.9**	**7.7**	**84.3**	**0.5**
Export	15,931.3	1,063.2	6.7	11.7	0.1
Import	1,567.8	278.7	17.8	72.7	4.6
South Sumatera	**4,479.2**	**611.3**	**13.6**	**132.6**	**2.9**
Export	3,734.5	551.7	14.8	122.7	3.3
Import	744.7	59.6	8.0	9.9	1.3
Total EC3	**36,586.1**	**2,707.1**	**7.4**	**634.7**	**1.7**

EC = economic corridor.
Source: BPS-Statistics Indonesia, 2019.

---

[18] Sea lanes of communication (SLOC) is a term describing the primary maritime routes between ports used for trade, logistics, and naval forces. The first SLOC is the Strait of Malacca. https://www.files.ethz.ch/isn/23243/Management%20of%20the%20Sea%20Lanes%20of%20Communication%20in%20SE%20Asia.pdf accessed on October 16, 2020.

Domestic trade is reflected in terms of purchases (imports) and sales (exports) among the four provinces. The pattern of domestic trade indicates strong partnerships between Aceh and North Sumatera and North Sumatera and Riau. Meanwhile, South Sumatera has stronger ties with Jakarta and West Java in Java Island, as well as with Lampung and Jambi in the southern part of Sumatera. The presence of Dumai Port in Riau and Belawan Port in North Sumatera is a key factor driving the sale and purchase of goods among these provinces. As the four provinces produce similar products, mainly palm oil and rubber, commodities traded are largely directed to the ports for exports rather than to the domestic market for consumption or further processing.

Domestic trade activities are conducted mainly by land as the Trans-Sumatera Toll Road has shortened the distances between the provinces, thereby contributing to increased economic activities between them. In North Sumatera, South Sumatera, and Riau, some trading activities still use inland water transportation (rivers).

Tourism

North Sumatera had the highest foreign visitor arrivals among the four EC3 provinces in 2018, while South Sumatera had the lowest. Malaysians dominated the foreign visitor composition in all four provinces because of good air connectivity between major cities in Sumatera and other parts of Indonesia, with Penang and Kuala Lumpur (plus Melaka through Riau). In 2018, foreign tourist arrivals in Kualanamu International Airport, Medan reached 236,431 an increase of almost 7% from the previous year. Almost 60% of tourist arrivals were from Malaysia (Table 15).

Thai tourists that visited North Sumatera were much less at 3,605 (1.5%). The low number of Thai visitors to the EC3 provinces in Sumatera is partly due to the limited number of carriers flying to Southern Thailand, except a few flying to Phuket and a Lion Air direct flight from Medan to Bangkok. As for Riau Province and Malaysia connectivity, there are international ferry services going to Dumai Port from MIFT, Port of Port Dickson, Muar Port and Port Klang.

Table 15: Economic Corridor 3: Foreign Visitor Arrivals in Economic Corridor 3 Provinces in Sumatera, 2018

Province	Total	Malaysia		Thailand	
		Number	Share (%)	Number	Share (%)
Aceh	29,213[a]	24,210	82.9	268	0.9
North Sumatera	236,431	139,878	59.2	3,605	1.5
Riau	146,935	31,915[b]	21.7	286	0.2
South Sumatera	13,862	7,817[c]	56.4	195	1.4

[a] Only through Sultan Iskandar Muda International Airport.
[b] Only through Sultan Syarif Kasim II International Airport (19,006) + through Dumai Port (12,909).
[c] Only through Sultan Mahmud Badaruddin II International Airport.
Sources: BPS-Statistics Indonesia, 2019; Ministry of Tourism and Creative Economy, 2019 (Ministry of Tourism and Creative Economy. *Data Kunjungan Wisatawan Mancanegara Bulan Desember Tahun 2018.* http://www.kemenpar.go.id/asset_admin/assets/uploads/media/pdf/media_1564113468_Laporan_Wisman_Bulan_Desember_2018_V_2_-_Klasik_12.pdf.

Development Strategies

Under the RPJMN 2020–2024, the government plans to develop a growth corridor in Sumatera Island covering all its 10 provinces. The single corridor in the eastern region is the "growth corridor" and comprises six provinces: (i) Aceh, (ii) North Sumatera, (iii) Riau, (iv) Jambi, (v) South Sumatera, and (vi) Lampung. The four other provinces would constitute the so-called "equalization or distribution branches" linking with the growth corridor. The equalization branches include: (i) West Sumatera, and (ii) Bengkulu located in the west coast region; and (iii) Riau Islands, and (iv) Bangka Belitung Islands, which are separate island groups in the eastern orientation of Sumatera. This configuration requires all provincial capitals to be connected to each other by the Trans-Sumatera toll road. In addition to the provincial capital, the growth corridor also highlights the catalytic role of SEZs, industrial zones, and national strategic tourism zones. Growth areas in different parts of Sumatera will be developed during 2020–2024.

Sumatera Island development will focus on developing downstream activities in agriculture, fisheries, and mining-based industries to create added value through the processing of raw materials into semi-finished and finished products. These activities will leverage the benefits of connectivity from the Trans-Sumatera toll road as well as port and airports improvements that will facilitate the movement of goods and reduce the costs of transport and logistics. Connectivity between the provinces in Sumatera will link production, processing, and logistics activities more efficiently for more competitive exports. Moreover, the development of economic zones along the eastern coast of Sumatera will further promote processing of leading commodities that could be exported at strategically located gateway ports. The leading commodities in Sumatera identified in the RPJMN 2020–2024 are cacao, coconut, palm oil, rubber, coffee, pepper, nutmeg, sugarcane, gold, tin, petroleum, natural gas, coal, capture fisheries, and aquaculture.

Reconfiguration of EC3

To align with the government's development plan for Sumatera, EC3 has been expanded to eight provinces—with their respective capitals as nodes—along the Trans-Sumatera toll road. The eight provinces in the expanded EC3 will comprise

- four provinces along the eastern coast under the existing corridor—Aceh, Riau, North Sumatera, and South Sumatera;
- two additional provinces along the western coast—West Sumatera and Bengkulu; and
- two additional provinces in the southeastern part of Sumatera—Lampung and Jambi.

As the EC3 will now comprise the eight provinces in Sumatera Island, **EC3 has been renamed Trans-Sumatera Economic Corridor** (Map 7).

Map 7: Trans-Sumatera Economic Corridor
(Reconfigured Economic Corridor 3)

INDONESIA–MALAYSIA–THAILAND
GROWTH TRIANGLE

THAILAND

Chumphon
Ranong
CHUMPHON
RANONG
Andaman Sea
PHANGNGA
Surat Thani
SURAT THANI
Phangnga
Nakhon Si Thammarat
Krabi
NAKHON SI THAMMARAT
PHUKET
Phuket
KRABI
Phatthalung
Trang
PHATTHALUNG
TRANG
Songkhla
SATUN
Satun
Pattani
Kuah
Yala
PATTANI
SONGKHLA
Kangar
NARATHIWAT
Narathiwat
LANGKAWI ISLAND
PERLIS
Kota Bharu
Alor Setar
KEDAH

Banda Aceh
Sigli
Arun Lhokseumawe SEZ
Lhokseumawe
Kuala Terengganu
Butterworth
Kulim
PENANG ISLAND
George Town
Gerik
Marang
Rimba Raya
Langsa
PENANG
KELANTAN
TERENGGANU
ACEH
Kuala Sepetang
Gua Musang
Belawan Port
Strait of Malacca
Ipoh
Kemasik
Belawan
PERAK
Kuala Lipis
Medan
Kuala
Bagan Datuk
PAHANG
Binjai
Tanjung Port
Sei Mangkei SEZ
Tebingtinggi
SELANGOR
Kuantan
Kisaran
Shah Alam
PENINSULAR
Pematangsiantar
KUALA LUMPUR
MALAYSIA
Lake Toba
Port Klang
NEGERI SEMBILAN
Temerloh
SIMEULUE
Rantau Prapat
Seremban
Port Dickson
Mersing
NORTH SUMATERA
Sibolga
MELAKA
Melaka
Dumai
Muar
JOHOR
Kota Tinggi
NIAS
Aek Kanopan
Johor Bahru
SINGAPORE
Tanjung Buton Port
BATU
Pekanbaru
Tanjungpinang
RIAU ISLANDS
Pariaman
RIAU
LINGGA
Bukittinggi
Rengat
Teluk Kuantan
Padang
WEST SUMATERA
INDONESIA
SIBERUT
BANGKA
JAMBI
Jambi
Pangkalpinang
PAGAI
BANGKA BELITUNG ISLANDS
Belitung
Tanjung Api-Api Port
BELITUNG
SOUTH SUMATERA
Palembang
Lahat
Bengkulu
Baturaja
Java Sea
BENGKULU
LAMPUNG
Lampung
Bandar Lampung
ENGGANO
Bakauheni Port
INDIAN OCEAN

0 50 100 150 200 250
Kilometers

Legend
- National Capital
- Provincial/State Capital
- City/Town
- Economic Corridor 3
- Economic Corridor 3 (reconfiguration)
- National Road
- Other Road
- Provincial Boundary
- International Boundary
- **SEZ** = special economic zone
- Boundaries are not necessarily authoritative.

This map was produced by the cartography unit of the Asian Development Bank. The boundaries, colors, denominations, and any other information shown on this map do not imply, on the part of the Asian Development Bank, any judgment on the legal status of any territory, or any endorsement or acceptance of such boundaries, colors, denominations, or information.

Source: Asian Development Bank.

The main industrial/commercial areas and ports in the eight provinces have been included in the expanded EC3. These are

- Arun Lhokseumawe SEZ (Aceh)

- Sei Mangkei SEZ and Kuala Tanjung Port (North Sumatera)

- Tanjung Buton (Riau Province)

- Padang and Bukittinggi (West Sumatera)

- Tanjung Api-Api (South Sumatera)

- Bengkulu City (Bengkulu Province)

- Bandar Lampung and Bakauheni Port (Lampung Province)

The expansion of EC3 would provide more opportunities to develop value chain linkages between the eastern, western, and southeastern provinces of Sumatera. These activities can leverage the benefits of connectivity from the Trans-Sumatera toll road connecting all provincial capitals, as well as port and airport improvements that will facilitate the movement of goods and reduce the costs of transport and logistics. Connectivity between eight provinces in Sumatera will link production, processing, and logistics activities more efficiently for more competitive exports. Moreover, the development of economic zones along the eastern coast of Sumatera will further promote processing of leading commodities for exports at strategically located gateway ports along the Strait of Malacca.

West Sumatera. West Sumatera's location along the western coast facing the Indian Ocean makes it distant from the concentration of economic activities along the eastern coast. West Sumatera's GRDP per capita is $2,104—the fourth lowest in Sumatera over Bengkulu, Lampung, and Aceh. The province's GRDP has been growing at an average of 1.38% from 2014–2018 and contributed 7.4% to Sumatera's GRDP in 2018. Padang, the capital city has a population of about 940,000 or 17.45% of the province's total population of 5.4 million.

West Sumatera belongs to the equalization corridor under the National Indicative Plan for Sumatera. West Sumatera's inclusion in EC3 will expand its opportunities to link with more mature supply chains in palm oil and rubber in Riau Province. Its inclusion in EC4 will open trade opportunities with Malaysia through Dumai Port. Moreover, Padang, which is part of the National Strategic Tourism Zone, can collaborate with other tourist destinations in EC3 in the packaging, promotion, and marketing of tourism products.

The National Development Plan for Sumatera 2020–2024 includes the Padang–Pekanbaru segment (2,544 km) and Padang–Sicincin[19] segment (36 km) as part of the Trans-Sumatera Toll Road. For maritime transport, Teluk Bayur/Padang Port in Padang City is the main export gateway of West Sumatera to India and the United States. Trade with Malaysia comprised 4.3% of West Sumatera's total trade, while trade with Thailand comprised 0.47%. The main commodities traded with Malaysia are palm oil, oil cake and residues, and fresh captured fish. Minangkabau International Airport in Padang serves domestic routes to Batam, Medan, Pekanbaru, Jambi, Palembang, and Bengkulu, as well as international routes to Kuala Lumpur and Singapore.

Bukittinggi is a well-known tourist destination in the Sumatera region. Under the RPJM 2020–2024, the city has been designated as part of the National Strategic Tourism Zone. West of Padang is the Mentawai Island, which has chosen as an Integrated Marine and Fishery Center in Sumatera, together with Sabang in

---

[19]   Sicincin is part of Padang Pariaman Regency, West Sumatera.

Aceh. Some famous tourist attractions include the Sianok Canyon and the Bukittinggi Clock Tower. The city is also famous as a center for ethnic Minangkabau souvenirs. The city is most famous for its authentic culinary delights, such as *Nasi Kapau*, which is hard to find in other areas.

Bengkulu Province, located along the western coast, is the third smallest province in Sumatera, occupying 19,919 square kilometers (km^2) or 4.1% of Sumatera's total land area. In 2018, its share to Sumatera's GRDP was 1.98% and its per capita GRDP of $1,553 is the lowest among the EC3 provinces. Bengkulu City, the provincial capital, has a population of 376,000 or 19.18% of Bengkulu Province's population.

Bengkulu's main resource is captured fish from the Indian Ocean, but it also has abundant rubber, wood, and palm oil. Grouper and tuna are exported to Malaysia, while palm oil shells are exported to Thailand and the PRC. Pulau Balai Port, 16 km from Bengkulu city, is the main gateway for Bengkulu's exports (49.3%), followed by Teluk Bayur Port in West Sumatera (24.0%), and Boom Baru Port in South Sumatera (1.2%). Bengkulu's exports contributed 16.7% (Malaysia) and 7.3% (Thailand) of Bengkulu's total export volume. For domestic trade, Bengkulu sells CPO, kernel, and coffee to West Sumatera, Jakarta, South Sumatera, and other provinces in Indonesia. Under the RPJMN 2020–2024, Bengkulu will be connected to Palembang through the Trans-Sumatera Toll Road, under the Lubuklinggau–Curup–Bengkulu section covering 95.8 km. This section is expected to be operational by 2022.

Lampung Province is the second most populous province in Sumatera after North Sumatera. In 2018, it contributed 10.4% to Sumatera's GRDP, but its per capita GRDP of $1,915 is one of the lowest in Sumatera. Bandar Lampung, the provincial capital, is located near Sunda Strait, a strategic waterway under the Indonesian sea lane of communication.[20] Lampung is part of Sumatera's growth corridor where four industrial zones—Tanggamus, Pesawaran, Way Pisang, and Katibung—which are being developed.

The sugar industry in Lampung is a primary sector, contributing an average of 38% to national sugar production (750,000–800,000 tons per year).[21] Sugar is widely traded in the domestic market; it was also Lampung's fourth biggest export in 2018. Panjang and Tarahan Ports (specifically for coal exports from PT Bukit Asam) in Bandar Lampung are the two gateway ports of the province.

Lampung contributed 8.6% to Sumatera's foreign trade in 2018—the fourth largest contribution after Riau Islands, Riau, and North Sumatera. Trade with Malaysia contributed 3.1% to the province's total trade, with CPO and coffee as the main export commodities, as well as oil and gas as the main import commodities. Meanwhile, trade with Thailand contributed higher at 7.20% by exporting coffee and paper while importing sugar and rice. For domestic trade, Lampung's biggest markets are Jakarta and South Sumatera. Tapioca flour, instant coffee, and rubber latex are the main products sold in the domestic market. Lampung's domestic trade contributed 11.3% of Sumatera's total domestic trade value in 2018.

The Trans-Sumatera toll road ends at Bakauheni in Lampung. The Bakauheni Port is the point of connectivity between Sumatera and Java Islands. There are Ro-Ro ferry services from Bakauheni Port to Merak Port (Banten Province) in Java Island. There are direct flights from the Radin Inten II Airport in Bandar Lampung to Kuala Lumpur.

---

[20]   Under the United Nations Convention on the Law of the Sea 1982, Indonesia as a littoral state, should provide a safe transit and innocent (international) passage in its (sea) water area. Indonesia has designated three sea lanes of communication. One of them is the Sunda Strait between Sumatera and Java and connects the Java Sea with the Indian Ocean.

[21]   Established sugarcane plantations in Lampung can be found in Lampung Tengah, Tulang Bawang, and Lampung Utara regencies, while developing plantations can be found in Mesuji and Lampung Timur regencies

Jambi Province in the eastern coast of central Sumatera is the fifth largest province in Sumatera (in terms of land area). It contributed 6.41% to Sumatera's GRDP in 2018 and its per capita GRDP of $2,766 is the third highest in Sumatera after the Riau Islands and Riau. Jambi City, the provincial capital, has a population of close to 600,000, or 6.75% of Jambi's total population. The city is part of Sumatera's growth corridor with plans to develop the Kemingking Industrial Zone for the agriculture industry. The zone covers about 2,000 ha and is located 20 km from Jambi City.

Jambi province has the third largest rubber plantation area in Indonesia after South Sumatera and North Sumatera. These three provinces pay an important role in placing Indonesia as the second largest rubber exporter after Thailand. Muara Sabak and Talang Duku are the province's major gateway ports. Jambi contributed 3.7% to Sumatera's total trade in 2018, with its export volume significantly higher than imports. Exports to Malaysia and Thailand were 5.9% and 5.5%, respectively of Jambi's total exports. Vegetable oil, mineral fuels, and coal are the main exports to Malaysia, while betel nut, mineral fuels, and coal are the main exports to Thailand. Malaysia is Jambi's third biggest import source (15.2%) after Canada and the PRC. Major imports from Malaysia are parts of machinery plant, soya beans, and ethylene polymers aseptic bag.

Jambi city is part of the main Eastern Trans-Sumatera National Highway, connecting Pekanbaru and Palembang and is also part of the Trans-Sumatera toll road. There are no direct flights to Malaysia, Singapore, and Thailand from Sultan Thaha Airport in Jambi City.

Apart from the additional four provinces, several commercial and industrial nodes and gateway ports have been added in the existing provinces in EC3.

Arun Lhokseumawe is an SEZ located in the eastern coast of Aceh Province and currently hosts global companies engaged in the production of petrochemicals, fertilizers, gas, and energy.[22] It also has the potential to develop a capture fisheries industry and showcase a productive aquatic ecosystem. The plan for 2020–2024 is to develop Arun Lhokseumawe SEZ, together with five other SEZs in Sumatera, as growth centers for key industries such as agro-processing (involving leading commodities such as palm oil, coffee, cocoa, rubber, coconut, and essential oils) energy, petrochemicals, and logistics. For the energy sector (oil and gas subsector), the the major initiatives will include liquified natural gas regasification, hub operations, and trading; liquified petroleum gas hub operations and trading; as well as the development of environmentally friendly power plants and clean energy solutions. Logistics infrastructure in the ports will be developed to support the requirements of the growth industries. In 2018, the port in Lhokseumawe handled 5.5% of Aceh's total exports (the second largest contributor after Meulaboh Port) and 36.5% of the province's imports (the top contributor, followed by Sabang Port).

Sei Mangkei SEZ is in Simalungun Regency on the eastern coast of North Sumatera, adjacent to the Strait of Malacca, covering 2,002 ha of land. The SEZ caters mainly to the palm oil and rubber industries. Raw materials from palm oil plantations are transported to Sei Mangkei SEZ for processing to fatty acid, fatty alcohol, surfactant, biodiesel, biogas, and other downstream products for exports. In 2019, the total export value of products from Sei Mangkei is $228.6 million. Sei Mangkei SEZ also supports ancillary industries such

---

[22]   Some companies located in Arun Lhokseumawe SEZ include PT Pupuk Iskandar Muda (petrochemical, fertilizer), PT Pertamina (gas and energy), PT Pelindo I (logistics), and PT Pembangunan Aceh (agro-industry).

as logistics, energy, electronics, and tourism.[23] Sei Mangkei is one of the five SEZs in Sumatera Island that are being developed as part of the growth corridor. Sei Mangkei SEZ is 40 km away from Kuala Tanjung Port.

Kuala Tanjung Port is in Batubara Regency, approximately 114 km from Medan. In the next 5 years, it will be developed as an international port hub to handle liquid bulk (CPO), dry bulk, container, and general cargo for North Sumatera and Aceh.[24] Palm oil plantations dominate the Kuala Tanjung Port's hinterlands, which include Asahan, Simalungun, Labuhan Batu, and the surrounding areas. Once completed, the port can accommodate 600 million TEUs per year and can facilitate the export of CPO and CPO-based upstream and downstream products from the hinterlands. At present, Kuala Tanjung Port handles 11% of North Sumatera's total export value (16.15% in trade volume) since it is not yet fully operational. Kuala Tanjung Port has been designed to serve as an outlet and inlet for Sei Mangkei SEZ which is only 40 km from Kuala Tanjung, compared to 148 km from Belawan Port.

Tanjung Buton is a designated industrial zone with a cargo port facility located in Siak Regency, Riau Province occupying 5,000 ha of land. Tanjung Buton supports industries around Riau Province, namely CPO, forest products, pulp and its derivatives, petrochemicals, coconut-based products, rubber products, fisheries, and oil and gas supporting industries, as well as other SMEs. It is a gateway for transporting coal which is a major industry in Siak Regency catering mostly to the domestic market. Export–import activities handled at the port are estimated at around 5.9 million tons per year.[25] Tanjung Buton (located in the mainland) operates ferry routes to Selat Panjang and other islands in Riau Province; Batam and Karimun in Riau Islands Province; as well as Belitung in Bangka Belitung Islands Province.[26] Tanjung Buton is one of the designated industrial zones that is being developed.

Tanjung Api-Api is an SEZ in Banyuasin Regency, about 67.9 km from Palembang and 2.5 km from Tanjung Api-Api Port. It was established in 2014 but as of December 2019, it has not operated yet. The government of South Sumatera proposes to integrate the existing area of 67 ha with the Sriwijaya Patria Authority area (2,170 ha), which is located about 12 km north of the designated SEZ location. The plan is for Tanjung Api-Api SEZ to be a downstream industrial center for resource-based industries such as seed rubber, palm oil, and coal. The port adjacent to Tanjung Api-Api SEZ would serve as an international gateway port since existing ports in Boom Baru Port in the Musi River are facing challenges of siltation from time to time. Tanjung Api-Api is one of the five SEZs in Sumatera Island identified as a growth area under the national development plan for 2020–2024.

Bakauheni Port connects Sumatera and Java Islands, which are separated by the Sunda Strait by about 14.7 miles. The Bakauheni Port services Ro-Ro ferry routes to Merak Port in Banten Province in the northwestern tip of Java. This link enables Sumatera to be a strategic supplier of raw materials and food to Java, the center of the Indonesian economy, where 57.45% of Indonesia's population live. In 2015, there were 52 ferries serving the Bakauheni–Merak route, with a combined capacity for taking 112 trips, and loading 11,400 vehicles, per day. In 2014, Bakauheni Port ferried almost 2 million vehicles, dominated by trucks (42.27%), across the Sunda Strait going to Java. In the same year, 1,652,565 passengers transited through the port. As of November 2018, there

---

23   Sei Mangkei SEZ investors include PT Unilever Oleochemical Indonesia, PT Industri Nabati Lestari, PTPN III, PT PLN, PT Pertamina, PTPN III & Posco Energy, and PT Pertagas & Alternatif Protein. PT Unilever Oleochemical Indonesia has exported its products to 42 countries, while PT Industri Nabati Lestari exported olein, refined bleached palm oil, stearin, and fatty acid to Argentina, Bangladesh, India, Papua New Guinea, the PRC, Senegal, and the US.

24   The policy was stated in Presidential Regulation No. 26/2012 on the Blueprint for National Logistics System Development, and later mentioned in National Medium-Term Development Plan (RPJMN) 2020–2024 (Annex I, p. III.39).

25   Dinas Penanaman Modal dan Pelayanan Terpadu Satu Pintu Kabupaten Siak. *Kawasan Industri Tanjung Buton.* https://web.siakkab.go.id/peluang-investasi/.

26   Government of Siak Regency, Riau. Pelabuhan Tg. Buton-Siak.

were 71 ferries, 51 of them above 5,000 GT, which can serve 17,280 vehicles per day.[27] The role of Bakauheni Port has become more important with the cancellation of the previous plan to construct the Sunda Strait Bridge connecting Sumatera and Java Islands. The existing and additional provinces and nodes in EC3 are summarized in Table 16.

Table 16: Economic Corridor 3: Existing and Additional Provinces and Nodes, by Type

Province	Node	Type				
		CAP	COM	INT	MGP	TOUR
INDONESIA						
Aceh	Banda Aceh	✓	✓	✓		✓
	Arun Lhokseumawe SEZ*		✓		✓	
North Sumatera	Medan	✓	✓	✓		✓
	Belawan Port				✓	
	Sei Mangkei SEZ		✓			
	Kuala Tanjung Port*		✓		✓	
Riau	Pekanbaru	✓	✓	✓		
	Dumai				✓	
	Tanjung Buton Port*		✓		✓	
West Sumatera*	Padang*	✓	✓			✓
	Bukittinggi*		✓			✓
Jambi*	Jambi*	✓	✓			
South Sumatera	Palembang	✓	✓			✓
	Tanjung Api-Api Port		✓		✓	✓
Bengkulu*	Bengkulu*	✓	✓			
Lampung*	Bandar Lampung*	✓	✓			
	Bakauheni Port*				✓	

CAP = capital, COM = commercial, INT = interchange, MGP = maritime gateway port, SEZ = special economic zone, TOUR = tourism.
Note: * denotes additional provinces and nodes.
Source: Study team.

Findings and Recommendations

Connectivity among the four EC3 provinces (Aceh, Riau, North Sumatera, and South Sumatera) is adequate, but the quality of roads is uneven, with most of the segments having two lanes and classified as Class II. The road surface is smooth but travel in some segments can be slow due to congestion and occasional potholes resulting from poor maintenance. The ongoing Trans-Sumatera Toll Road Project will eventually connect all provincial capitals including those under EC3. As of August 2020, around 22% of the 2,704-km stretch has been completed. With this progress, the target of completing the eight priority sections by 2019 as stated in the Presidential Regulation No.117/2015, has not been achieved. For the next phase, the government should prioritize key sections that connect key nodes in EC3 including sections along Medan–Pekanbaru–Palembang.

---

[27]　D. M. Hutauruk. 2018. Kemenhub: Jumlah kapal di lintasan Merak-Bakauheni resmi dibatasi (accessed 1 September 2020).

As external trade expands and value chains develop in Sumatera, railways as an alternative and more efficient mode of transport will become increasingly important. There is no single railway line that connects the provinces in Sumatera Islands although there is a plan to construct a Trans-Sumatera Railway in the Strategic Plan of Ministry of Transport 2020–2024. At present, there are only partial railway links that facilitate transport of goods from production centers to the ports. Given that railways are highly capital-intensive, the railway routes or sections should be prioritized according to the strategic requirements of supply chains for particular products.

The development of EC3 should focus not only on land connectivity between provinces in Sumatera, but also in developing transportation systems and links between industrial zones and ports. Investments in land-based infrastructure (both road and rail) should be leveraged with improvements in the services and performance of ports to make them competitive with other Asian ports, notably Port Klang and Singapore. Since most provinces in Sumatera produce similar products, mainly rubber and palm oil, commodities transported across these provinces either undergo further processing as part of value chains or are directed to gateway ports. A number of provinces in EC3 have their own international ports located in the vicinity of the capital city and SEZs or industrial zones. Land and port bottlenecks in these areas should be addressed as a priority to reduce logistics cost—estimated to be about 26% of overall GDP for Indonesia—to boost the efficiency of the transport sector. This can potentially create a more efficient supply chain, especially for palm-oil based and rubber-based products that could make a difference in achieving the goals of economic growth in the region.

Economic Corridor 4. The Melaka–Dumai Economic Corridor

Overview

The Melaka–Dumai Economic Corridor (EC4) is a maritime corridor linking Riau Province in Sumatera to the state of Melaka in Peninsular Malaysia. The underpinning economic rationale for this link is based on the strategic location of Dumai Port and Tanjung Bruas Port located opposite each other in one of the narrowest stretches of the Strait of Malacca thus having the shortest distance between them across the Straits (Map 8).

Riau and Melaka have a long tradition of freight and passenger traffic driven by the dynamism of their respective economies. Riau Province is the second richest province of Indonesia with abundant palm oil plantations and onshore oil and gas resources. Melaka, located at the southern tip of the Strait of Malacca, is Riau's major gateway to the peninsula and is a major destination for local and international tourists. The MIFT has recently become a popular port of call for cruise ships.

Since 2013, proposals have been mooted to establish a "fixed link" between Sumatera and Malaysia across the Strait of Malacca. These proposals include the Melaka–Dumai Bridge, the Batam–Singapore Bridge, and the Riau–Johor Link—a 17.5-km sea tunnel that will connect Riau in Sumatera to Kukup in Pontian Johor.[28]

---

[28]   The University Teknologi Malaysia and the Pelalawan Regency have conducted the feasibility study for the Riau–Johor link. The tunnel will link Karimun Island in Riau to Kukup Pontian near the existing ferry in Pontian district. The study showed that that link would create higher economic impact between Riau and Johor and has a lower risk level and disturbing effect compared to the development of Dumai–Melaka and Batam–Singapore bridges.

**Map 8: Melaka–Dumai Economic Corridor
(Economic Corridor 4)**

INDONESIA–MALAYSIA–THAILAND
GROWTH TRIANGLE

Source: Asian Development Bank.

Existing Provinces and Nodes

Riau Province is a resource-based economy in Sumatera rich in crude oil, palm oil, rubber trees, and other forest products. In 2018, Riau Province contributed 21.6% to Sumatera's GRDP and had the highest GRDP per capita in Sumatera of $4,861. The province's population was estimated at 6.8 million in 2018 or 11.8% of Sumatera's population. The islands of Bengkalis, Rupat, and Rangsang are part of Riau Province.

EC4 involves two key cities in Riau Province—Pekanbaru and Dumai.[29] Pekanbaru is the capital and commercial center of Riau Province. The city's population was 1.1 million in 2018, or 16.4% of the total population in Riau Province.[30] Pekanbaru is strategically located at the center of Sumatera's most dynamic economies—Padang in West Sumatera, Medan in North Sumatera, Dumai in the east, and Jambi City, Jambi Province in the south. Connectivity with these provinces is through the existing Eastern Trans-Sumatera National Highway and will further be improved with the completion of the Trans-Sumatera toll road. It is linked to the province's outermost islands through three ports—Perawang, Pekanbaru, and Rumbai—that are used for trade by the surrounding regencies. It is among the cities included in the Trans-Sumatera growth corridor under the RPJMN 2020–2024. The Riau provincial government is contemplating on establishing an SEZ for tourism in North Rupat Island and Pekanbaru.

Dumai City is a small port city located along the Strait of Malacca and serves as a commercial and gateway node for goods and passengers. Although Dumai City comprises only 1.9% of Riau Province's land area, it contributed 5.8% of Riau Province's total revenue in 2017. The city has well-developed oil refinery and palm oil processing industries generated by five industrial estate areas, namely Pelintung, Lubuk Gaung, Dock Yard, Bukit Kapur, and Bukit Timah. The presence of large oil companies such as Caltex/Chevron and Pertamina, as well as palm oil processing companies (PT Bukit Kapur Reksa, Asian Agri, Sinarmas, and Energi Unggul Persada) has earned for Dumai the label of *kota minyak* (oil city). These companies export their products to various international destinations through Dumai Port.

Dumai Port is the main international gateway for goods and passengers and a central port for CPO exports to international markets including Malaysia and Thailand. It has the advantage of having a shorter distance to Peninsular Malaysia (approximately 107.8 km) compared to other major ports in Sumatera. CPO from the regencies of Rokan Hulu, Rokan Hilir, Kampar, Kuantan Singingi, Bengkalis, Siak, Pelalawan, Indragiri Hulu, and Indragiri Hilir are all shipped through Dumai Port, making it the largest gateway for CPO exports in Sumatera. Its strategic location has made it the center for at least five feeder ports—Bagansiapiapi, Tanjung Lumba-Lumba, Tanjung Medang, Sinaboi, and Panipahan. Dumai Port services international ferries from Malaysia (MIFT, Port of Port Dickson, Muar Port, and Port Klang).

The EC4 node in Malaysia is Tanjung Bruas Port in Melaka. The port is the main trade gateway to Melaka and other states in the peninsula from Riau Province. Situated within a large hinterland drawn from Melaka, Negeri Sembilan and northern Johor, Tanjung Bruas Port is surrounded by more than 500 companies that ship both conventional and container cargoes through the port. Comprehensive improvements are being planned to develop the port as a hub for sea–air cargoes. The implementation of the Dumai–Melaka Ro-Ro Ferry Project will boost cargo freight between the Dumai and Tanjung Bruas ports. In addition, the MIFT is affiliated with the Port of Bandar Sri Laksamana in Bengkalis Regency, which provides ferry services from Melaka to Riau.

---

[29]   The other 10 areas in the province are classified as regencies.

[30]   BPS-Statistics Indonesia. *Provinsi Riau dalam Angka 2019*. Pekanbaru: BPS Provinsi Riau, 2019, p. 67.

Status of Physical Connectivity

Road Connectivity

There are two alternative routes between Pekanbaru and Dumai: (i) the 177 km non-toll road as part of the Trans-Sumatera Highway, and (ii) the 131.5 km toll road which is ongoing construction as part of the Trans-Sumatera Toll Road. Most of the roads in the Trans-Sumatera Highway are paved, but some sections| are in a poor condition due to the large number of trucks transporting palm oil crops from Riau to North Sumatera and vice versa.

From Port Klang, the road to Tanjung Bruas Port is via Simpang Ampat (Alor Gajah) on Expressway E2 and Alor Gajah–Melaka–Jasin Highway. Roads to Tanjung Bruas Port are in good condition with two-way federal and state roads. Tanjung Bruas Port is accessible from the city of Melaka via Federal route 5 with a distance of 14 km.

Rail Connectivity

There is currently no active railway line in Riau after the Pekanbaru Railway was abandoned at the end of World War II. Projects are being planned to reactivate the Pekanbaru–Padang (West Sumatera) railway; establish the Pekanbaru–Duri-Rantau Prapat railway connecting Riau with the existing railway in North Sumatera; and build the missing rail link from Pekabanru to Jambi. These projects are currently in various stages of design and feasibility study.

Melaka City is covered by the Southern Zone Line, along with Negeri Sembilan, Johor, and Singapore. There is no train connection between Tanjung Bruas Port and Pulau Sebang/Tampin Melaka and Batang Melaka. Tanjung Bruas is only accessible by federal and state roads. The railway route from Pulau Sebang–Tampin Melaka would continue up to Johor Bahru.

Maritime Connectivity

Despite the proximity between Dumai Port and Tanjung Bruas Port, there are no direct trade links between these ports. Exports of stearin from Dumai Port are shipped to Port Klang. Dumai Port's maritime link with Malaysia is through ferry services to Port Klang, Port Dickson (Negeri Sembilan) MIFT, and Muar Port (Johor).

Sri Junjungan Port is the designated port in Riau for the Ro-Ro Ferry Project that would link to Tanjung Bruas Port. The Ro-Ro ferry will transport goods in lorries directly to traders in 5 hours compared to 1 week using regular cargo ports services. A Ro-Ro can transport 20 lorries as well as 20 cars at any one time. The Ro-Ro service can also be used as an alternative mode of transport by Malaysian tourists going to Sumatera. Harmonization of rules for permitting trucks to operate in foreign territory is one of the main issues waiting to be resolved before the Ro-Ro ferry services can start operations. Other infrastructure-related issues include the designation of Sri Junjungan as an international port; and upgrade of infrastructure facilities in Sri Junjungan Port to accommodate cargoes since it is mainly a ferry port.

Tanjung Bruas Port is in one of the busiest trade routes at the center and narrowest point in the Strait of Malacca. As a secondary port, the volume of cargo handled in the port is relatively small. Tanjung Bruas has maritime trade links with ports in Sumatera, particularly Palembang (South Sumatera) and Lhokseumawe (Aceh). The MIFT (Banda Hilir) is affiliated with the Port of Bandar Sri Laksamana in Bengkalis Regency (Riau Province), which provides ferry services for passengers from Melaka to the Riau Province (Table 17).

Table 17: Economic Corridor 4: Port Linkages Between Ports in Melaka and Ports in Sumatera

Ports in EC4	Maritime Links	Type
Tanjung Bruas Port, Alor Gajah	Palembang (South Sumatera) Lhoksuemawe (Aceh)	Cargo (steam coal, gypsum) Cargo (ammonia gas)
Melaka International Ferry Terminal, Bandar Hilir	Bandar Sri Laksamana (Bengkalis, Riau)	Ferry

Source: Study team.

Air Linkages

Sultan Syarif Kasim II International Airport[31] in Pekanbaru is the international airport of Riau Province. The airport serves flights to and from several cities and towns in Indonesia as well as Malaysia (there are direct flights to Melaka), Singapore, Sri Lanka, and Saudi Arabia. Melaka International Airport (formerly Batu Berendam Airport) services AirAsia and Malindo flights to Penang and Pekanbaru. Other than these, flights to Sumatera are very limited.

Malaysian visitors arriving in Riau Province through the airport averaged 19,495 (62% of total arrivals) during 2014–2018. Visitors from Thailand are small in comparison, averaging only 372 passengers or 1.17% of total arrivals during 2014–2018.

Overall, the status of land connectivity in EC4 is adequate although some road segments along the Trans-Sumatera highway are in poor condition. Railway links are adequate in Malaysia. There is no maritime trade link between Dumai and Tanjung Bruas Ports but there are trade links with other ports in Malaysia, as well as ferry links (Table 18).

Table 18: Economic Corridor 4: Status of Physical Connectivity

	Road	Rail	Maritime	Air
Indonesia	Adequate but with some segments in poor condition	No rail links between nodes	No maritime trade links between Dumai and Tanjung Bruas ports, but there are trade links with other Malaysia ports, as well as ferry links	Adequate
Malaysia	Good, safe, and efficient	Adequate		Adequate

Source: Study team.

---

[31]   Sultan Syarif Kasim II International Airport is often referred to as SSK II, SSK, or Sultan Syarif Kasim II International Airport (SSQ II), and formerly known as Simpang Tiga Airport.

Maritime Trade

Riau Province's total foreign trade averaged 32.0 million tons or 26.2% of Sumatera's total foreign trade during 2014–2018. Although Riau's total exports comprised about 89% of its total trade, it decreased by 3.2% from 32.2 tons in 2014 to 28.3 tons in 2018. Imports on the other hand, although comprising only 10.6% of total trade, increased by 9.9% during the period (Table 19).

Riau's trade volume with Malaysia grew by an average of 14.6% during 2014–2018. The volume of exports was consistently higher than imports although Riau's imports grew by 36.0%, compared to exports, which grew at a much slower pace of 5.4% (Table 19).

Table 19: Economic Corridor 4: Riau Province's Foreign Trade Volume
(million tons)

	2014	2015	2016	2017	2018	Average 2014–2018	Compounded Average Growth Rate 2014–2018 (%)
Total Sumatera	**116.7**	**119.1**	**108.2**	**125.7**	**140.5**	**122.0**	**4.8**
Exports	94.5	97.4	87.7	101.6	113.8	99.0	4.8
Imports	22.2	21.8	20.5	24.1	26.7	23.0	4.7
Riau	**35.1**	**30.33**	**30.04**	**32.0**	**32.5**	**32.0**	**(1.9)**
Exports	32.2	27.62	26.81	28.3	28.3	28.6	(3.2)
Imports	2.9	2.71	3.23	3.7	4.2	3.4	9.9
Share of Riau to SumateraTrade (%)	**30.0**	**25.5**	**27.8**	**25.5**	**23.1**	**26.2**	**–**
Exports	1.5	3.0	3.1	3.2	3.3	29.0	–
Imports	13	12.5	15.7	15.4	15.7	14.5	–
Trade with Malaysia	**1.8**	**1.7**	**2.8**	**2.8**	**3.1**	**2.4**	**14.6**
Exports	1.4	1.4	2.3	1.7	1.7	1.7	5.4
Imports	0.4	0.3	0.5	1.1	1.4	0.7	35.9
Share of Malaysia to Riau Trade (%)	**5.1**	**5.8**	**9.5**	**8.8**	**9.5**	**7.8**	
Exports	0.7	1.5	5.3	1.1	4.1	6.0	–
Imports	14.1	11.1	15.5	29.6	33.4	20.9	–

– = not applicable, ( ) = negative.
Source: BPS - Statistics Indonesia – various publications .

At the provincial level, Riau's trade with Thailand averaged less than 1% of the province's total foreign trade during the period 2014–2018. Exports to Thailand decreased by 70% between 2014 and 2018; in contrast, imports increased by 66.2%.

Dumai Port accounts for almost 80% of Riau Province's exports and 42% of its imports (Table 20). Dumai Port handles the largest volume of CPO exports from Indonesia destined for the PRC, India, and Saudi Arabia. Dumai Port handles exports of stearin—a CPO derivative—to Port Klang in Malaysia, as well as palm kernel oil and palm kernel shell to Thailand.

Table 20: Economic Corridor 4: Main Trading Ports in Riau Province, 2018

Port	Trade Volume (million tons)				Trade Value ($ million)			
	Export	Share (%)	Import	Share	Export	Share (%)	Import	Share
Dumai	22.6	80.0	1.8	42.1	12,497.7	78.5	557.6	35.6
Buatan (Siak)	2.7	9.5	0.8	18.8	1,463.0	9.2	399.5	25.5
Perawang (Siak)	1.5	5.4	1.4	34.0	1,366.0	8.6	436.9	27.9

Source: BPS-Statistics Indonesia, 2018.

Although Dumai Port is the largest exporter of CPO in Indonesia, there is no SEZ in the province related to the palm oil industry. Only a few companies are engaged in the processing of CPO derivative products (e.g., PT Kuala Lumpur Kepong and Kreasi Jaya Adikarya, which are Malaysian-invested companies). Presently, the provincial government is planning to establish an SEZ to boost declining export levels. Under the National Logistics System Blueprint 2012, Dumai Port will be developed as the main port for CPO-based commodities.

The volume of trade activities in Tanjung Bruas in Melaka, being a secondary port, is small—less than 1% of the total throughput in all Malaysian ports. There is no trade link between Tanjung Bruas Port and Dumai Port pending the implementation of the Ro-Ro Ferry Project. However, Tanjung Bruas Port has trade links with other ports in Sumatera, particularly Palembang (South Sumatera) and Lhokseumawe (Aceh). Commodities imported from Palembang are gypsum and coal; from Aceh, ammonia gas.

Development Strategies

A key strategy in Indonesia's National Development Plan 2020–2024 is to develop regions in order to reduce inequality and promote a more equitable distribution of the benefits of economic growth. The two main approaches for regional development are (i) the growth approach, and (ii) the equity approach under which growth corridors and island-based equalization and equal distribution corridors have been designated.[32]

Malaysia is currently focused on Tanjung Bruas Port in Melaka. However, developments in the last 5 years have opened other opportunities for Melaka to develop economic links between the southern part of the peninsula and Sumatera. These developments include massive infrastructure developments in Melaka's neighboring state of Johor as it gears up to become an innovation-driven regional hub; the sustained growth in Melaka's tourism industry and the increasing popularity of cruise tourism; and the high impact railway projects between Malaysia and Singapore that will likely affect growth patterns in areas traversed by the railway routes.

Reconfiguration of EC4

Riau's role as part of Sumatera's growth corridor can be enhanced by (i) mainstreaming Riau Province's outer islands into the mainland economy of the province and to EC4 as a means to promote a more balanced distribution of the benefits of growth, and (ii) promoting connectivity between Riau and West Sumatera to enhance value linkages and expand trade opportunities along Sumatera's eastern coast.

---

[32] Indonesia's RPJMN 2020–2024 identified a growth corridor in Sumatera comprising six provinces, namely: Aceh (Banda Aceh), North Sumatera (Medan), Riau (Pekanbaru), Jambi (Jambi City), Palembang (South Sumatera), and Lampung (Bandar Lampung).

Taking these strategies into account, EC4 has been expanded as follows:

- In Sumatera, the inclusion of (i) the outermost islands of Riau Province (Rupat Isalnds), (ii) Sri Junjungan Port, and (iii) West Sumatera; and

- In Malaysia, the inclusion of (i) the state of Johor, (ii) Tanjung Pelepas Port (Gelang Patah) and Johor Port (Pasir Gudang), both in the state of Johor; and (iii) Melaka City and the MIFT.

To reflect these additional provinces/states and nodes, **EC4 has been renamed Central Sumatera–Southern Malaysia Economic Corridor** (Map 9).

The expansion of EC4 to include the outermost islands of Riau (Rupat Islands)[33] will open new opportunities to develop Riau Province's tourism potential through closer collaboration with Melaka. The government's plan to develop an SEZ for tourism in north Rupat can tap into Melaka's plans to develop cruise tourism along the Strait of Malacca.

The inclusion of West Sumatera in EC4 will enhance the province's economic status through improved productivity and expanded trade opportunities. West Sumatera, located in the west coast facing the Indian Ocean, belongs to the equalization corridor under the National Indicative Plan for Sumatera. The Trans-Sumatera Highway connects Padang, West Sumatera's capital, with Pekanbaru and Dumai. Once completed, the Padang–Pekanbaru segment of the Trans-Sumatera Toll Road will enable faster and more efficient transport between the two cities.

Connectivity with Riau Province will enable West Sumatera to tap into more developed palm oil and rubber supply chains and expand trade with Malaysia through Dumai Port. Padang can also potentially benefit from the development of the tourism SEZ being planned at Rupat. Both Rupat and Padang are part of the National Strategic Tourism Zone and can collaborate in the packaging, promotion, and marketing of tourism products in their territories as well as in Melaka.

Sri Junjungan Port in Dumai City is the designated port for the Melaka–Dumai Ro-Ro ferry project. At present, it serves as the logistics gateway to Rupat Island transporting agricultural products, especially rice. Even though there are palm oil plantations in Rupat, its contribution to the CPO supply chain through Dumai is not significant. Sri Junjungan Port provides Ro-Ro ferry services to Rupat Island, but it will eventually extend these services to Tanjung Bruas (Melaka) once the Dumai–Melaka Ro-Ro Ferry Project is implemented.

In Malaysia, EC4 has been expanded to include the state of Johor.[34] Johor Bahru, the capital city, is a growth center of the Iskandar Malaysia corridor where high impact infrastructure investments, industrial expansion, urban development, and innovation-driven growth will be taking place over the next 5 years. The planned Johor Bahru–Singapore Rapid Transit System is envisaged to stimulate economic activities in the intermediate cities traversed by the railway, which in turn could have spillover effects on the provinces and states in EC2. Johor can enable the link to Riau Islands (in particular Batam) and Bangka Belitung Islands, which are part of the proposed route for EC6.

---

[33] Rupat Island belongs to an island group under the administration of Bengkalis Regency, Riau Province and is in front of Dumai City. The islands of Rupat, Bengkalis, and Ransang have been designated as priority locations for development

[34] Johor is not a participating state in the IMT-GT. Involvement of Johor in the IMT-GT economic corridors will require approval by the Government of Malaysia.

**Map 9: Central Sumatera–Southern Malaysia Economic Corridor
(Reconfigured Economic Corridor 4)**

INDONESIA–MALAYSIA–THAILAND
GROWTH TRIANGLE

98°00'E   104°00'E

Andaman Sea

THAILAND

Chumphon
CHUMPHON
Ranong
RANONG
Surat Thani
SURAT THANI
PHANGNGA
Phangnga
Nakhon Si Thammarat
NAKHON SI THAMMARAT
Krabi
KRABI
Phuket
PHUKET
Phatthalung
PHATTHALUNG
Trang
TRANG
Songkhla
SONGKHLA
Pattani
PATTANI
Satun
SATUN
Yala
YALA
Narathiwat
NARATHIWAT
Kuah
Kangar
PERLIS
Alor Setar
KEDAH
Kota Bharu

8°00'N   8°00'N

N

0 50 100 150 200 250
Kilometers

Banda Aceh
Sigli
Lhokseumawe
Kuala Terengganu
KELANTAN
Marang
TERENGGANU
Butterworth
PENANG ISLAND
George Town
PENANG
Kulim
Gerik
Gua Musang
Kuala Sepetang
Ipoh
PERAK
Kuala Lipis
PAHANG
Kemasik
Rimba Raya
Langsa
ACEH
LANGKAWI ISLAND
Strait of Malacca
Belawan
Medan
Binjai
Tebingtinggi
Bagan Datuk
Kuantan
Kisaran
Pematangsiantar
Lake Toba
SELANGOR
Shah Alam
KUALA LUMPUR
Port Klang
Seremban
NEGERI SEMBILAN
Temerloh
PENINSULAR MALAYSIA
Rantau Prapat
NORTH SUMATERA
Sibolga
SIMEULUE
NIAS
Mersing
Tanjung Bruas Port
Melaka
MELAKA
MIFT
Muar
JOHOR
Kota Tinggi
Sri Junjungan Port
Dumai Port
Dumai
Johor Bahru
Johor Port
SINGAPORE
Tanjung Pelepas Port
Batam
Tanjungpinang
RIAU ISLANDS
LINGGA
Aek Kanopan
Rekanbaru
RIAU
BATU
Pariaman
Rengat
Teluk Kuantan
0°   0°
Padang
WEST SUMATERA
INDONESIA
BANGKA
SIBERUT
Jambi
JAMBI
Pangkalpinang
BANGKA BELITUNG ISLANDS
Belitung
PAGAI
BELITUNG
Palembang
SOUTH SUMATERA
4°00'S   4°00'S
Bengkulu
Lahat
Baturaja
BENGKULU
LAMPUNG
Java Sea
Lampung
Bandar Lampung
ENGGANO
INDIAN OCEAN

Legend

✪ National Capital
◉ Provincial/State Capital
● City/Town
▬ Economic Corridor 4
▬ Economic Corridor 4 (reconfiguration)
— National Road
— Other Road
— Provincial Boundary
—·— International Boundary
MIFT = Melaka International Ferry Terminal
Boundaries are not necessarily authoritative.

This map was produced by the cartography unit of the Asian Development Bank.
The boundaries, colors, denominations, and any other information shown on this map do not imply, on the part of the Asian Development Bank, any judgment on the legal status of any territory, or any endorsement or acceptance of such boundaries, colors, denominations, or information.

98°00'E   104°00'E

Source: Asian Development Bank.

The nodes in Johor include the Tanjung Pelepas Port (Gelang Patah) and Johor Port (Pasir Gudang). These two ports in the Strait of Malacca are important maritime gateways to the southern peninsula and to international destinations. The Tanjung Pelepas Port has a direct rail link to Malaysia's national rail grid which connects to Singapore and Southern Thailand.

Melaka City and the MIFT have been included as nodes in EC4, in addition to Tanjung Bruas Port. Melaka City has a huge domestic and international tourism market that could link to tourism initiatives of Rupat and Padang that belong to Sumatera's national strategic tourism zones. The MIFT is a passenger terminal ferry and is the main gateway to Riau Province. In 2018, 98% of passengers that arrived at the port were from Indonesia. Many tourists from Dumai have made Melaka a health tourism destination. The MIFT is also a port of call for cruise tourism in the Strait of Malacca. In 2018, about 13,500 cruise ship passengers arrived at this port of call which is the fourth most important port of call in the country. There are plans to make the MIFT a home port for cruise ships. The existing and additional provinces/states and nodes are summarized in Table 21.

Table 21: Economic Corridor 4: Existing and Additional Provinces and Nodes, by Type

Province/State	Node/Type	Type			
		CAP	COM	MGP	TOUR
INDONESIA					
Riau	Dumai Port			✓	
	Dumai City		✓		
	Sri Junjungan Port*			✓	
	Rupat Island*				✓
	Pekanbaru	✓	✓		
West Sumatera*	Padang*	✓	✓		
MALAYSIA					
Melaka	Tanjung Bruas Port (Port of Melaka)			✓	
	Melaka International Ferry Terminal*			✓	✓
	Melaka City*	✓	✓		✓
Johor*	Johor Bahru*	✓	✓		
	Tanjung Pelepas Port, Gelang Patah*			✓	
	Johor Port, Pasir Gudang*			✓	

CAP = capital, COM = commercial, MGP = maritime gateway port, TOUR = tourism.
Note: * denotes additional provinces and nodes.
Source: Study team.

Findings and Recommendations

Road connectivity between Dumai and Pekanbaru is adequate. Currently, access between the two nodes is through the Trans-Sumatera Highway with paved roads but there are some sections that are in poor condition possibly due to the large number of trucks carrying palm oil crops passing from Riau to North Sumatera or vice versa. Connectivity between the two cities will be enhanced once the segment in the Trans-Sumatera Toll Road is completed. **In Malaysia, the road access from Melaka City to Tanjung Bruas Port is adequate and in good condition** with two-way federal and state roads, as well as an expressway from Port Klang.

There is currently no active railway line in Riau after the Pekanbaru Railway was abandoned at the end of World War II. However, there have been proposals to reactivate the Pekanbaru–West Sumatera railway connecting Pekanbaru and Padang on the western coast of Sumatera. If realized, this rail link can further enhance economic activities between the two provinces as West Sumatera becomes part of EC4. In Malaysia, there is no rail link between Pulau Sebang and Tanjung Bruas Port. This is a last mile connectivity problem facing the domestic railroad network.

To take advantage of the short distance between Dumai Port and Tanjung Bruas Port across each other in the Strait of Malacca, the Dumai–Melaka Ro-Ro Ferry Project needs to be expedited. The Ro-Ro ferry service was scheduled to start in 2021 but the operating procedures have yet to be mutually agreed upon by the relevant authorities in Indonesia and Malaysia. This project will significantly reduce transport costs and travel time since lories from Sumatera will reach Malaysian traders directly through the Ro-Ro service. This project will boost trade between Riau Province and Melaka and will especially benefit the micro, small, and medium-sized enterprises that use trucks mainly to transport their goods. At present, although Dumai Port is a major gateway for CPO, there is no palm oil trade between this port and Tanjung Bruas. Dumai Port's maritime links with ports in Malaysia (MIFT at Bandar Hilir, and Port of Port Dickson, Negeri Sembilan) are mostly for passenger ferry services.

Riau Province should develop palm oil processing industries to produce higher value-added exports for CPO. Although Dumai Port is the largest exporter of CPO in Indonesia, there is no SEZ in the province related to the palm oil industry. The establishment of SEZ for this purpose, as planned by the provincial government, will be an important catalyst to boost Riau Province's declining export levels, compared to rapidly increasing imports in trade with Malaysia.

The inclusion of Johor in EC4 will open important links to Riau Islands (in particular Batam) and Bangka Belitung Islands which are part of the proposed route for EC6. Johor's rapid urban and industrial transformation as part of the Iskandar Malaysia SEZ, as well as major railway projects being planned to enhance connectivity with the rest of the peninsula and Singapore, will generate positive spillover effects throughout the region. The Tanjung Pelepas Port and Johor Port are important maritime gateways to the southern peninsula and to international destinations. The Tanjung Pelepas Port in particular has a direct rail link to Malaysia's national rail grid that connects to Singapore and Southern Thailand.

Economic Corridor 5. The Ranong–Phuket–Aceh Economic Corridor

Overview

The Ranong–Phuket–Aceh Economic Corridor (EC5) is mainly a maritime corridor linking ports in the northern part of Sumatera (mainly Ulee Lheue and Malahayati in Aceh Province) with Southern Thailand along its western coast facing the Andaman Sea, with the aim of exploiting tourism potentials. In Sumatera, Aceh Province is part of the corridor and Banda Aceh, the capital, and Sabang (located in the adjacent We Island) are the gateway and tourism nodes, respectively (Map 10).

Map 10: Ranong–Phuket–Aceh Economic Corridor
(Economic Corridor 5)

Source: Asian Development Bank.

Ranong and Phuket are the two Thailand provinces in EC5. Ranong Port is a cargo and container port and is the main maritime gateway in the Andaman Sea connecting to trade routes with South Asia, Middle East, Europe, and Africa. It is Thailand's Indian Ocean Port. Phuket Port is mainly a pier for goods. Recently, cruise ships have made regular calls to the port, which has led to plans to develop Phuket as a home port for cruises. Phuket also serves as a connecting route to South Asia, Middle East, Africa, and Europe. Both ports are accessible from Bangkok. The land route between the two ports is 305 km.

Existing Provinces and Nodes

Aceh is located at the northern tip of Sumatera and belongs to the islands' "growth corridor." Banda Aceh, the capital of the province, is a base for processing companies of yellowfin tuna tuna coming from Meulaboh, Pulau Aceh, Laweng, and Ulee Lheue. The frozen tuna and tuna loin are sold mainly in the domestic market and some are exported to Japan, the Republic of Korea, and Thailand. Coffee bean processing is also a thriving industry in Banda Aceh. The coffee products are marketed to North Sumatera along with other products such as betel nut and CPO. Aceh exports coal to India and Thailand. Banda Aceh is also popular for halal tourism.

There are two ports in Banda Aceh: **Ulee Lheue** services fast craft services to Sabang, while **Malahayati** (Aceh Besar) serves as an international gateway port for container freight. In Sabang, **Balohan Port** serves as a passenger port, and **Sabang Port** (under Badan Pengusahaan Kawasan Sabang) serves as a free port and free trade zone. Sabang has the potential to be a strategic transshipment port to the west.

Ranong is the northernmost province on Thailand's Andaman seacoast, located 568 km from Bangkok. Ranong's main resources are fisheries and tin. The SEC project, approved by the Government of Thailand in 2018, emphasizes development of Ranong Port as a gateway to trade with Bangladesh, India, Myanmar, and Sri Lanka. Ranong Port, which is nearer to Kolkata compared with Bangkok and Laem Chabang, has been operational but the (export–import) activities have been less. Improvements in Ranong Port are underway to improve connectivity with Kolkata and Chennai ports in India to save distance and boost trade.

Phuket, one of the southern provinces of Thailand, consists of the island of Phuket, the country's largest island, and some 32 smaller islands on Thailand's west coast facing the Andaman Sea. The closest provinces are Krabi to the east, and Phangnga to the north, which is connected to Phuket by the Sarasin Bridge. Its economy is based on tourism, although it also produces rubber and tin.

Status of Physical Connectivity

Land Connectivity

The road from Ranong to Phuket in Thailand covering 326 km is in good condition and safe. At present, the entire route from Ranong to Phuket is being upgraded to four traffic lanes and is expected to be completed in 2024. Apart from roads, goods can also be transported by rail at the container yard at Wisai Railway Station in Chumphon. From Chumphon, goods can be further transported by road to Ranong Port covering 110 kms. Ranong and Phuket can also be traveled through maritime transport.

Maritime Connectivity

Maritime connectivity between Sumatera and Thailand in EC5 is limited. Banda Aceh and Sabang, which are on separate islands are linked by ferry services but there is no onward connection to Thailand. There are no shipping routes for cargo from Malahayati Port to Phuket and Ranong Ports, although the port services routes to other destinations (Table 22).

Ulee Lheue Port in Banda Aceh city is a ferry port serving the Ulee Lheue Port–Balohan Port (Sabang) route. Express ferries are operated by private vessels.[35] A Ro-Ro service between Ulee Lheue and Phuket Port is being planned.

Malahayati Port in Aceh Besar regency serves domestic containers in the shipping routes from Tanjung Priok–Belawan–Malahayati and Tanjung Priok–Belawan–Lhokseumawe–Malahayati. The port is part of Indonesia's sea highways (*tol laut*) program. Malahayati Port is used to export pozzolan (a mixture of cement) to India and Dubai and to import liquid asphalt from Singapore.

Balohan Port is in Sabang, We Island. In June 2019, the government initiated a port revitalization project with a budget of Rp221 billion to make Balohan an international ferry port.[36]

Sabang Port is in Sabang Bay, We Island, located in the northern end of the Strait of Malacca and sits only 90 miles away from the southern tip of India's Andaman and Nicobar Islands in the Pacific Ocean. It has two container terminals and a dock for cruise ships and yachts and is part of the Sabang Free Port and Free Trade Zone. It has the potential to be a strategic transshipment port.

Ranong Port is Thailand's principal Indian Ocean port situated on the east side of the estuary of Kraburi River on the Andaman Sea coast. It connects to trade routes with South Asia, the Middle East, Europe, and Africa. The port serves as a supply base for oil and offshore gas exploration and can accommodate limited container service to Port Blair, Yangon, and Chennai. The potential for further developing the port is constrained by the absence of a significant hinterland and rail connection. In August 2019, the Port Authority of Thailand signed a memorandum of understanding (MOU) with Navayuga Container Terminal and Krishnapatnam Port of India on port-to-port cooperation covering 2019–2022.[37] Thailand and India have also agreed to promote a new maritime route in the Andaman Sea toward South Asia.

Phuket Deep Sea Port is on the coast of the Andaman Sea on the southeast of Phuket Island. The port is an embankment and accommodates cargo and passenger ships. Although Phuket Deep Sea Port has been designed mainly as a pier for goods, cruise ships have increasingly used the port in recent years. There are plans to develop Phuket Port from a port of call to a home port to accommodate large cruise ships. Phuket is a popular tourist destination with a huge potential to attract more tourists from South Asia, Middle East, Africa, and Europe to the Andaman Sea.

---

[35] Private vessels operating in Ulee Lheue are: KM Bahari 3, Km Cantika 89, Bahari 89, and Bahari 2F. Meanwhile, ASDP (a state-owned enterprise) is operating two Ro-Ro ferries: (i) KMP BRR, 911 GT in capacity, which can load 450 passengers, 25 cars, and 100 motorcycles; and (ii) KMP Tanjung Burang, 507 GT in capacity ehich can load 200 passengers, 15 cars, and 50 motorcycles. Maftuh Ihsan. 2019. Tambah Jadwal Penyeberangan Banda Aceh-Sabang. *ASDP*. 6 June.

[36] Terminal Baru Balohan Mulai Dioperasikan. *Bakri*. 2019. 16 April.

[37] The MOU was signed the under the framework of the BIMSTEC, which groups Bangladesh, Bhutan, India, Myanmar, Nepal, Sri Lanka, and Thailand. The MOU involves (i) exchange of information and news on port management, (ii) port internal operations, (iii) promotion of marketing and investments in business related to port operations, (iv) information technology systems, (v) communication and linkage of port networks, and (vi) industries related to port business.

Table 22: Economic Corridor 5: Maritime Activities of Ports

Ports	Maritime Activities
Banda Aceh, Sumatera	
Ulee Lheue	• express ferry services to Sabang (We Island)
Malahayati Port	• no commercial ferry and no shipping routes for cargo that connects Malahayati Port in Aceh with Phuket and Ranong Ports • international gateway port for container freight • exports pozzolan to India and Dubai; entry point of asphalt from Singapore • container facilities for loading/unloading on domestic routes
Sabang, We Island	
Balohan Port	• passenger port • sea transport infrastructure to support tourism from Aceh Province in the mainland to Sabang Island
Sabang Port	• serves as a free port and free trade zone • serves as unloading dock for imports, no exports recorded • potential to be a strategic transshipment port to the west • has two container terminals and a dock for cruise ships and yachts
Southern Thailand	
Ranong Port	• container port; can accommodate limited container service to Port Blair, Yangon, and Chennai • connects to trade routes with South Asia, the Middle East, Europe, and Africa • serves as a supply base for oil and offshore gas exploration • signed an MOU on port-to-port cooperation with India
Phuket Port	• pier for goods • serves as a supply base for oil and gas exploration • accommodates cargo and passenger ships • being developed to become a homeport for cruise ships

MOU = memorandum of understanding.
Source: Study team.

Air Linkages

Air connectivity in EC5 is limited. There are three airports in EC5: (i) Sultan Iskandar Muda (Banda Aceh International Airport), (ii) Ranong Airport, and (iii) Phuket International Airport. There are no direct flights from Banda Aceh International Airport to Ranong and Phuket, and vice versa. Flights to reach these destinations are through the capital cities. Banda Aceh International Airport has no direct flights to Phuket, Ranong, or other parts of Thailand. Phuket International Airport has direct flights to Kuala Lumpur but none to Aceh or other parts of Indonesia. Ranong Airport is basically a domestic airport connecting Don Mueang Airport in Bangkok.

Maritime Trade

Maritime trade links in EC5 ports have not developed, with the very limited trade between Ranong and Phuket provinces, and Aceh. Thailand does not have a land border with Aceh and maritime links are mostly in passenger ferry services. In tourism, the potential for Aceh and Sabang to tap into the burgeoning tourism market of Phuket has not been realized. For 2014–2018, Aceh's total trade with Thailand increased by an average of 38%, with exports peaking to $18.3 million in 2018 from $4.4 million the previous year. Imports also increased but at a much slower rate than exports (Table 23). Coal is Aceh's major export to Thailand (97% in 2018), while oats (78%) and salt, sulfur, and lime (16.5% combined) are the major imports.

Table 23: Economic Corridor 5: Aceh's Trade with Thailand through Ports in Aceh, 2014–2018
($ million)

Item	2014	2015	2016	2017	2018	Average 2014–2018 (%)	Compounded Annual Growth Rate (%)
Aceh with Thailand	**7.6**	**10.0**	**2.6**	**6.2**	**27.4**	**10.8**	**38.0**
Exports	0.035	5.8	0.6	4.4	18.3	5.8	377.2
Imports	7.5	4.3	2.0	1.8	9.1	4.9	4.9
Total Aceh	**547.9**	**210.2**	**51.9**	**117.0**	**168.3**	**219.1**	**(25.6)**
Exports	507.4	93.3	22.9	77.7	138.6	168.0	(27.7)
Imports	40.5	116.8	29.0	39.3	29.7	51.1	(7.5)
Share of Aceh's Trade with Thailand to Total Aceh (%)							
Total Trade	1.38	4.8	4.9	5.3	16.3	4.9	16.3
Exports	nil	6.2	2.5	5.6	13.2	3.4	13.2
Imports	18.62	3.6	6.9	4.5	30.7	9.5	30.7

( ) = negative.
Sources: BPS-Statistics Indonesia. BPS-Statistics Indonesia, Statistik Perdagangan Luar Negeri Aceh 2018 Banda Aceh: 2019; BPS-Statistics Indonesia, Statistik Perdagangan Luar Negeri Aceh 2017 Banda Aceh: 2018; BPS-Statistics Indonesia, Statistik Perdagangan Luar Negeri Aceh 2016 Banda Aceh: 2017; BPS-Statistics Indonesia, Statistik Perdagangan Luar Negeri Aceh 2015 Banda Aceh: 2016; BPS-Statistics Indonesia, Statistik Perdagangan Luar Negeri Aceh 2014 Banda Aceh: 2015.

There are no commercial shipping routes for cargo from Malahayati Port to Phuket and Ranong ports. Malahayati Port services routes to other international destinations such as Dubai and India for the export of pozzolan and serves as a loading dock for imports of asphalt from Singapore. Exports going through Malahayati Port is less than 1% of Aceh's exports. The port that actively trades with Thailand is Meulaboh Port, located in the western part of Aceh, which has become the main gateway for coal exports. In 2018, coal exports through Meulaboh Port comprised 93.7% of total exports to Thailand. More than 90% of exports to Thailand go through Meulaboh Port in the western coast of Sumatera, while 36.5% of imports go through Lhokseumawe Port located near the SEZ.

Development Strategies

Aceh is among six provinces[38] belonging to the growth corridor of Sumatera along the eastern coast where industrial and tourism zones are being developed. Banda Aceh is at the northern tip of the Trans-Sumatera Toll Road that extends to Bakauheni as its end point. Aceh hosts the Arun Lhoksuemawe SEZ,[39] where a consortium of companies participating in global value chains is located. Arun Lhokseumawe has the potential to become one of the richest and productive aquatic ecosystems that would be the basis for the development of capture fisheries industry. Arun Lhoksuemawe is poised to develop alongside the development of several countries in the South Asia region through the revitalization of the Maritime Silk Road.

---

[38] The six provinces are Aceh, North Sumatera, Riau, Jambi, South Sumatera, and Lampung.

[39] Arun Lhoksuemawe has been proposed as an additional node in EC3.

Aceh plays an important role in the supply chain for tuna and coffee. The capital city of Banda Aceh is home to several processing companies of yellowfin tuna coming from Meulaboh, Pulau Aceh, Laweng, and Ulee Lheue. The tuna is processed and frozen for the domestic and international markets that includes Japan, the Republic of Korea, and Thailand. Tuna processing has a huge potential for expansion since 90% of captured tuna are sent to Medan unprocessed. Banda Aceh is also a base for coffee bean processing, especially for Robusta coffee produced in Ulee Kareng in Banda Aceh, and Arabica coffee produced in Gayo Highland (Aceh Tengah and Bener Meriah Regencies). The coffee products are marketed to other Sumatera provinces and Kalimantan.

Sabang complements the development of the fisheries industry in Aceh because of its comparative advantage in marine tourism and fisheries. As a small island, Sabang has no natural resources for export. There is no record of export activities in Sabang Port in 2018. Sabang is a free port and is being developed as an integrated fisheries center and marine tourism destination. In recent years, Sabang Port has become part of the route of cruise ships that call on Phuket. In 2018, seven cruise ships and 96 yachts called on the port. Tourist arrivals in Sabang Port have been increasing, reaching over 6,000 international visitors and close to 737,000 domestic visitors in 2017.

In Thailand, EC5 plays an important role in supporting the SEC strategy to develop a tourism gateway in the Gulf of Thailand and the Andaman Sea (Royal Coast and Andaman Route). The strategy aims to develop a network of tourist attractions between the two coastal areas by connecting them with a land bridge (Map 11). The high-potential inland tourist destinations, to form part of the tourist networks are Phuket, Phangnga, Krabi, Surat Thani (Ko Samui, Ko Pha-ngan, Ko Toa), Chumphon, and Nakhon Si Thammarat (Sichon and Khanom beaches). Apart from integrating tourism routes between the Gulf of Thailand and the Andaman Sea, the network in this collective area will also integrate provincial production networks (e.g., rubber latex, rubber wood, and halal food supply chains) along the EC5 and EC6.

Reconfiguration of EC5

The reconfiguration of EC5 involves the inclusion of (i) Krabi and Phangnga in Thailand, (ii) the island of Langkawi in Kedah in Malaysia, and (iii) Teluk Ewa Port within the island of Langkawi. No additional nodes are proposed in Sumatera.

The reconfigured EC5 has been renamed Southwestern Thailand–Northern Sumatera–Northwestern Malaysia Economic Corridor (Map 12).

The inclusion of **Phangnga and Krabi** in EC5 will support Thailand's strategy for the SEC to develop an inland tourism network between the coasts along the Gulf of Thailand and the Andaman Sea. The network will link high-potential tourist destinations, namely Phuket, Phangnga, Krabi, Surat Thani (Ko Samui, Ko Pha-ngan, Ko Toa), Chumphon, and Nakhon Si Thammarat (Sichon and Khanom beaches). This collective area will also integrate provincial production networks for rubber latex, rubber wood, and halal food supply chains in EC5 and EC6.

Thailand has lined up several projects in EC5 including improvements in Ranong Port and Ranong Airport, improvements in Phuket Deep Sea Ports, and the construction of a light rail as part of Phuket's mass transit system between Phuket International Airport and Chalong intersection. Thailand will use Ranong Port to link with BIMSTEC countries via the new port in Sri Lanka and various ports in the Bay of Bengal.

Map 11: Land Bridge between the Gulf of Thailand and the Andaman Sea

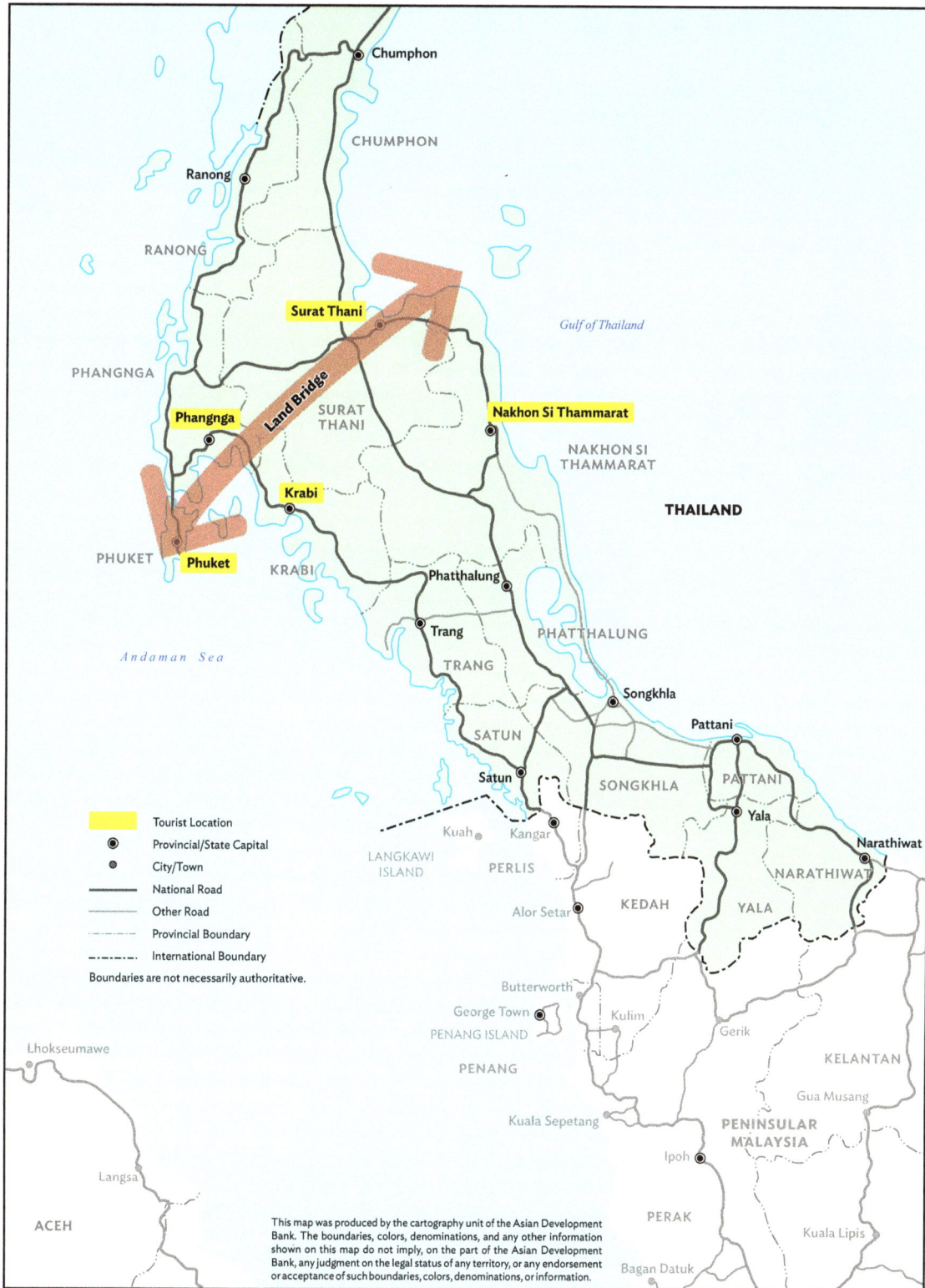

Source: Asian Development Bank.

Map 12: Southwestern Thailand–Northern Sumatera–Northwestern Malaysia Economic Corridor (Reconfigured Economic Corridor 5)

Source: Asian Development Bank.

Langkawi's inclusion in EC5 would enable Malaysia to tap into the tourism opportunities in the corridor. The island will serve as a new link between Sabang and Phuket to develop the Sabang–Phuket–Langkawi (SAPULA) Tourism Development Belt. Langkawi's economy is based on tourism, which is an important source of income for the state. The island has had a duty free status since 1987 and is one of the most popular tourist destinations among local and international tourists. The SAPULA "golden triangle" is expected to create business opportunities in EC5 related to cruise and yacht tourism. The MOU on Marine Tourism Triangle Cooperation signed between the governments of Malaysia and Indonesia in April 2007 can be used as a platform to further develop the cruise and yacht tourism industry in the corridor.

Within Langkawi Island, the central district of Kuah connects by road to the Kuah Jetty, the International Airport at Padang Matsirat, Langkawi Port, the Star Cruise Jetty at Kedawang, and **Teluk Ewa Port**. Teluk Ewa Port has links with the Port of Palembang (South Sumatera) through the imports of coal. For Southern Thailand, Teluk Ewa Port imports iron ore from the Port of Krabi (Satun). The port is designed to handle petroleum products, coal, and general cargo. The major exports include cement and clinker. There have been proposals to expand Teluk Ewa Port. The port would enable Langkawi to connect to and shorten the trade passageway, which currently passes through Singapore.

As regards maritime connectivity, Langkawi can be accessed by ferry from Penang (Penang Port), Perlis (Kuala Perlis), and mainland Kedah (Kuala Kedah). The island can also be accessed from Thailand via Ko Lipe and Satun. Key entry points for passengers to Langkawi are through Kuah Jetty, Port of Langkawi (Tanjung Lembong Port), Telaga Harbor Jetty, and Star Cruise Jetty. The Port of Langkawi operates a Ro-Ro ferry service (cars and passengers) from Kuala Kedah and Kuala Perlis to Teluk Ewa Port (Ayer Hangat), a trading port.

Air connectivity is through Langkawi International Airport at Padang Matsirat. There are flights to Kuala Lumpur, Penang, Johor Bahru, Subang, Singapore, and Medan, but there are no flights from Langkawi to Aceh and Phuket/Ranong. The airport handled 3 million visitors on average from 2014–2018, 87% are from domestic origins and 13% are international visitors.

The expansion of the corridor will generate synergies in tourism between Thailand's provinces along the Andaman Sea coast and the islands of Sabang and Langkawi that can help generate demand for maritime transport to develop. The expansion will also support plans of Indonesia and Thailand to build ties with South Asia through the development of Sabang and Ranong ports, having recently discussed cooperation initiatives with India for port-to-port cooperation involving Ranong, and the development of infrastructure and economic zones in Sabang.

Although no additional nodes are proposed in Sumatera, it should be able to expand tourism opportunities with Langkawi, in addition to Phuket, to revitalize the corridor. The collaboration between SAPULA for cruise tourism has been initiated under the IMT-GT framework. Table 24 summarizes the existing and additional provinces in the reconfigured EC5.

Table 24: Economic Corridor 5: Existing and Additional Provinces and Nodes, by Type

Province/State	Node	Type			
		CAP	COM	MGP	TOUR
INDONESIA					
Aceh	Banda Aceh	✓			
	Sabang City		✓		
	Ulee Lheue Port			✓	
	Malahayati Port			✓	
	Sabang Port		✓	✓	✓
	Balohan Port			✓	
MALAYSIA					
Kedah	Langkawi*				✓
	Teluk Ewa Port*			✓	
THAILAND					
Ranong	Ranong City	✓	✓		✓
	Ranong Port			✓	
Phuket	Phuket City	✓	✓		✓
	Phuket Port			✓	
Krabi*	Krabi City*	✓	✓		
Phangnga*	Phangnga City*	✓			

CAP = capital, COM = commercial, MGP = maritime gateway port, TOUR = tourism.
Note: * denotes additional provinces and nodes.
Source: Study team.

Findings and Recommendations

Maritime links in EC5 have not developed as originally intended and trade links have been limited. There are no commercial shipping routes for cargo from Malahayati Port to Phuket and Ranong ports, although Malahayati Port services routes to other international destinations such as Dubai and India for the export of pozzolan and is a loading dock for imports of asphalt from Singapore. Malahayati Port's potential to become a loading port for coffee, processed tuna, halal foods, and other exports to Thailand should be developed because of its proximity to Arun Lhoksuemawe SEZ. Arun Lhoksuemawe SEZ, located 235 km from Malahayati Port, hosts a consortium of companies participating in global value chains. Lhokseumawe Port can be developed in EC3 and linked with EC5.

In tourism, the potential for Aceh and Sabang to tap into the burgeoning tourism market of Phuket has not been realized and was not able to generate the demand for ferry services. Part of this could be due to the lack of deliberate efforts on the part of national tourism organizations and private tour operators to design attractive tour packages to promote the area. At present, ferry services at Balohan Port are limited to serving tourists from Aceh only up to Sabang in the absence of tourist demand to travel to Phuket and vice versa.

Collaboration between SAPULA for cruise tourism should be pursued. To further exploit the tourism potential of the corridor, Sabang can leverage on Phuket's and Langkawi's popularity as a tourist destination through collaboration in the design and promotion of attractive tourism packages for ship cruises and yachts. The increasing number of cruise ships and yachts docked in Sabang Port signifies a promising opportunity for collaboration with Phuket given plans to make Phuket a home port for cruise tourism. As Sabang is relatively small, Aceh can also be included in the tourism packages featuring the province's authentic culinary and cultural heritage. National or provincial tourist organizations and private tour operators should make deliberate efforts to develop tourism packages and conduct joint marketing activities. This could increase the demand for ferry services at Balohan Port to cater to visitors traveling to Phuket and Langkawi and vice versa.

The inclusion of Phangnga and Krabi in EC5 will support Thailand's strategy to develop an inland tourism network between the coasts along the Gulf of Thailand and the Andaman Sea. The network will link high-potential tourist destinations, namely Phuket, Phangnga, Krabi, Surat Thani (Ko Samui, Ko Pha-ngan, Ko Tao), Chumphon, and Nakhon Si Thammarat (Sichon and Khanom beaches). This collective area will also integrate provincial production networks (e.g., rubber latex, rubber wood, and halal food supply chains) in EC5 and EC6.

The concept of an IMT-GT integrated tourism corridor should be explored to leverage on the subregion's comparative advantage in tourism and optimize its investments in tourism infrastructure. EC2 and EC5 can serve as the backbone of this integrated corridor. EC5, through Krabi and Phangnga, can link with (i) Chumphon and Surat Thani (the Gulf of Thailand and the Andaman Sea routes) in EC1; and (ii) Satun and Trang in EC2 to feed into tourism routes in Malaysia (e.g., Langkawi in Kedah) and Indonesia (e.g., Medan and Lake Toba in North Sumatera) along the Strait of Malacca. Both Phuket and Melaka plan to develop their respective ports into home ports for cruise ships. Air linkages within the corridor, which are currently limited, can be further developed with an increase in travel demand.

CHAPTER

4

PROPOSED ROUTE FOR ECONOMIC CORRIDOR 6

Background

The sixth economic corridor (EC6) is a new corridor proposed by Thailand during the 24th IMT-GT Ministerial Meeting held on 1 October 2018 in Melaka, Malaysia. The proposed EC6 is envisaged to open new trade routes between Southern Thailand and Malaysia through the ECRL. The ECRL, which is part of the PRC's BRI, will connect Peninsular Malaysia's east and west coasts. The proposed corridor is perceived to be a game changer for IMT-GT as it creates opportunities for expanded trade with the PRC and Europe through ports in the eastern coast. Malaysia is currently undertaking rapid and massive development of its eastern coast to create catalytic growth centers that could leverage on infrastructure expansion in the next 10 years.

In configuring the route for EC6, the following factors were considered: (i) the development strategy of the countries in the areas to be traversed by the route, (ii) the existing connectivity between provinces or states and nodes along the route, and (iii) the economic opportunities and potential value chain linkages.

Development Strategies

Thailand's strategy for EC6 is to integrate provincial production networks in the three provinces—Pattani, Yala, and Narathiwat—with halal and other food supply chains in Songkhla and nearby areas (EC1). Because of security issues in these provinces that limit outside investments, agricultural produce is transported to nearby factories or exported directly through the Thai–Malaysian borders. Enhancing the domestic value chain will boost the productivity and economic resiliency of provinces in Southern Thailand. The three provinces can also leverage their shared culture and history to expand opportunities for tourism.

Malaysia's strategy for EC6 is aligned with the government's strategy to develop the ECER by enhancing value chains, increasing knowledge and capacity innovation, addressing socioeconomic inequalities and improving the quality of life. To realize these goals, the ECER Blueprint 2.0 (2018–2025) identified seven priority development areas: (i) tourism; (ii) oil, gas, and petrochemicals; (iii) manufacturing; (iv) agribusiness; (v) human capital development; (vi) logistics; and (vii) services. These clusters would be supported by developments in transportation, infrastructure, property development, and environmental protection to make the region an ideal destination for business, investments, and quality living.

The development of the eastern region will be boosted with the construction of the ECRL, which will provide the peninsula's eastern coast with a more efficient means of access to the west coast along the Strait of Malacca. There are two alternative routes in Malaysia from Kelantan: one passes through Terengganu, Pahang along the eastern coast, crossing to Selangor (EC2) and Melaka (EC4) and onward to Johor (EC4); the other route links Kota Bahru (the starting point of ECRL) and passes through Perak, Selangor (Port Klang, which is the end point of ECRL) and up to Melaka and Johor.

Indonesia's strategy for EC6 is to link Riau Islands and Bangka Belitung Islands with rapid developments in Malaysia. Riau Islands and Bangka Belitung Islands are strategic nodes in Sumatera's growth corridor (Batam, Tanjungpinang, and Pangkalpinang) and equalization corridor (*koridor pemerataan*) (Natuna and Tanjung Pandan). Riau Islands is one of Indonesia's prosperous southernmost provinces. It is the fourth largest province after East Kalimantan, Jakarta, and Riau. Bangka Belitung Islands is known to have the largest tin deposit in the world, but while its economy is growing, the distribution of the benefits of growth has lagged. The SEZs in these territories are spurring industrial development that benefit from their strategic locations—in the case of Riau Islands, to Singapore and Malaysia; and in the case of Bangka Belitung Islands, to South Sumatera.

The SEZs in these territories include Galang Batang SEZ (Batam) and the Tanjung Kelayang SEZ (Belitug) Moreover, Batam–Bintan and Bangka Belitung also have been designated as national tourism zones in the RPJMN 2020–2024, with the increasing popularity and attraction of these areas to cruise ships and yachts. Batam and Tanjungpinang (Riau Islands) have maritime links to Dumai and Pekanbaru (Riau Province), Jambi (a proposed addition to EC3), and Bangka Belitung Islands, while Pangkalpinang and Tanjung Pandan (Bangka Belitung Islands) have maritime links to Palembang (South Sumatera), Lampung (proposed addition to EC3), Dumai and Pekanbaru (Riau), Batam and Tanjungpinang (Riau Islands), and Belawan (North Sumatera).

The Proposed Route for EC6

The proposed route involves 17 provinces and states, covering almost the entire span of the IMT-GT triangle. It covers three provinces in Southern Thailand, eight states in Malaysia in two alternative routes, and the six provinces in Sumatera—four provinces in mainland Sumatera, and two archipelagic provinces in the southeastern part. Of the eight states in Malaysia proposed to be traversed by EC6, three are currently not participating states in IMT-GT: Johor, Terengganu, and Pahang—and would thus require a decision by the government.

EC6 would be called Southeastern Thailand–Eastern Malaysia–Southern Sumatera Economic Corridor (Map 13).

Map 13: Southeastern Thailand–Eastern Malaysia–Southern Sumatera Economic Corridor (Proposed Route for Economic Corridor 6)

Source: Asian Development Bank.

Table 25: Provinces, States, and Nodes in the Proposed Economic Corridor 6, by Type

Province/State	Node	CAP	COM	BCP	MGP	TOUR
INDONESIA						
South Sumatera	Palembang	✓	✓			✓
Jambi	Jambi	✓	✓			
Lampung	Bandar Lampung	✓	✓		✓	
Bengkulu	Bengkulu	✓	✓		✓	
Riau Islands	Batam		✓		✓	
	Tanjungpinang	✓			✓	
Bangka Belitung Islands	Tanjung Pandan		✓			✓
	Pangkalpinang	✓				
MALAYSIA						
Kelantan	Rantau Panjang			✓		✓
	Bukit Bunga			✓		✓
	Pengkalan Kubor			✓		✓
	Kota Bharu	✓				
	Tok Bali Port		✓		✓	
Terengganu	Kuala Terengganu	✓				
	Kemaman Port		✓			
Pahang	Kuantan	✓	✓	✓		
	Kuantan Port		✓			
Perak	Ipoh	✓				
	Lumut Port				✓	
Selangor	Port Klang				✓	
Melaka	Melaka City	✓				
	Tanjung Bruas Port (Port of Melaka)				✓	
	Melaka International Ferry Terminal				✓	
Johor	Johor Bahru	✓				
	Tanjung Pelepas Port, Gelang Patah				✓	
	Johor Port, Pasir Gudang				✓	
Negeri Sembilan	Seremban	✓				
	Port Dickson				✓	✓
THAILAND						
Pattani	Pattani City	✓				
Yala	Yala City	✓				
	Betong			✓		✓
Narathiwat	Narathiwat City	✓	✓			
	Su-ngai Kolok		✓	✓		
	Buketa			✓		
	Tak Bai		✓	✓		

BCP = border crossing point, CAP = capital, COM = commercial, MGP = maritime gateway port, TOUR = tourism.
Source: Study team.

The configuration of EC6 was designed to link with other IMT-GT corridors, thus creating a network of transport links that impacts on the regional allocation and distribution of resources and benefits. Chapter 4 discusses the subject in detail. The resulting network of economic corridors interact dynamically and create new patterns of regional economic development. This dynamic can contribute to balanced development between lagging areas and growth centers, allowing poorer areas to benefit from corridor development spillovers to promote inclusive growth. The provinces, states, and nodes proposed for EC6[40] are summarized in Table 25 and are discussed below.

Thailand

The EC6 route will start from Pattani, continuing south to Yala and Narathiwat. Narathiwat will connect with Kelantan. In Narathiwat, there are three BCPs at the border with Kelantan, namely Su-ngai Kolok, Buketa, and Tak Bai (Map 14). Narathiwat links with Kelantan through a bridge across the Kolok River, at Tak Bai (Narathiwat) and Tumpat (Kelantan), and a second bridge at the border of Su-ngai Kolok (Narathiwat) and Rantau Panjang (Kelantan). The rail link at Su-ngai Kolok–Rantau Panjang–Pasir Mas–Tumpat, which is currently dormant, will be reactivated. Narathiwat is connected to Kota Bharu (Kelantan) through Asian Highway No. 17 (Thailand) and No. 7 (Malaysia). There are existing overland routes from Songkhla to Penang Port and further to Port Klang which is the end point of ECRL on the west coast.

Narathiwat is the only province that shares a border with Kelantan. There are three BCPs at the Narathiwat–Kelantan borders:

- Su-ngai Kolok–Rantau Panjang
- Ban Buketa–Bukit Bunga/Tanah Merah
- Tak Bai–Pengkalan Kubor

Another entry point to Malaysia is at Betong (Yala) connecting to Pengkalan Kubor (Perak). This link is part of EC2.

---

40   The study team's proposed routes for EC6 considered the views expressed during the consultations with the IMT governments through the IMT–GT national secretariats and other stakeholders during the team's field visits.

Map 14: Economic Corridor 6: Proposed Route in Thailand

INDONESIA–MALAYSIA–THAILAND
GROWTH TRIANGLE

Chumphon

CHUMPHON

Ranong

RANONG

PHANGNGA

Surat Thani

SURAT
THANI

Phangnga

Nakhon Si Thammarat

NAKHON SI
THAMMARAT

Krabi

THAILAND

PHUKET

Phuket

KRABI

Phatthalung

Trang

PHATTHALUNG

TRANG

Songkhla

Pattani

PATTANI

SATUN

Satun

SONGKHLA

NARATHIWAT

Yala

Tak Bai

Kuah   Kangar

LANGKAWI
ISLAND

PERLIS

Narathiwat

Su-ngai Koloke

Alor Setar

KEDAH

YALA

Buketa

Betong

Butterworth

George Town

Kulim

Gerik

KELANTAN

PENANG ISLAND

Gua Musang

Lhokseumawe

PENANG

Kuala Sepetang

PENINSULAR
MALAYSIA

Ipoh

Langsa

PERAK

Kuala Lipis

ACEH

Bagan Datuk

Legend:

- ◉ Provincial/State Capital
- ● City/Town
- ▬ Economic Corridor 6 (proposed)
- ── National Road
- ┄┄ Other Road
- ─·─ Provincial Boundary
- ─··─ International Boundary

Boundaries are not necessarily authoritative.

This map was produced by the cartography unit of the Asian Development Bank. The boundaries, colors, denominations, and any other information shown on this map do not imply, on the part of the Asian Development Bank, any judgment on the legal status of any territory, or any endorsement or acceptance of such boundaries, colors, denominations, or information.

Source: Asian Development Bank.

The link between Su-ngai Kolok and Rantau Panjang, and between Ban Buketa and Bukit Bunga, is a bridge, while the link between Tak Bai and Pengkalan Kubor is by ferry. The roads connecting the first two BCPs are in good condition and the CIQ facilities are adequate and well-maintained.

- **Su-ngai Kolok–Rantau Panjang**. The Asian Highway (AH18) connects the border towns of Su-ngai Kolok (Su-ngai Kolok District, Narathiwat) with Rantau Panjang (Pasir Mas District, Kelantan). The two towns are connected by the Friendship Bridge (*Jambatan Muhibbah*) over the Kolok River. The 110-meter-long bridge was built in 1971 and opened to the public in 1973.

- **The Ban Buketa–Bukit Bunga**. A second bridge is from the border at Ban Buketa (Waeng District, Narathiwat) to the border gateway in Jeli (Kelantan), the commercial node of the Tanah Merah district, near the Bukit Bunga border. The 120-meter Friendship Bridge connects Bukit Bunga and Ban Buketa. The bridge was built in 2004 and opened to the public in 2007. The distance from Jeli to Tanjung Bruas Port (Melaka) is 882 km.

- **Tak Bai–Pengkalan Kubor**. A third route is from Tak Bai (Narathiwat) to the border at Pengkalan Kubor, Tumpat (Kelantan). Tumpat is a commercial node near the Pengkalan Kubor border. The Kolok River separates the border of Pengkalan Kubor and Tak Bai. The two bordering towns are linked via ferry service. The distance from Pengkalan Kubor to Tanjung Bruas Port (Melaka) is 809 km.

Malaysia

The EC6 route in Malaysia will start from the BCPs in Kelantan (bordering Thailand) extending southwards to Melaka (Tanjung Bruas Port) and Johor. Melaka will link to Dumai (Riau Province) under EC4. Johor will link with Batam (Riau Islands), which Indonesia has proposed to be part of EC6.

There are two alternative routes from Kelantan to Melaka. These routes are henceforth referred to as EC6 Malaysia Route 1 (EC6-MR1), and EC6 Malaysia Route 2 (EC6-MR2).

EC6-MR1. From the BCPs in Kelantan, this route links with Kota Bahru—the starting point of ECRL—and passes through Tok Bali, Kuala Terengganu, Kemaman Port, Kuantan City, Kuantan Port up to Tanjung Bruas Port in Melaka (Map 15). The total distance is 832 km from Kota Bahru to Tanjung Bruas Port in Melaka. This route has an eastward orientation.

The key maritime gateway in EC6-MR1 is Kuantan Port (Pahang). Kuantan Port is the designated port for the PRC–Malaysia BRI and plays a strategic role in expanding trade with the PRC and Europe. Kuantan Port has maritime links to Songkhla Port (Thailand), Cambodia, the Lao PDR, and Viet Nam, and the northeast Asia region. There is no maritime connectivity between Kuantan Port (Pahang) and Sumatera ports but Kuantan Port has connectivity with Laem Chabang Port in Bangkok.

Two other ports along this route are Kemaman Port (Terengganu) and Tok Bali Port (Kelantan). Kemaman Port is one of the deepest seaports in Malaysia and fast emerging as the new gateway to the Asia and Pacific region. Tok Bali Port (Kelantan) is a minor fishing port. Under the ECER Blueprint 2.0 (2018–2025), this port will be expanded to serve as a feeder to Kuantan Port.

Map 15: Economic Corridor 6: Proposed Malaysia Route 1

INDONESIA–MALAYSIA–THAILAND GROWTH TRIANGLE

Legend:
- National Capital
- Provincial/State Capital
- City/Town
- Economic Corridor 6 (proposed)
- National Road
- Other Road
- Provincial Boundary
- International Boundary
- **MIFT** = Melaka International Ferry Terminal

Boundaries are not necessarily authoritative.

This map was produced by the cartography unit of the Asian Development Bank. The boundaries, colors, denominations, and any other information shown on this map do not imply, on the part of the Asian Development Bank, any judgment on the legal status of any territory, or any endorsement or acceptance of such boundaries, colors, denominations, or information.

Source: Asian Development Bank.

EC6-MR2. From the BCPs in Kelantan, this route links with Kota Bahru—the starting point of ECRL—and passes through Perak (Gerik, Ipoh City, Lumut Port), Port Klang and up to Tanjung Bruas Port in Melaka (Map 16). The total distance is 794 km. This route has a westward orientation.

The key maritime gateways in EC6-MR2 are Lumut Port (Pahang), Port Klang (Selangor), and Tanjung Bruas Port (Melaka).

- Port Klang is the end point of ECRL and is expected to significantly increase its cargo traffic volume when the rail project is completed. As Malaysia's premier port, its service routes to various international destinations. It links with other Malaysia ports along western coast of the peninsula, as well as with Sumatera ports across the Strait of Malacca, including Belawan (EC2), Palembang (EC3), and Dumai (EC4).

- Lumut Port is a maritime gateway to trade with Southeast Asia, India, the Middle East, the PRC, Australia, and the Atlantic Basin. There is an overland route from Songkhla Port to Lumut Port up to Port Klang.

- Tanjung Bruas Port, which is a secondary port, has trade links with ports in Sumatera, especially with Palembang and Lhokseumawe. It also has links with ports in Bangkok (Thailand); Jurong (Singapore); Kaohsiung (Taipei,China); Saiki (Japan); and Humen (the PRC). Tanjung Bruas Port in Dumai is a major node in EC4.

Table 26 compares the features of EC6-MR1 and EC6-MR2 in terms of distance, missing links; road, rail, and ferry links; trade links and development impact.

Melaka and Johor as part of EC6. Melaka and Johor, which are under the Extended EC4, will play an important role in EC6 for enabling connectivity with provinces in Sumatera, in particular, for provinces proposed by Indonesia to be part of EC6. These provinces are Riau Islands (Batam and Tanjungpinang in Bintan); Bangka Belitung Islands (Pangkalpinang in Bangka and Tanjung Pandan in Belitung); and South Sumatera (Palembang).

There are existing maritime trade links between Tanjung Bruas Port (Melaka) and Dumai (Riau). Once fully implemented, the Melaka–Dumai Ro-Ro project will further boost exports and imports of cargo freights between the two provinces. In addition, the MICT is affiliated with the Port of Bandar Sri Laksamana, Bengkalis, which provides ferry services for passengers from Melaka to the Riau Province.

Johor Port (Pasir Gudang) has trade links with ports in Palembang (South Sumatera) and Belawan (North Sumatera). There are also ferry links with Batam (Riau Islands). Passenger arrivals from Batam at Johor's ferry terminal port, which is the main entry port from Batam and Bintan Island, averaged 576,000 people a year during 2014-2018. However, Tanjung Pelepas Port (Johor), which is a container port, does not possess trade connectivity with ports in Sumatera.

Johor is also an important node in the planned rail link projects between Malaysia and Singapore, namely the Johor Bahru–Singapore Rapid Transit System (RTS) project.

Map 16: Economic Corridor 6: Proposed Malaysia Route 2

INDONESIA–MALAYSIA–THAILAND
GROWTH TRIANGLE

PENINSULAR
MALAYSIA

Legend:
- ✪ National Capital
- ◉ Provincial/State Capital
- ● City/Town
- Economic Corridor (proposed)
- National Road
- Other Road
- Provincial Boundary
- International Boundary
- **MIFT** = Melaka International Ferry Terminal

Boundaries are not necessarily authoritative.

This map was produced by the cartography unit of the Asian Development Bank. The boundaries, colors, denominations, and any other information shown on this map do not imply, on the part of the Asian Development Bank, any judgment on the legal status of any territory, or any endorsement or acceptance of such boundaries, colors, denominations, or information.

Source: Asian Development Bank.

Table 26: Economic Corridor 6: Features of EC6-MR1 and EC6-MR2

	EC6-MR1 (Kelantan–Terengganu–Pahang)	EC6-MR2 (Kelantan–Perak)
Distance (km) and travel time (hrs) from Kota Bahru (Kelantan) to Port Klang (Selangor)	Distance: 832 km Travel time: 7.6 hours (based on speed of 110km/hr)	Distance: 794 km Travel time: 7.2 hours (based on speed of 110km/hr)
Distance (km) and travel time (hrs) from Port Klang to:		
Lumut Port	—	Distance: 201 km Travel time: 1.9 hours
Tanjung Bruas	Distance: 173 km Travel time: 1.6 hours	Distance: 173 km Travel time: 1.6 hours
Missing links at entry point from Narathiwat to Kelantan road links	No train service from Su-ngai Kolok to Pasir Mas • Good access roads to the Bukit Bunga and Rantau Panjang BCPs between Narathiwat and Kelantan • Good access conditions to ports and BCPs provided by expressways and federal roads that connect states on the east coast and west coast of the peninsula	— • Good access roads to the Pengkalan Hulu BCP between Yala and Perak • Good access conditions to ports provided by expressway and federal road on the west coast of peninsula
Ferry links	Adequate ferry link to Pengkalan Kubor BCP between Narathiwat and Kelantan	—
Rail links with Thailand	The revival of Su-ngai Kolok to Pasir Mas rail link will connect the train network from Kunming–Bangkok–Su-ngai Kolok/Pasir Mas–Tumpat–Kota Bharu and via the ECRL to Port Klang.	No spur rail link from Ipoh to Yala via Pengkalan Hulu–Betong BCP.
Maritime trade links with Sumatera	• Kemaman Port: No links with Sumatera • Kuantan Port: No links with Sumatera	• Lumut Port: Riau, Riau Islands, Jambi, Bengkulu, South Sumatera • Port Klang: North Sumatera, Riau, West Sumatera, Jambi, South Sumatera, Lampung • Tanjung Bruas: Riau, Aceh, South Sumatera
International destinations of major maritime gateway ports	• Kuantan Port: Thailand, Cambodia, the Lao PDR, Viet Nam, the PRC, and Europe • Port Klang: Asia, the US, Europe, Middle East • Tanjung Bruas Port: Sumatera, Thailand, northeast Asia	• Lumut Port: Southeast Asia, India, the Middle East, the PRC, Australia, and the Atlantic Basin • Port Klang: Asia, the US, Europe, Middle East • Tanjung Bruas Port: Sumatera, Thailand, northeast Asia
Development Impact	• Strong catalytic effect on Kelantan, which is one of the less-developed regions in the eastern coast. ECRL provides new cross-border trade opportunity trade with Sumatera via Melaka–Dumai Ro-Ro Project • The proposed bridge Su-ngai Kolok–Rantau Panjang and Tak Bai–Pengkalan Hulu will promote cross-border economic activities (including tourism)	The Baling–Pengkalan Hulu–Betong Border Zone will further strengthen cross-border development between Perak and Yala and has transcending border effects toward Kelantan, particularly the Bukit Bunga–Rantau Panjang–Pengkalan Kubor tourism corridor.

— = not applicable, BCP = border crossing points, ECRL = East Coast Rail Link, EC6-MR1 = Economic Corridor 6– Malaysia Route 1, EC6-MR2 = Economic Corridor 6–Malaysia Route 2, hr = hour, km = kilometer, Lao PDR = Lao People's Democratic Republic, PRC = People's Republic of China, US = United States. Source: Study team.

Indonesia

Sumatera's link with Malaysia is primarily through the maritime mode across the Strait of Malacca, and with Thailand through multimodal links via the Malaysian Peninsula. Sumatera will connect with EC6 in

- Jambi City, Jambi Province
- Palembang, South Sumatera
- Bengkulu City, Bengkulu Province
- Bandar Laumpung, Lampung Province
- Batam, Riau Islands
- Tanjungpinang, Bintan, Riau Islands
- Pangkalpinang, Bangka Islands
- Tanjung Pandan. Belitung Islands (Map 17)

Map 17: Economic Corridor 6: Proposed Route in Sumatera

Source: Asian Development Bank.

Palembang (South Sumatera). The capital of South Sumatera Province, Palembang is part of the existing Eastern Trans-Sumatera National Highway and the ongoing Trans-Sumatera Toll Road, connecting Palembang with Jambi and Pekanbaru in the north, Bakauheni Port in Lampung as the gateway to Java Island in the south, as well as Bengkulu in the west. To the east, Palembang connects with Bangka Belitung Islands through maritime and air transportation. It also connects with Kuala Lumpur and Singapore via direct air routes. Palembang is part of both EC6 and EC3. Based on the RPJMN 2020–2024, Palembang will be developed as Metropolitan Palembang, together with Medan.

Jambi City (Jambi Province). Jambi City, the capital of Jambi Province, is part of the Sumatera growth corridor under RPJMN 2020–2024. The Kemingking Industrial Zone, 20 km from Jambi City, will be developed for the agriculture industry. Jambi Province has the third largest rubber plantation area in Indonesia and is a center for rubber processing for midstream products for exports. Jambi's largest export gateway is Belakang Padang Port in Riau Islands, followed by Muara Sabak and Talang Duku in Jambi. Other export gateways include Belawan Port and Kualanamu Airport in North Sumatera, Teluk Bayur port in West Sumatera, Musi River and Plaju in South Sumatera, and Panjang Port in Lampung. Jambi plays a significant role in developing Indonesia as the second largest rubber exporter worldwide, after Thailand.

Bengkulu City (Bengkulu Province) . Bengkulu City is in the less-developed western coast of Sumatera. Bengkulu's main products include fish from the Indian Ocean, rubber, wood, and palm oil. Grouper and tuna are exported to Malaysia, while palm oil shells are exported to Thailand and the PRC. In addition to the existing national non-toll road, Bengkulu City, the province's capital, will also connect to Palembang through Trans-Sumatera Toll Road. Before the COVID-19 pandemic, Bengkulu City was also connected to Batam in Riau Islands through regular direct flights twice a day.[41]

Bandar Lampung (Lampung Province). Bandar Lampung, the province's capital, is part of Sumatera's growth corridor where four industrial zones are planned to be developed, namely Tanggamus, Pesawaran, Way Pisang, and Katibung. Bandar Lampung is well connected to Palembang (South Sumatera) through Trans-Sumatera National Highway, Trans-Sumatera toll road, and with regular flights (four times a day before the COVID-19 pandemic).

Batam (Riau Islands). Batam is the biggest city in Riau Islands Province even though the administrative capital is Tanjungpinang. Located adjacent to the Singapore Strait, Batam serves as an industrial base for shipbuilding, apparel, plastic-based products, tooling and stamping, and emergency lanterns. These industries are hosted in many industrial estates such as Kabil Integrated Industrial Park, Bintan Inti Industrial Estate, Batamindo Industrial Park, and West Point Batam Industrial Park. The raw materials for these industries come not only from Sumatera and other regions in Indonesia (especially mineral fuel and CPO), but also from other countries shipped through Batu Ampar, Sekupang, Kabil/Panau, and Pulau Sambu ports.

Major development initiatives are being planned for Batam under the RPJMN 2020–2024. The Trans-Sumatera Toll Road will run from Batu Ampar Port to Hang Nadim Airport. Batam–Bintan–Karimun has been designated as a free trade zone and free port. Batam–Bintan has been designated as a National Strategic Tourism Zone.

---

[41] https://radityoaufar.blogspot.com/2016/08/jadwal-penerbangan-bandara-fatmawati.html.

Batam has six gateways for its export–import activities: Belakang Padang, Batu Ampar, Sekupang, Kabil/Panau, Pulau Sambu, and Hang Nadim. For maritime passenger transport, Batam has ferry routes from Batam Center, Sekupang, and Harbour Bay ports to HarbourFront in Singapore, as well as from Batam Center to Stulang Laut Jetty in Johor Bahru.

Tanjungpinang (Bintan, Riau Islands). Tanjungpinang, located in Bintan Islands, is the capital of Riau Islands Province. Tanjungpinang is connected with Batam through Ro-Ro ferry and air transport. The Raja Haji Fisabilillah Airport services flights to Medan and Pekanbaru. For international routes, Tanjungpinang is connected to Stulang Laut jetty in Johor and HarbourFront Singapore via express ferry. Bintan has logged the highest number of cruise ship calls in Indonesia during 2015–2019 due to the "Genting Dream" weekly cruises.

Pangkalpinang (Bangka Island). Pangkalpinang is the capital of Bangka Belitung Islands Province, located in Bangka Island. The main gateway ports for Bangka Island are Muntok, Pangkal Balam, and Belinyu. Pangkalpinang is connected to Palembang (South Sumatera) and Tanjung Pandan via ferry, as well as via air transport through Depati Amir Airport. Pangkalpinang is also connected via air transport to Batam and Jakarta.

Tanjung Pandan (Belitung Island). Tanjung Pandan is the capital of Belitung regency in Belitung Island. Belitung is a popular tourism destination in Indonesia and recently some cruise lines have proposed to call on the island. Tanjung Pandan is connected to Pangkalpinang via ferry and air transport. It is also connected with Jakarta, Palembang, Singapore, and Kuala Lumpur through H.A.S. Hanandjoeddin International Airport. Some cruise lines are also proposing to have cruise call in Belitung Island.

Status of Physical Connectivity in the Proposed Route

Land Connectivity

Thailand. The proposed EC6 route in Thailand convers the provinces of Pattani, Yala, and Narathiwat (also called the Deep South) linking with Malaysia at Kelantan and Perak. Road connectivity starts at Mueang District in Pattani and ends at the Thai–Malaysian border in Yala and Narathiwat. The route is divided into six sections: (i) Pattani Mueang District, Yala Mueang District; (ii) Yala Mueang District–Betong Border Checkpoint; (iii) Pattani Mueang District–Narathiwat Mueang District; (iv) Narathiwat Mueang District–Tak Bai Border Checkpoint; (v) Narathiwat Mueang District–Su-ngai Kolok Border Checkpoint; and (vi) Narathiwat Mueang District–Buketa Border Checkpoint.

The routes in these six sections cover the distance between 38.2 and 131 kms depending on the start and end points and with two or four traffic lanes (Table 27). The entire route is safe, equipped with traffic signs, traffic lines, complete and undamaged safety equipment, curved guideposts, and complete guard rail in good condition. The road is smooth in the entire section.

Table 27: Economic Corridor 6: Start and End Points in Thailand

Start Point	End Point	Route	Distance (kilometer)	Traffic Lane	Road Classification
Pattani	Yala	410	42	2	Class II
Yala	Betong	410	131	2–4	Class II/I
Patani	Narathiwat	42	94.8	2–4	Class II/I
Narathiwat	Tak Bai	4084/42	38.2	4	Class I
Narathiwat	Su-ngai Kolok	4084/42	64.5	4	Class I
Narathiwat	Buketa	4055/4056/4193/4057	79.2	2–4	Class II/I

Source: Study team.

Malaysia. The road conditions in both EC6-MR1 and EC6-MR2 routes are well-maintained, efficient, and safe as they are part of federal and state road systems including the East Coast Expressway 1 and 2 and the East–West Highway 1 and 2 (Tables 28 and 29).

Table 28: Economic Corridor 6: Malaysia Route 1-Connectivity Route from Border Crossing Points in Kelantan to Tanjung Bruas (Melaka) via Terengganu and Pahang

Start Point	End Point	Route	Distance (kilometer)	Traffic Lane	Road Class
Bukit Bunga BCP, Tanah Merah, Kelantan		4, 8, D14	83	2	Federal and state road
Rantau Panjang BCP, Pasir Mas, Kelantan	Kota Bharu, Kelantan	AH18, 196, D23, 134, 3	40	2	Federal road
Pengkalan Kubor BCP, Tumpat Kelantan		D21, 3	18	2	Federal and state road
Kota Bharu, Kelantan	Tok Bali, Kelantan	3, D10, D141	46	2	Federal and state road
Tok Bali, Kelantan	Kuala Terengganu, Terengganu	T3, 3685, T147, 3, 65	118	2	Federal and state road
Kuala Terengganu, Terengganu	Kemaman Port, Terengganu	14, E8, 3	157	2–4	Federal road and expressway
Kemaman Port, Terengganu	Kuantan Port, Pahang	3	45	2	Federal and state road
Kuantan Port, Pahang	Kuantan, Pahang	3	42	2	Federal road
Kuantan, Pahang	Tanjung Bruas Port, Melaka	E8, 68, E2/AH2, 19, M6, M9,5	372	2–4	Federal road, state road, and expressway
Port of Tanjung Bruas, Melaka	Port of Bandar Sri Junjungan, Dumai Riau, Sumatera	Sea routes	177 (or 96 nautical miles)	Shipping Route	Ferry (Ro-Ro)

BCP = border crossing point.
Source: Study team.

Table 29: Economic Corridor 6: Malaysia Route 2–Connectivity of Border Crossing Points in Kelantan to Tanjung Bruas Port (Melaka) via Ipoh and Lumut Port (Perak)

Starting Point	End Point	Route	Distance (kilometer)	Traffic Lane	Road Class
Pengkalan Kubor BCP, Kelantan	Ipoh, Perak	EW-1(4), 76, E1/AH2	339	2–4	Federal road and expressway
Rantau Panjang BCP, Pasir Mas Panjang, Kelantan		EW-1(4), 76, E1/AH2	304	2–4	Federal road and expressway
Bukit Bunga BCP, Tanah Merah, Kelantan		EW-1(4), 76, E1/AH2	271	2–4	Federal road and expressway
Ipoh, Perak	Lumut Port, Perak	5, 3145	79	2	Federal road
Lumut Port, Perak	Port Klang, Selangor	5, 58, NSE1/AH2	250	2	Federal and state road
Port Klang, Selangor	Tanjung Bruas, Port, Melaka	182, E5, E1/AH2, 19, M9, 5	157	2–4	Federal road and expressway
Port of Tanjung Bruas, Melaka	Port of Bandar Sri Junjungan, Dumai Riau, Sumatera	Sea routes	177 (or 96 nautical miles)	Shipping Route	Ferry (Ro-Ro)

BCP = border crossing point; Ro-Ro = roll on, roll off.
Source: Study team.

Indonesia. The four provinces in mainland Sumatera are connected to each other by the existing national highway and the ongoing Trans-Sumatera toll road that traverses their capital cities.

- Palembang connects with Jambi in the north, Bengkulu in the west, and Bandar Lampung in the South. Palembang serves as an interchange node between EC6 and EC3.

- Jambi City is located along the main eastern Trans-Sumatera National Highway, connecting to Palembang, and is also covered by the Trans-Sumatera toll road under the section Jambi–Rengat (198 km) and Betung–Tempino–Jambi (190 km).

- Bengkulu City is connected to Padang and Bandar Lampung through the western Trans-Sumatera National Highway. In the Trans Sumatera toll road, the city will be connected to Palembang under Lubuklinggau–Curup–Bengkulu section (95.8 km).

- Bandar Lampung is connected to other cities in Sumatera via western Trans-Sumatera National Highway, especially Bengkulu. It is also indirectly connected to Palembang via the Trans-Sumatera toll road under the sections of Bakauheni–Terbanggi Besar (140 km) and Terbanggi Besar–Pematang Panggang–Kayu Agung (185 km).

Rail Connectivity

Thailand. The main rail route goes southeast from Hat Yai (Songkhla) to the Su-ngai Kolok border in Narathiwat covering 214 kms (Map 18). There is a rail link at Su-ngai Kolok (last station on the southeast branch) across the Kolok River to Rantau Panjang (Malaysia), but there are no cross-border passenger train services there. The railway service between Su-ngai Kolok and Pasir Mas stations, which has been operating since 1954, was terminated in 1999 due to smuggling and human trafficking activities.

Map 18: Rail Routes in Thailand

Map showing rail routes in Thailand. Cities labeled include: Kanchanaburi, Pathum Thani, Nakhon Nayok, Nonthaburi, Prachin Buri, Nakhon Pathom, BANGKOK, Sa Kaeo, Samut Sakhon, Chachoengsao, Ratchaburi, Samut Prakan, Chon Buri, Samut Songkhram, Phetchaburi, Rayong, Chanthaburi, Cha-am, Hua Hin, Trat, Prachuap Khiri Khan, Chumphon, Ko Tao, Ranong, Lang Suan, Ko Pha-ngan, Ko Samui, Chaiya, Surat Thani, Phangnga, Nakhon Si Thammarat, Krabi, Thung Song, Phuket, Trang, Phatthalung, Kantang, Songkhla, Hat Yai, Pattani, Padang Besa, Satun, Yala, Narathiwat, Su-ngai Kolok.

Distances shown: 122 km, 59 km, 72 km, 89 km, 84 km, 45 km, 110 km, 104 km.

THAILAND

Legend:
- National Capital
- Provincial Capital
- Other City
- Railway
- Ferry Route
- River
- Provincial Boundary
- International Boundary
- km = kilometer
- Boundaries are not necessarily authoritative.

This map was produced by the cartography unit of the Asian Development Bank. The boundaries, colors, denominations, and any other information shown on this map do not imply, on the part of the Asian Development Bank, any judgment on the legal status of any territory, or any endorsement or acceptance of such boundaries, colors, denominations, or information.

Source: Asian Development Bank.

There are also no cross-border bus services between Thailand and Malaysia on the southeast coast of the Thai–Malaysian border. From Su-ngai Kolok Rail Station (Thailand), access to the Thai–Malaysian Border is by taxi or by foot (1 km) over the Friendship Bridge to Rantau Panjang. From Rantau Panjang, it is possible to get a bus, motorbike, or taxi to the nearest Pasir Mas Station.

The absence of train services from Su-ngai Kolok Railway Station to Pasir Mas Railway Station, is a critical missing link to connect Narathiwat with Kelantan as part of EC6. The train route covers 20 km (18 km in Thailand and 2 km in Malaysia). The resumption of rail services will make it possible to connect Thailand to Malaysia's ECRL, which will connect Malaysia's east and west coasts. Land connectivity between the east and west coast of the peninsula will transform the current trade route in the subregion since the transport of goods will no longer have to go through the Strait of Malacca. Moreover, Kuantan Port (Pahang) is the designated port for the PRC–Malaysia Belt and Road Initiative, which together with Port Klang, connects to European trade routes. The entire ECRL route covers 620 km and the land bridge in Malaysia covers 250 km.

Malaysia. The rail link with the south of Thailand is via the Southern Thailand Line, which runs from Bangkok to Hat Yai, connects to Padang Besar Station and continues to Johor Bahru and Singapore (Woodlands CIQ) (Map 19). The Southern Thailand Line that connects to the east coast of the peninsula ends in Su-ngai Kolok (Narathiwat) in the absence of rail links with Pasir Mas.

The railway network in Peninsular Malaysia is operated by the KTMB, which provides both passenger and cargo services. The same railroad tracks are used for passenger and cargo. The railroad network consists of a double-track and single-track route. For cargo services, KTMB has established connections with other container terminals by having rail links to their depots. Most rail facilities link to the seaports.

Major railway projects. Malaysia has two major railway projects that will have a significant impact on EC6: (i) ECRL, and (ii) the Johor Bahru–Singapore Rapid Transit System (RTS).[42] The ECRL Project passes through three states in EC6. The RTS project involves Johor and Singapore. The RTS project will improve transport connectivity between the southern region (from Johor Bahru/Singapore) while the ECRL will improve connectivity along the peninsula's west coast, as well as between the west coast and the east coast via connectivity with the ECRL in Kuala Lumpur.

The East Coast Rail Link. The ECRL is a 640-km, double-track railway connecting Kota Bahru in Kelantan and the east coast states of Terengganu and Pahang to Port Klang in Selangor on the Strait of Malacca (Map 20). It cuts across the central region of Peninsular Malaysia connecting the east coast to the west coast. The project is a joint venture between Malaysia Rail Link Sdn Bhd and the China Communications Construction Company.

The ECRL service covers both freight and passengers with a projected revenue share of 70% and 30%, respectively. Passenger trains will travel at a speed of 160km/hour, cutting travel time from Kota Bharu to Putrajaya to approximately 4 hours. The railway will have 20 stations. Construction began in August 2017, suspended for a brief period in July 2018, and resumed in April 2019 after the signing of a supplementary agreement between Malaysia Rail Link Sdn Bhd and the China Communications Construction Company on the revised construction cost and southern alignment of the rail link. The project cost is estimated at RM44 billion. The ECRL Project is expected to be completed by the end of 2026.

---

[42] The ECRL will be implemented by the Malaysia Rail Link Sdn. Bhd and RTS will be implemented by Johor Bharu Singapore Rapid Transit System.

Map 19: Rail Routes in Malaysia

THAILAND

NAKHON SI THAMMARAT

TRANG

PHATTHALUNG

SATUN

Hat Yai

SONGKHLA

PATTANI

NARATHIWAT

YALA

Padang Besar

Arau

Alor Setar

KEDAH

PERLIS

LANGKAWI ISLAND

Su-ngai Kolok

Tumpat

Kota Bharu

Wakaf Bharu

Tanah Merah

Gurun

Sungai Petani

Kuala Krai

Butterworth

Bukit Mertajam

PENANG ISLAND

Dabong

KELANTAN

PENANG

Taiping

Gua Musang

TERENGGANU

Kuala Kangsar

Ipoh

PENINSULAR MALAYSIA

Batu Gajah

PERAK

Padang Tengku

Kuala Lipis

PAHANG

Sungkai

Jerantut

Strait of Malacca

Tanjong Malim

SELANGOR

Mentakab

Triang

KUALA LUMPUR

Port Klang

NEGERI SEMBILAN

Seremban

Bahau

Gemas

Tampin

Segamat

MELAKA

JOHOR

Melaka

INDONESIA

Kluang

Kulai

Johor Bahru

Woodlands

SINGAPORE

Legend

⊛ National Capital
◉ Provincial/State Capital
▭▭▭ SRT Southern Line
▭▭▭ KTMB West Coast Line
▭▭▭ KTMB East Coast Line
▭▭▭ KTMB Kargo Line
━━━ National Road
─── Other Road
─·─·─ Provincial Boundary
──── International Boundary
Boundaries are not necessarily authoritative.

State Railway of Thailand (SRT)
• Southern Line: Bangkok–Hat Yai–Padang Besa/Su-ngai Kolok

Keretapi Tanah Melayu Berhad (KTMB)/ Malayan Railways Limited
• West Coast Line
  ◦ North Line: Padang Besar–Tanjong Malim
  ◦ Central Line: Tanjong Malim–Kuala Lumpur
  ◦ South Line: Seremban–Woodlands
• East Coast Line: Tumpat–Gemas
• Kargo Line: Kuala Lumpur–Port Klang

This map was produced by the cartography unit of the Asian Development Bank. The boundaries, colors, denominations, and any other information shown on this map do not imply, on the part of the Asian Development Bank, any judgment on the legal status of any territory, or any endorsement or acceptance of such boundaries, colors, denominations, or information.

Source: Asian Development Bank.

Map 20: East Coast Rail Line

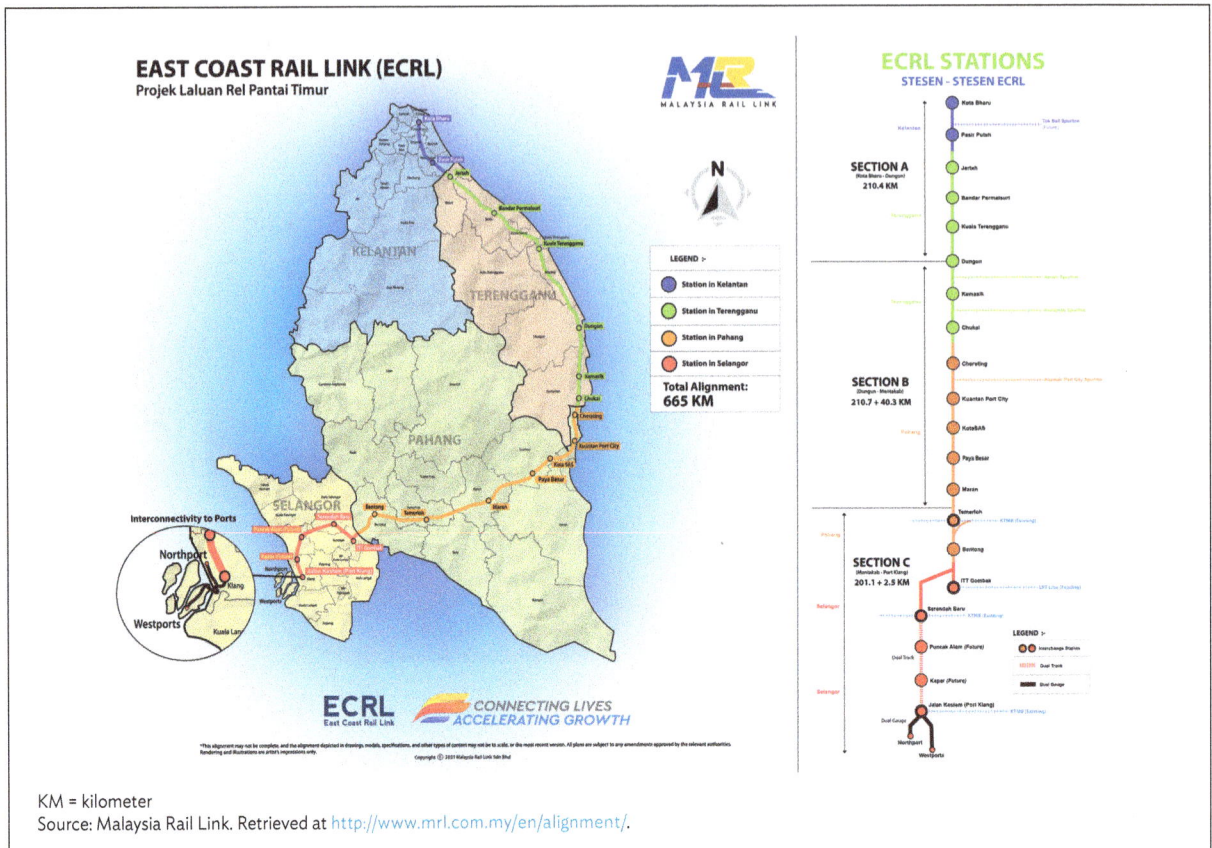

KM = kilometer
Source: Malaysia Rail Link. Retrieved at http://www.mrl.com.my/en/alignment/.

Johor Bahru–Singapore Rapid Transit System. The RTS is a cross-border rapid transit system that would connect Johor Bahru with Woodlands, Singapore crossing the Strait of Johor. The RTS will have two stations—the Singapore terminus located at Woodlands North station and the Malaysia terminus at Bukit Chagar station. Both stations will have co-located Singaporean and Malaysian CIQ facilities. The RTS link is expected to replace the railway line and shuttle train services between Johor Bahru Sentral and Woodlands Train Checkpoint. The RTS link will significantly ease causeway congestion and facilitate business and tourism. The RTS link will have a capacity of 10,000 passengers. The starting date for the project construction has not been announced. The original cost of the project is about RM5 billion.[43]

Land Bridge Services

Since 1999, a land bridge service has been operating from Sri Setia, Selangor, to Bangsue, Thailand. KTMB operates the land bridge service in collaboration with the SRT, and in partnership with transport operators, vessel operators, and freight forwarders. The land bridge service permits cross-border movement of containers between Malaysia and Thailand by railways; the containers are sealed once for the entire trip and cargo clears both Malaysian and Thai Customs at the point of origin. It is a more cost-effective alternative to transportation services entirely by sea providing shorter travel time: 2.5 days by land bridge compared to

---

[43]   *Business Insider.* 2019. Singapore-JB RTS Link Agreement Signing Delayed Again as Malaysia Now Wants an LRT System Instead. 5 November.

5–7 days by sea (e.g., Port Klang to Bangkok) or 3–4 days (Port Klang to Bangkok) by truck. The seamless border, cheaper freight rates, and guaranteed security makes Malaysia's land bridge service an attractive alternative transport mode. The land bridge service also provides an overland transit link from Malaysian ports to Cambodia, the Lao PDR, and Viet Nam.

The land bridge service operates 28 weekly services between[44]

- Port Klang–Bangkok–Port Klang
- Port Klang–Hat Yai–Port Klang
- Singapore–Surat Thani–Singapore
- Singapore–Bangkok–Singapore

A total of 80 TEUs/40 wagons of cargo can be moved per trip, with an average of 4,500 TEUs monthly. Cargoes normally transported using this service include steel, chemical, gypsum boards, machinery, electronic products, and consumer goods.[45]

Maritime Connectivity

Thailand. There are no major maritime routes for Thailand in EC6. The ports along the coast of Narathiwat and Pattani are used mainly as fishers' pier. There is no commercial port for transport of goods and passengers.

Malaysia. The important maritime gateway ports are:

- Kuantan Port (Pahang), Kemaman Port (Terengganu), and Tok Bali Port (Kelantan) along the eastern coast; and
- Lumut Port (Perak), Port Klang (Port Klang), Tanjung Bruas (Melaka), Tanjung Pelepas and Pasir Gudang (Johor) along the Strait of Malacca.

Kuantan Port (Pahang). Kuantan Port is a multi-cargo deep seaport situated at Tanjung Gelang on the eastern seaboard of Peninsular Malaysia some 25 km north of Kuantan, the state capital of Pahang.[46] Kuantan Port is well connected by road and rail to other parts of Peninsular Malaysia as well as by air to major world destinations via Kuala Lumpur.[47] Kuantan Port serves primarily the PRC, Cambodia, the Lao PDR, and Viet Nam. It has developed into a major container terminal for the east coast region with its excellent port facilities and services, a vast market outreach and a strong network of global shipping connections. Kuantan Port is positioned to be a catalyst for the rapid expansion of the industrial and manufacturing activities in the East Coast Industrial Corridor, given its location in the heartland of the petrochemical industry. Upon completion of the New Deep-Water Terminal, Kuantan Port is envisaged to be the main gateway to the PRC and the Far East and will serve as a transshipment hub for minor ports in the region. There is a road link between Songkhla Port and Kuantan Port via Highway 43 in Thailand and Highway AH18 in Malaysia (656 km). Kuantan Port also links to Penang Port using Highway E8 (306 km).

---

[44] D. M. Lowtan. 2004. Rail Systems in Malaysia. Final Report to Massachusetts Institute of Technology.

[45] Information adapted from KTMB. Landbridge. Retrieved at https://www.ktmb.com.my/Kargo.html.

[46] The information for Kuantan Port was compiled from http://www.kuantanport.com.my/en_GB/about-us/corporate-profile/.

[47] Located approximately 220 km away from Kuala Lumpur, Kuantan Port is accessible by road via the East Coast Expressway, with travel time of approximately 3 hours By air, it takes only 40 minutes from Kuala Lumpur International Airport to Kuantan Airport located approximately 38 km from Kuantan Port.

Kemaman Port (Terengganu). The Kemaman Port located on the east coast of Peninsular Malaysia, is one of the deepest seaports in Malaysia and a fast-emerging port acting as the new gateway to the Asia and Pacific region.[48] As a deep-sea all-weather port operating all year round, it is capable of handling vessels of up to 150,000 deadweight tonnes and various types of cargo ranging from general cargo, dry bulk, to liquid bulk. It serves as a feeder port for Kuantan Port, while serving the logistics requirements of the nearby Kemaman Heavy Industrial Park. The port will be complemented by ship building and repair facilities at the industrial park, and will leverage on the upstream and downstream developments in the oil and gas industry in nearby Kerteh.

Tok Bali Port (Kelantan). Tok Bali Port in Kelantan is a minor fishing port. Under the East Coast Economic Region Development Council (ECERDC) Blueprint 2.0, this port will be expanded to serve as a feeder port for Kuantan Port.[49] The Tok Bali Port has been identified as the regional distribution hub for movement of goods from Southern Thailand to Cambodia, the Lao PDR, and Viet Nam. Tok Bali Port will also act as the halal export hub, focusing on halal production–distribution with its links to Pasir Mas Halal Park. The port also serves as a supply base for offshore support activities in the oil and gas sector, playing the role of a one-stop center for multinationals operating in the Malaysia–Thailand Joint Development Area, North Malay Basin, and Malaysia–Viet Nam Commercial Arrangement Area.

Lumut Port (Perak). Lumut Port is a secondary port and strategically located off the Strait of Malacca, on the west coast of Peninsular Malaysia.[50] It was established as a State Port to serve as a catalyst for economic growth, development, and industrialization. Adjacent to the port is Lumut Industrial Park equipped with comprehensive utilities especially suitable for marine, heavy, medium, and light industries. Land is sold on a 99-year leasehold tenure only to investors who would utilize the facilities and services of the port.

Port Klang (Selangor). Port Klang is Malaysia's premier port and the world's 12th busiest port. The port's Northport Terminal is positioned as an intra-Asian transshipment and regional trading hub, serving domestic and coastal trade routes to ports in Sabah, Sarawak, and Brunei Darussalam as well as short-seaport destinations in Indonesia, Thailand, and Viet Nam. The Asa Niaga Harbor City Terminal is a regional passenger ferry terminal that serves high speed passenger ferries plying between Port Klang and the ports of Dumai and Tanjung Balai in Sumatera. Port Klang has maritime links with 10 large and small ports in Sumatera. Its trading is concentrated in the North Sumatera, Riau, West Sumatera, Jambi, South Sumatera, and Lampung regions.

Tanjung Bruas Port (Melaka). The port is the main trade gateway to Melaka and to other states in the Peninsula from Riau Province in Sumatera. Tanjung Bruas is one of the world's busiest trade routes at the center and narrowest point of the Strait of Malacca. Situated within a large, developed hinterland drawn from Melaka, Negeri Sembilan, and northern Johor, Tanjung Bruas Port is surrounded by more than 500 manufacturing companies that ship both conventional and container cargoes through the port. Comprehensive improvements are being planned to develop the port as a hub for sea–air cargoes. Tanjung Bruas Port has trade links with Dumai Port (Riau Province). The implementation of the Melaka–Dumai Ro-Ro project (EC4) will further boost exports and imports of cargo freights between Melaka and the Riau Province. In addition, the MIFT is affiliated with the Port of Bandar Sri Laksamana, Bengkalis, which provides ferry services for passengers from Melaka to

---

[48]   The information for Kemaman Port was compiled from EPIC Group - Subsidiaries | Konsortium Pelabuhan Kemaman Sdn Bhd. https://www.epicgroup.com.my/subsidiaries/kpk.php.

[49]   The information for Tok Bali port was compiled from Tok Bali Integrated Fisheries Park (TBIFP) - ECERDC. https://www.ecerdc.com.my/investment-opportunity/ecer-an-ideal-investment-destination/thematic-industrial-parks/tok-bali-integrated-fisheries-park/.

[50]   The information for Lumut Port was compiled from http://lumutport.com/about/.

the Riau Province. Tanjung Bruas Port is a node linking EC1 and EC2 in the Peninsula with EC3 in Sumatera via Dumai.

Tanjung Pelepas Port (Johor). The Tanjung Pelepas Port is a deep seaport located along the Strait of Malacca and is the international gateway for the southern part of Malaysia.[51] The port provides transshipment services because of its proximity to international shipping routes.[52] The Tanjung Pelepas Port is well connected to the hinterland. Cargo movement from major industrial estates is convenient especially with Tanjung Pelepas Port's 5.04-km access road linking the port to the second Malaysia–Singapore expressway and the north–south highway that connects all the way up north of Peninsular Malaysia and the Thai border. The rail line that runs through Tanjung Pelepas Port is directly linked to the national rail grid, which connects Singapore and the southern area of Thailand. The 1,500-acre Pelepas free-zone land located directly behind the port makes it ideal for manufacturing and commercial activities including value adding activities such as cargo consolidation, international procurement centers, and regional distribution operations. The Tanjung Pelepas Port is also located within the 2,200 km² development area of Iskandar Malaysia, and plays a key role in the development of Johor as one of Malaysia's new regional economic growth centers. The Tanjung Pelepas Port provides the south of Malaysia with a high level of both national and international accessibility and mobility through its well-developed integrated port and free zone.

Johor Port Pasir Gudang. Located at the southern tip of Peninsular Malaysia, Johor Port is the southern gateway and multipurpose port in Malaysia.[53] It is strategically positioned at the heart of the sprawling 8,000-acre Pasir Gudang Industrial Estate across the causeway from Singapore. It is the first port in Malaysia to be accorded a free zone status. Johor Port is the largest palm oil terminal in the world and was designated as an approved London Metal Exchange location in 2004. It is also one of the largest in the region for the hubbing of nonferrous metals, the largest discharging point for rice and cocoa in Malaysia, and one of the biggest terminals in Malaysia for fertilizer and cement.[54]

Links of Malaysia Ports with Sumatera. Maritime links between the EC6 ports in Malaysia and Riau Islands and Bangka Belitung Islands—the two Sumatera provinces proposed for EC6—are limited. Only Lumut Port has maritime trade links with Batam, Batu Ampar in Riau Islands for dry bulk cargo, mostly coal. However, Lumut has links with other ports in Sumatera at Jambi and Palembang.

Other maritime links are for passenger ferry services. There are ferry services from Tanjung Pelepas (Stulang Ferry Terminal Berjaya Waterfront Ferry Terminal) and Johor Port Pasir Gudang (Pasir Gudang Ferry Terminal) to Batam and Tanjungpinang in Riau Islands. Tanjung Pelepas Port, which is a container port, does not have maritime trade links with Sumatera. Johor Port (Pasir Gudang) has maritime trade links with Belawan (Medan, North Sumatera) and Palembang (South Sumatera) (Table 30).

---

[51] The information for Tanjung Pelepas Port was compiled from http://www.ptp.com.my/home.

[52] It takes vessels accessing Tanjung Pelepas Port only 45 minutes to divert to the port. The draft of the port ranging between 15–19m allows it to service the new generation of mega container vessels with capacity of more than 18,000 TEUs. Behind the port's 14 berths is a container yard—one of the largest container storage facilities in the region with the capacity to handle up to 10.5 million TEUs annually.

[53] The information for Johor Port was compiled from http://www.johorport.com.my/.

[54] Multinational clients at the port include companies such as Shell, Chevron, Holcim/LaFarge, BASF, and FJB.

Table 30: Economic Corridor 6: Maritime Links of Malaysia Ports with Sumatera Ports

Malaysia Port	Maritime Links with Sumatera Province	Sumatera Port	Type of Maritime Activities	Remarks
Port Klang, Selangor	North Sumatera	Belawan, Medan	Cargo and container	
		Tanjung Balai	Cargo	
	Riau	Buatan	Container	
		Dumai	Cargo and container	
		Pekanbaru	Cargo and container	
		Perawang	Container	
	West Sumatera	Padang, Teluk Bayur	Cargo and container	
	Jambi	Jambi	Cargo	
	South Sumatera	Palembang	Cargo and container	
	Lampung	Panjang	Container	
Tok Bali Port	No trade links	—	Fishing port	To be expanded into secondary port and feeder to Kuantan Port)
Kemaman Port, Terengganu	No trade links	—	Feeder port	Feeder port to Kuantan Port
Kuantan Port, Pahang	No trade links	—	Cargo	Has connectivity with Laem Chabang Port (Thailand) and focusing on northeast Asia ports
Lumut Port, Perak	Riau	Pelintung	Barge	
	Riau Islands	Batam, Batu Ampar	Barge	
	Jambi	Jambi	Barge	
		Kuala Tunggal	Barge	
	Bengkulu	Bengkulu	Barge	
	South Sumatera	Muara Lematang	Barge	
		Palembang	Barge	
Port of Port Dickson	Riau	Dumai Port	Ferry passenger	Ferry passenger terminal
Tanjung Bruas Port, Melaka	Riau	Dumai Port	Cargo	Ro-Ro ferry for cargo, as part of the Melaka–Dumai Ro-Ro Ferry Project
	South Sumatera Province	Palembang	Cargo	
	Aceh	Lhokseumawe	Cargo	
Melaka International Cruise Terminal, Melaka	Riau	Port of Bandar Sri Laksamana, Bengkalis	Ferry passenger	Ferry passenger terminal
Johor Port (Pasir Gudang), Johor	South Sumatera	Palembang	Cargo and container	
	North Sumatera	Belawan, Medan	Cargo and container	
Tanjung Pelepas, Johor	North Sumatera	Port of Belawan	Cargo and container	
Stulang Ferry Terminal (Berjaya Waterfront Ferry Terminal, Tanjung Pelepas, Johor)	Riau Islands	Batam Tanjungpinang	Ferry passenger	Ferry passenger terminal
Pasir Gudang Ferry Terminal, Pasir Gudang, Johor		Batam		

— = not applicable; Ro-Ro = roll on, roll off.
Source: Study team.

Indonesia. Direct maritime links between Sumatera ports in Riau Islands and Bangka Belitung Islands with Malaysia are limited. For Riau Islands, Batu Ampar Port in Batam has a trade link with Lumut Port in Perak and Johor Port (Pasir Gudang). Due to the limited capacity of ports in Batam, export commodities from Batam would undergo double and triple handling. Some of Batam's export commodities will be transferred from Johor Port to Jurong Port in Singapore. There are also passenger ferries from some ports in Batam and Tanjungpinang to Stulang Laut and Pasir Gudang Ports in Johor. The Port of Tanjung Pandan (under Pelindo II) in Belitung Island serves direct export activities to Malaysia. As of December 2019, there were 20 ships that exported kaolin directly to Port Klang in Malaysia. The Port of Pangkal Balam in Tanjungpinang City has a small capacity, which can only accommodate ships under 3,000 GT. Export–import activities are thus carried out through other ports, especially Jakarta (Sunda Kelapa Port and Tanjung Priok Port), Riau (Dumai Port), North Sumatera (Belawan Port), and Lampung (Panjang Port) (Table 31).

Table 31: Economic Corridor 6: Maritime Links of Sumatera Ports with Malaysia Ports

Sumatera Port	Maritime Links with Malaysia States	Malaysia Port	Type of Maritime Activity	Remarks
Batu Ampar, Batam	Perak	Lumut Port	Cargo	
Batam	Johor	Stulang Laut	Passenger ferry	
Tanjungpinang	Johor	Pasir Gudang	Passenger ferry	
Tanjung Pandang, Belitung Islands	Selangor	Port Klang		Mainly for exports of kaolin

Source: Study team.

Air Linkages

Air connectivity within EC6 is limited, with no direct flights between the capital cities of the provinces and states in the corridor. Destinations in EC6 can be reached through low-cost carrier flights originating from the national capital cities and other economic centers.

Thailand airports located in EC6 are Narathiwat Airport and Betong Airport (Yala). Narathiwat Airport services mainly domestic flights by Thai Smile Airways and Thai AirAsia, except for international flights by Thai Airways to Mecca during the period of the Hajj. The Betong Airport (Yala) which opened in April 2021, will help alleviate the difficulty of land travel in Yala's mountainous terrain, and support tourism.

In **Malaysia**, there are three airports located in EC6 states: Sultan Ismail Petra Airport (Kota Bharu, Kelantan), Sultan Mahmud Airport (Kuala Terengganu), and Sultan Haji Ahmad Shah Airport (Kuantan, Pahang). LCCs operating in these airports serve only domestic routes to Kuala Lumpur, Subang, Penang, and Johor Bahru. There are no international flights to Sumatera and Thailand.

In **Indonesia**, there are eight airports in the EC6 provinces: (i) Hang Nadim Airport (Batam, Riau Islands); (ii) Raja Haji Fisabilillah Airport (Bintan, Tanjungpinang, Riau Islands); (iii) Depati Amir Airport (Pangkalpinang, Bangka Belitung Islands); (iv) H.A.S. Hanandjoeddin International Airport (Tanjung Pandan, Belitung Island); (v) Sultan Mahmud Badaruddin II International Airport (Palembang, South Sumatera); (vi) Sultan Thaha Airport (Jambi City); (vii) Fatmawati Soekarno Airport (Bengkulu City); and (viii) Radin Inten II Airport (Bandar Lampung). These airports service mostly LCCs in domestic flights, including to Jakarta. Airports in Batam and Palembang have flights to Kuala Lumpur.

In summary, the road and rail connectivity between Malaysia and Thailand are adequate although there are gaps in certain segments that need to be addressed. Maritime and air connectivity, however, need to be developed further. While major ports in Malaysia have maritime trade links with ports in Sumatera and Southern Thailand, maritime links with ports in Riau Islands and Bangka Belitung Islands are limited to ferry services rather than commerce (Table 32).

**Table 32: Economic Corridor 6: Status of Proposed Connectivity
in the Proposed Economic Corridor 6 Routes**

	Road	Rail	Maritime	Air
Indonesia	Adequate	Not applicable	Limited links of Riau Islands and Bangka Belitung Islands with Malaysia	Mostly domestic flights to capital cities; no direct flights to EC6 nodes
Malaysia	Good, efficient, and safe	Adequate		
Thailand	Good, efficient, and safe	Adequate	There are no major maritime routes for Thailand in EC6	
	Gap: Construction of second bridge at Su-ngai Kolok; Construction of new bridge at Tak Bai	Gap: Improvement of railway route between Su-ngai Kolok–Rantau Panjang–Tumpat		

Source: Study team.

Overland and Maritime Trade

Thailand. Total trade of BCPs in Pattani, Yala, and Narathiwat at the border of Malaysia averaged $216.0 million during 2014–2018 (Table 33). This amount represents only 1.3% of Thailand's total BCP trade with Malaysia.

Thailand has enjoyed a trade surplus on overall border trade with Malaysia over the 5-year period. Exports comprised an average of 61%, driven by Yala's exports which accounted for almost 96% of its border trade with Malaysia. In Narathiwat, imports were higher—more than twice the level of exports. During 2014–2018, the average value of Narathiwat's imports was about $79.0 million, compared to exports of about $35 million.

Among the three Customs Houses in Narathiwat, about 78% of the trade goes through Su-ngai Kolok, of which around 84% are imports. In 2018, top export commodities via Su-ngai Kolok Customs House were frozen short mackerel, cup lump, tapioca flour, fabric woven, and colored Roman tiles. The top imports were processed wood, frozen longtail tunas, asphalt, peeled coconuts, and bread (Table 34).

Thailand's main exports at the BCPs with Malaysia are rice, fruits, and rubber products while imports consist mainly of peeled coconuts, liquid ammonia, and processed wood (Table 34).

Table 33: Economic Corridor 6: Trade Values at Thailand's Malaysian Border Crossing Points, 2014–2018
(million $)

Provinces	2014	2015	2016	2017	2018	Average 2014–2018	CAGR (%)
Pattani	**0.02**	**0.08**	**1.0**	**7.7**	**3.9**	**2.5**	**291.5**
Export	0.01	0	0	3.6	3.1	1.3	286.5
Import	0.003	0.08	1.0	4.1	0.8	1.2	312.6
Yala	**108.8**	**77.1**	**78.8**	**122.9**	**111.1**	**99.7**	**0.53**
Export	103.3	74.0	75.8	119.4	107.2	95.9	0.92
Import	5.5	3.1	3.0	3.5	3.9	3.8	(7.9)
Narathiwat	**95.6**	**94.8**	**135.3**	**128.5**	**114.1**	**113.7**	**4.51**
Export	32.9	32.9	40.9	33.9	33.0	34.7	0.08
Import	62.7	61.9	94.4	94.6	81.1	78.9	6.6
Total (3 BCPs)	**204.4**	**172.0**	**215.1**	**259.1**	**229.1**	**215.9**	**2.31**
Export	136.2	106.9	116.7	156.9	143.3	132.0	1.3
Import	68.2	65.1	98.4	102.2	85.8	83.9	5.9
Trade Balance	**68.01**	**41.82**	**18.30**	**54.7**	**57.50**	**48.1**	**(4.1)**
All BCPs Thai–Mal	**15,866.0**	**15,076.6**	**15,606.2**	**17,568.6**	**17,830.0**	**16,389.5**	**2.36**
Export	8,601.0	7,782.9	8,046.1	9,728.8	9,161.8	8,664.1	1.27
Import	7,265.0	7,293.7	7,560.1	7,839.8	8,668.2	7,725.4	3.59

( ) = negative, BCP = border crossing point, CAGR = compound annual growth rate, NESDC = National Economic and Social Development Council, Mal = Malaysia, Thai = Thailand.
Sources: Pattani: Department of Foreign Trade, Yala: Department of Foreign Trade, 2019; Bank of Thailand. Retrieved from https://www.bot.or.th/App/BTWS_STAT/statistics/ReportPage.aspx?reportID=123&language=th; Narathiwat: Department of Foreign Trade, 2019; Bank of Thailand. Retrieved from https://www.bot.or.th/App/BTWS_STAT/statistics/ReportPage.aspx?reportID=123&language=th; NESDC: Retrieved from https://www.nesdc.go.th/ewt_dl_link.php?nid=9491.

Table 34: Economic Corridor 6: Top Five Export and Import Commodities at Thailand's Malaysian Border Crossing Points, 2018

	Pattani		Yala		Narathiwat (Su-ngai Kolok)	
Rank	Exports	Imports	Exports	Imports	Exports	Imports
1	Rice (white rice 5%)	Peeled coconuts	Rubber products	Liquid ammonia	Frozen short mackerel in whole	Processed wood
2	Shallots		Finished rubber (rubber mixed with chemicals)	Styrene butadiene rubber	Cup lump	Frozen longtail tunas in whole
3	Corn seeds		Durians, langsats, rambutans, rose apples, cempedaks	Other lubricants used for rubber industry	Finished tapioca flour	Asphalt
4	Sacks		Plywood	Formalin	Fabric woven with synthetic fiber	Peeled coconuts
5			Mangoes, mangosteens, guavas	Used centrifuge for concentrated latex	Colored Roman tiles made from cellulose fiber cement	Bread

Sources: Pattani: Pattani Customs House, 2019, Bank of Thailand. Retrieved from https://www.bot.or.th/App/BTWS_STAT/statistics/ReportPage.aspx?reportID=123&language=th, Yala - Betong Customs House, 2019, Bank of Thailand. Retrieved from https://www.bot.or.th/App/BTWS_STAT/statistics/ReportPage.aspx?reportID=123&language=th, Narathiwat Su-ngai Kolok BCP: Su-ngai Kolok Customs House, 2019. Bank of Thailand. Retrieved from https://www.bot.or.th/App/BTWS_STAT/statistics/ReportPage.aspx?reportID=123&language=th.

Malaysia. During 2015–2018, total cross-border trade through the three BCPs in Kelantan—Rantau Panjang, Pengkalan Kubor, and Bukit Bunga—averaged $147 million and averaged a cross-border trade surplus of $35 million. Kelantan's contribution to the total trade of all Malaysia–Thailand's BCPs is 2%. The Rantau Panjang BCP, which is the main trade gateway between Kelantan and Narathiwat accounted for 86% of Kelantan's total trade for 2015–2018 (Table 35).

Table 35: Economic Corridor 6: Trade Values at Malaysia's Thai Border Crossing Points in Kelantan, 2015–2018 ($ million)

BCPs	2015	2016	2017	2018	Average (2015–2018)	Average Share to All Malaysia–Thai BCPs Trade (2015–2018) (%)	CAGR (2015–2018) (%)
Total Kelantan	147	152	145	145	147	2.3	0.7
Export	86	97	96	86	91	3.2	1.3
Import	61	55	49	58	56	1.5	(0.02)
BCPs in Kelantan							
Rantau Panjang	126	133	127	123	127	1.9	0.4
Export	82	92	90	80	86	3.0	0.5
Import	44	41	37	43	41	1.1	0.3
Pengkalan Kubor	19	17	14	16	16	0.3	(5.6)
Export	4	5	6	6	5	0.2	16.1
Import	15	12	8	10	11	0.3	(12.7)
Bukit Bunga	1.9	2.8	3.7	6.4	3.7	0.1	50.8
Export	0.2	0.1	0.0	0.1	0.1	0.0	(15.1)
Import	1.7	2.7	3.7	6.3	3.6	0.1	55.8
ALL Malaysia–Thailand BCP**	**6,515**	**6,420**	**6,574**	**6,620**	**6,532**		**1.6**
Export	2,792	2,848	2,904	2,985	2,882		3.4
Import	3,723	3,572	3,670	3,634	3,650		0.3

( ) = negative, BCP = border crossing point, CAGR = compound annual growth rate.
* Based on Malaysian ringgit.
**Includes border crossing points other than Rantau Panjang, Bukit Bunga, and Pengkalan Kubor.
Source: Royal Malaysian Customs Department, 2019.

The bulk of exports to Thailand at the Rantau Panjang BCP is composed of wood and wood products, contributing more than 90% of total exports in 2018. Imports are mainly rubber and plastics (34%) and vegetable products (30%).

Indonesia. Riau Islands' foreign trade in 2018 was the highest in Sumatera in terms of value (33.6%) and the second-highest in terms of volume (21.6%). Singapore, the PRC, and the US are the top export destinations in 2018, with Malaysia ranking 4th, and Thailand ranking 13th. For imports, Singapore, the PRC, and Malaysia are the top countries of origin, with Thailand ranking 17th. The share of of Riau Island's trade with Malaysia averaged 4.8% during the period 2014 to 2018 (Table 36).

Batam was the biggest contributor to Riau Island's foreign trade in 2018 (72.1%). Batam, the biggest city in Riau Islands, is the base for various industries such as shipbuilding, apparel, plastic-based products, tooling and stamping, and emergency lanterns. The raw materials for manufacturing are sourced not only from Sumatera and other regions in Indonesia but also from other countries. Raw material and intermediate product imports are processed in Batam's industrial estates and reexported through Singapore. Tanjungpinang (Bintan) recorded the biggest export volume in 2018 comprising 30% of the island's total exports.

Table 36: Economic Corridor 6: Trade between Riau Islands and Malaysia, 2014–2018
($ million)

Year	Riau Islands' Exports to Malaysia	Total Exports of Riau Islands	Share (%)	Riau Islands' Imports from Malaysia	Total Imports of Riau Islands	Share (%)
2014	912.3	15,707.3	5.8	869.2	10,877.4	8.0
2015	623.3	11,949.0	5.2	589.6	8,462.0	7.0
2016	397.3	11,030.4	3.6	581.8	7,749.7	7.5
2017	564.9	12,182.0	4.6	725.4	8,790.6	8.2
2018	645.5	13,193.0	4.9	923.2	11,423.5	8.1

Sources: BPS-Statistics Indonesia, 2015–2019 (BPS-Statistics Indonesia. 2019. *Kepulauan Riau dalam Angka 2019.* Tanjungpinang: BPS Provinsi Kepulauan Riau. p. 386; BPS-Statistics Indonesia. 2019. *Indikator Ekonomi Provinsi Kepulauan Riau 2019.* Tanjungpinang: BPS Provinsi Kepulauan Riau p. 76; BPS-Statistics Indonesia. 2019. *Statistik Ekspor Provinsi Kepulauan Riau 2018.* Tanjungpinang: BPS Provinsi Kepulauan Riau. p. 12; BPS-Statistics Indonesia. 2018. *Statistik Ekspor Provinsi Kepulauan Riau 2017.* Tanjungpinang: BPS Provinsi Kepulauan Riau. p. 12; BPS-Statistics Indonesia. 2017. *Statistik Ekspor Provinsi Kepulauan Riau 2016.* Tanjungpinang: BPS Provinsi Kepulauan Riau. p. 12; BPS-Statistics Indonesia. 2016. *Statistik Ekspor Provinsi Kepulauan Riau 2015.* Tanjungpinang: BPS Provinsi Kepulauan Riau. p. 12; BPS-Statistics Indonesia. 2015. *Statistik Ekspor Provinsi Kepulauan Riau 2014.* Tanjungpinang: BPS Provinsi Kepulauan Riau. p. 12–15. BPS-Statistics Indonesia. 2019. *Statistik Impor Provinsi Kepulauan Riau 2018.* Tanjungpinang: BPS Provinsi Kepulauan Riau. p. 12; BPS-Statistics Indonesia. 2018. *Statistik Impor Provinsi Kepulauan Riau 2017.* Tanjungpinang: BPS Provinsi Kepulauan Riau. p. 12; BPS-Statistics Indonesia. 2017. *Statistik Impor Provinsi Kepulauan Riau 2016.* Tanjungpinang: BPS Provinsi Kepulauan Riau. p. 12; BPS-Statistics Indonesia. 2016. *Statistik Impor Provinsi Kepulauan Riau 2015.* Tanjungpinang: BPS Provinsi Kepulauan Riau. pp. 14–17; BPS-Statistics Indonesia. 2016. *Statistik Impor Provinsi Kepulauan Riau 2015.* Tanjungpinang: BPS Provinsi Kepulauan Riau. pp. 10–13.

Riau Island's trade with Thailand is small: the share of exports to Thailand to the province's total trade averaged only 1.24% during 2014–2018, while the share of imports averaged less than 1%. Iron and steel articles were Riau Island's top exports, while electrical machinery and equipment were the top imports.

Bangka Belitung Islands contributed 2.62% of Sumatera's total foreign trade in 2018. Tin is the major export commodity, while fuel oil and other fuels are the main imports. Bangka Belitung Islands has an active trade with Malaysia. In 2018, about 75% of imports was sourced from Malaysia, while exports to Malaysia contributed about 13% of total exports in terms of volume. Kaolin is the major export commodity to Malaysia. Trade with Thailand contributed 3.68% of the province's total trade.

For South Sumatera, Malaysia is the second biggest trade partner after the PRC. In 2018, trade with Malaysia contributed 13.7% in volume or 13.9% in value. Meanwhile, South Sumatera's trade with Thailand is limited. It only contributed 2.7% in volume or 7.2% in value to Sumatera's total foreign trade. It is dominated by exports while import activity is very limited. Coal is the main export commodity from South Sumatera to Malaysia and Thailand.

Findings and Recommendations

The IMT-GT's endorsement in 2018 to have a sixth economic corridor was motivated by the need to respond to emerging changes in connectivity patterns in Asia with the launching of the PRC's BRI. Plans under the BRI to use the Strait of Malacca in opening new trade routes was perceived to be a game changer for the subregion. The ECRL Project in Malaysia was a major step in realizing this plan. The ECRL would connect the peninsula's east coast and west coast, providing the provinces of Southern Thailand with access to Malaysia's ports through Kelantan and Perak. It would also expand opportunities for Sumatera's provinces along the eastern coast to tap into new trade routes through expanded maritime links in the Strait of Malacca.

Roads connecting Pattani, Yala, and Narathiwat in Thailand are adequate, safe, and in good condition as they are part of the national road systems. The road conditions from Kelantan in Malaysia are also adequate, safe, and in good condition—both in EC6-MR1 (via Terengganu and Pahang) and in EC6-MR2 (via Perak) as they are part of federal or state roads systems. Road connectivity is complemented by rail links and land bridges. Access roads to BCPs at Narathiwat and Kelantan are adequate. The building and facilities at BCPs are well-maintained and adequate space is available for inspection and other formalities.

A number of infrastructure gaps require priority attention to make the proposed EC6 route viable. **Developing connectivity between Narathiwat and Kelantan is crucial** in enabling Thailand to connect with the ECRL and improve supply chain linkages between Southern Thailand and ECER Malaysia. The three projects that would enable this connection are as follows:

- **Improvement of the railway route between Su-ngai Kolok–Rantau Panjang–Tumpat**. This project would revive the missing rail link between Narathiwat to Kelantan. The rail link will complete the connection along the route from Kunming–Bangkok–Su-ngai Kolok/Pasir Mas–Tumpat–Kota Bharu and via the ECRL to Port Klang. This will form a land bridge mainly from Bangkok to Port Klang. This land bridge service can reduce logistic costs to manufacturers in Thailand who wish to export their products to Sumatera and the states in the peninsula. The route covers 20 km (2 km in Thailand and 18 km in Malaysia).

- **Construction of the second bridge over Kolok River at Su-ngai Kolok–Rantau Panjang**. This route is the most important inbound and outbound link for vehicles crossing the Malaysia–Thailand borders since 1972.

- **Construction of a new bridge over Kolok River at Tak Bai District**, which will directly connect Mueang District, Narathiwat, and Kota Bharu without having to travel by ferry and without having to make a detour via Su-ngai Kolok District (reducing the distance of 40 km).

Road, rail, and port interfaces will be a dominant feature of connectivity in EC6. The movement of goods across these modes should be further studied as connectivity projects are developed and implemented. Intermodal facilitation will be crucial and should be the focus of a second generation of trade facilitation initiatives in IMT-GT by way of moving forward from the present focus on land-based CIQ facilitation.

Road–rail connectivity infrastructure should be emphasized in planning for EC6. Rail transport has increasingly become an integral part of Malaysia–Thailand connectivity, as the demand for more efficient and cost-effective means of transporting goods intensifies. Road connectivity to main railway lines, ICDs, and land bridges that facilitate the container movement across borders would need to be planned to take advantage of these emerging developments. Road–rail connectivity that links the core to the periphery areas has an externality that can drive economic activity in the economic corridor. It can provide local producers with better access to markets and supply chains. For investors, such infrastructure links can facilitate raw materials sourcing, reduce logistics costs, and open new markets.

Maritime trade links between Riau Islands and Bangka Belitung Islands with Malaysia are limited and should be further developed. Due to limited capacity of ports in Batam, export commodities from Batam have to undergo double and triple handling with some of Batam's export commodities having to be transferred from the port in Johor to Jurong Port in Singapore. Meanwhile, export–import activities in Bangka Belitung Islands are carried out through other ports within Indonesia (e.g., Sunda Kelapa Port and Tanjung Priok Port in Jakarta, Dumai Port in Riau, Belawan Port in North Sumatera, and Panjang Port in Lampung) rather than with ports in Malaysia. This underscores the important role of Johor in enabling connectivity with provinces in Sumatera. Once the Dumai–Melaka Ro-Ro Project (EC4) is fully implemented, this can trigger an increase in exports and imports of cargo between the Riau and Melaka and further open transport of goods to Johor. Johor Port (Pasir Gudang) has trade links with ports in Palembang (South Sumatera) and Belawan (North Sumatera). There are also ferry links with Batam (Riau Islands).

CHAPTER

5

THE NETWORK OF IMT-GT ECONOMIC CORRIDORS

This chapter discusses the conceptual basis for the reconfiguration of the economic corridors to appreciate the perspective of the IMT-GT corridors as a network. It revisits the economic corridor concept, reviews the perspective on economic corridor development articulated in the IMT-GT strategic framework documents since 2007, and explains the importance of corridor networks in IMT-GT.

The latter part of the chapter illustrates some of the interlink corridors that have emerged from the expansion of the existing corridors.

Revisiting the Economic Corridor Concept

An economic corridor refers to a loosely defined geographic space that connects and integrates economic agents and facilitates the efficient movement of goods and services within that space, thereby linking the supply and demand sides of markets.[55] Economic corridors typically develop along a major transport backbone and expand to concentrations of economic activities or agglomerations that provide economies of scale and scope. Cities, urban centers, and industrial zones are associated with agglomerations given their concentration of economic activities, the associated skills, and higher productivity and incomes (Figure 8).

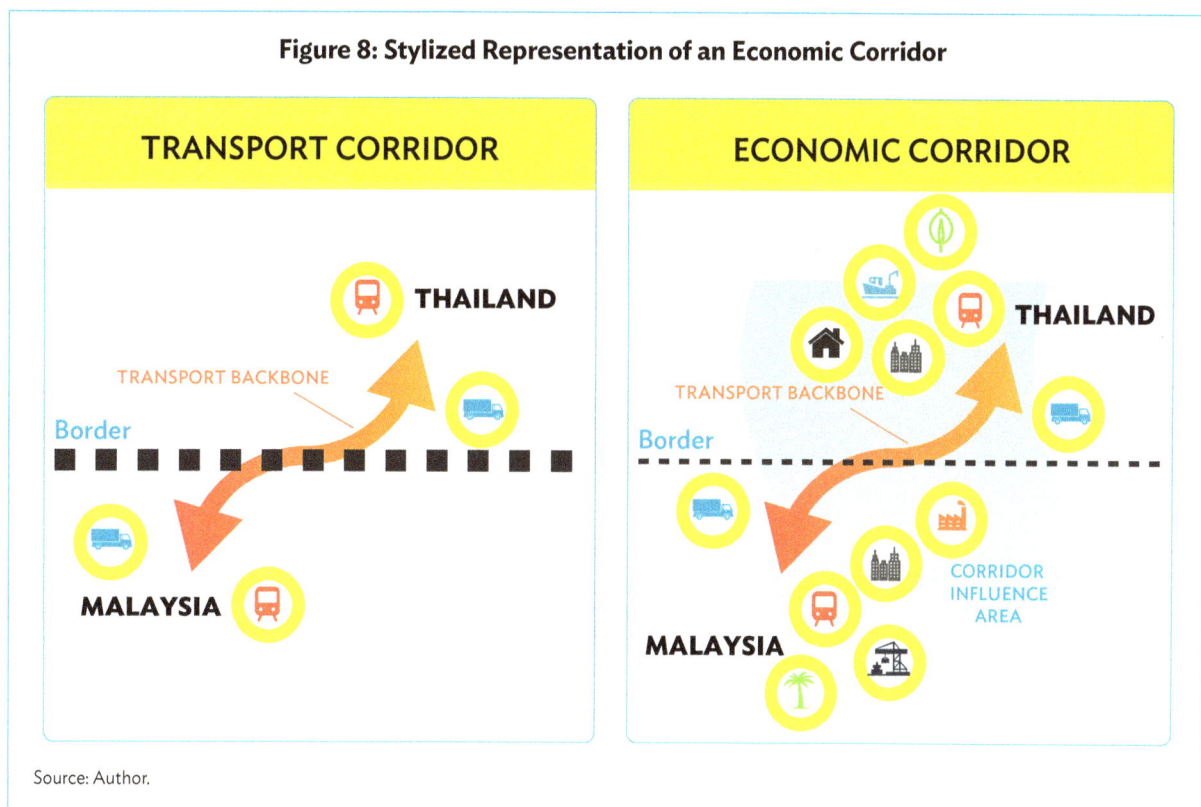

Figure 8: Stylized Representation of an Economic Corridor

Source: Author.

---

55   H. Hill and J. Menon. 2020. *Economic Corridors in Southeast Asia: Success Factors, Impacts and Policy*. Institute of Southeast Asian Studies-Yusof Ishak Institute. May.

Economic corridor development has become an attractive development strategy because of the externalities and beneficial spillovers they generate in the corridor's influence area. The spillovers can take the form of complementarities between adjacent cities or nodes or leading and lagging regions. In this manner, economic corridors can contribute to the balanced economic development of a country's economy as they spatially disaggregate economic activities in a given geographic space.

The development of economic corridors cannot be viewed in isolation from the larger economic environment where it operates. They are not mere transport connections along which people and goods move. Economic corridors are part of an integrated economic network that extends beyond the main transport backbone. Their role in regional economic development must be understood in terms of generating network effects that induce regional production networks resulting in spillover effects on the economy in terms of trade, investment, and employment.

The success factors for economic corridor development are wide-ranging (Figure 9). They include the following:

- Inherent geographic advantage such as proximity to gateways, cities, ports, or critical waterways and proximity to land and natural resources as foundation for an economic base.

- Physical infrastructure and connectivity through transport services (roads, railways, ports, bridges, airports) that facilitate the movement of goods, services, and people. This also encompasses intermodal connections across the various modes.

- Soft infrastructure or the set of policy and process interventions that facilitate economic exchanges, especially across international borders. It includes transport, trade, and investment facilitation which serves, to reduce the "thickness" of the borders by reducing the nonphysical barriers. On a larger scale, it also encompasses overall macroeconomic stability; the legal and regulatory frameworks that provide predictability, transparency, and fairness in commercial transactions; a conducive environment for attracting investment and easing the conduct of business and human resource development to build the required skills and innovation.

- Openness of the economy or the extent to which nondomestic actors can participate in the local economy to bring in the required resources and know-how.

- Governance mechanisms that promote effective and efficient planning and project implementation in all levels of jurisdiction of economic corridor development.

These success drivers are inextricably linked. Infrastructure provision builds on natural geographic advantages of strategically located cities, industrial enclaves, or access to the sea. These agglomerations induce people to cluster around these areas, creating human settlements as potential source of skills and innovation.

In a regional setting such as the IMT-GT, the interplay of these factors can be particularly challenging given the dynamics of political decision making at various levels (central and local governments), variations in policy orientation and strategic priorities, differences in the levels of financial resources and varying governance cultures and capacities. This notwithstanding, a regional approach is required to drive economic corridor success in a more coordinated fashion, transform national corridors that are merely juxtaposed at the borders, into fully-functioning economic corridors with seamless cross-border movements of goods. As discussed in this study, a truly regional approach to economic corridor development has not fully materialized and is an area that could be further strengthened in the next stage of economic corridor development in the IMT-GT. For the most part, Indonesia, Malaysia, and Thailand have been actively pursuing economic corridor development in their respective segments of the IMT-GT economic corridors.

Figure 9: Critical Success Factors for Economic Corridor Development

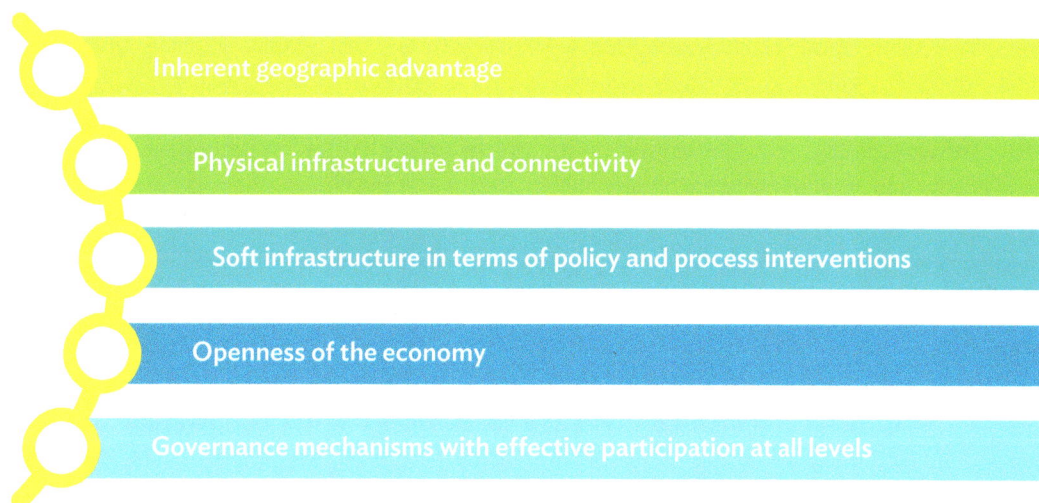

Inherent geographic advantage

Physical infrastructure and connectivity

Soft infrastructure in terms of policy and process interventions

Openness of the economy

Governance mechanisms with effective participation at all levels

Source: Author.

Economic Corridors as Focus of IMT-GT Cooperation

The literature on the economic rationale of the IMT-GT economic corridors is scant. A seminal book—*Indonesia–Malaysia–Thailand Growth Triangle: From Theory to Practice*[56]—published by ADB in 1996, provided a comprehensive treatise on the conceptual underpinnings of the growth triangle as a form of regional cooperation, the application of the concept, and the experience of growth triangles at that time,[57] and the opportunities and challenges for cooperation in the IMT-GT. Subsequent studies touched on specific aspects of corridor development. The Logistics Development Study of the IMT-GT[58] conducted in 2006 proposed a logistics development policy covering the five economic corridors to realize their potential. The Scoping Study for the Special Border Economic Zone in the IMT-GT[59] conducted in 2014 focused on Thailand–Malaysia land border crossings that happen to be part of the economic corridors.

The economic corridor approach was identified as a core strategy for the accelerated development of the IMT-GT and declared a flagship project at the 13th Ministerial Meeting of IMT-GT in Selangor in September 2006. This decision was reflected in the IMT-GT Road Map 2007–2011 where economic corridors were identified as a key anchor for clustering major economic activities in the subregion. The idea was for the corridors to serve as trunk lines from which development would radiate to neighboring areas through transport and economic linkages. The road map identified four economic corridors; subsequently, a fifth one was added for a total of five economic corridors at present covered in this study.

---

[56]   M. Thant and Min Tang. 1996. *Indonesia–Malaysia–Thailand Growth Triangle: From Theory to Practice.* Manila: ADB.

[57]   These included the growth triangle in the southern part of the People's Republic of China and the Singapore-Johor-Riau Growth Triangle. The Tumen Area Development Program and the Greater Mekong Subregion Economic Cooperation Program were also mentioned in the book although they do not fall strictly in the concept and definition of "growth triangle."

[58]   R. Banomyong. 2006. Logistics Development Study of the IMT-GT. Consultant's report.

[59]   M. Lord. 2014. *Scoping Study for the Special Border Economic Zone in the IMT-GT.* Manila: ADB.

The IB 2012–2016—the successor to the road map 2007–2011 focused on programs and projects in the economic corridors and included these among the flagship initiatives in the transport and energy sector. Vision 2036, launched in 2017, affirmed the relevance of economic corridors as trunk lines for regional development. While economic corridor development in the past focused on developing lagging regions, Vision 2036 advocated a regionwide strategy where corridor development would include both urban and rural areas in the periphery or outside the corridor to also benefit from spillovers. The vision called for the need to focus on the software deficits to optimize investment returns on the hardware components, develop industrial clusters and production networks, and encourage public–private partnerships in infrastructure. The IB 2017–2021, which operationalizes the first 5 years of the vision, considered economic corridors as a spatial focus to underpin the Vision's three priority goals of (i) sustainable, inclusive, and innovative agriculture sector; (ii) competitive, innovative, and advanced industrial base; and (iii) sustainable, competitive, and inclusive cross-border tourism (Figure 10).

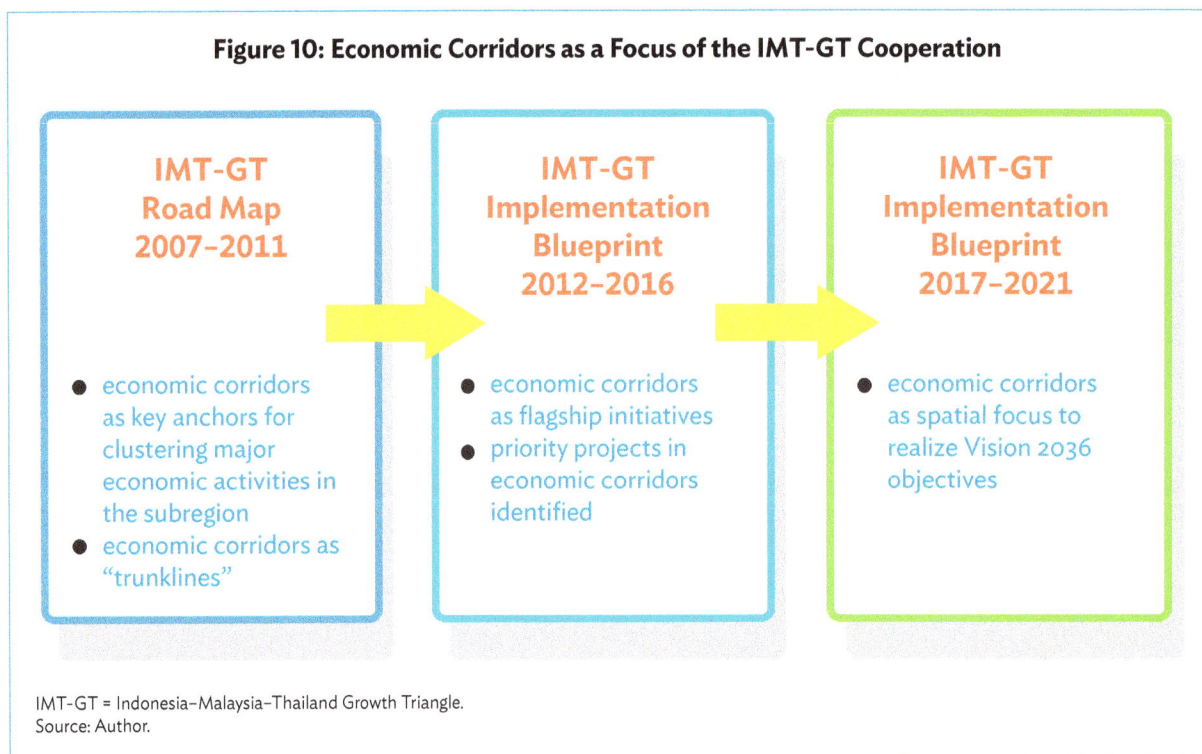

Figure 10: Economic Corridors as a Focus of the IMT-GT Cooperation

IMT-GT Road Map 2007–2011	**IMT-GT Implementation Blueprint 2012–2016**	**IMT-GT Implementation Blueprint 2017–2021**
• economic corridors as key anchors for clustering major economic activities in the subregion • economic corridors as "trunklines"	• economic corridors as flagship initiatives • priority projects in economic corridors identified	• economic corridors as spatial focus to realize Vision 2036 objectives

IMT-GT = Indonesia–Malaysia–Thailand Growth Triangle.
Source: Author.

Interlink Corridors and Corridor Networks

As explained in Chapter 3, nodes, broadly defined, are basically the points that connect different economic units. For a given corridor, the continuity of the different nodes and their interrelated roles are important, underscoring the need to carefully plan the juxtaposition or location of the different nodes. The corridor networks that have emerged from the reconfiguration of the existing corridors, as well as the proposed EC6, have expanded the links among the nodes, resulting in interlink corridors with significantly expanded potential.

An interlink corridor is the route that connects two or more points in different corridors. Interlink corridors can loop strategically positioned areas in different corridors to enable them to function as a network, rather than as single corridors. Corridors functioning as a network can change the pattern of mobility for both goods and people. They can facilitate access to a larger and more diverse base of inputs (raw materials, parts, energy, or labor) and broader markets for diverse outputs (intermediate and finished goods).

Interlink corridors can bring about network effects when they enable new interactions between economic units in the corridor. The development of economic corridor networks is a consequence of continuous improvements as opportunities arise. It is the outcome of deliberate strategies, such as providing access and mobility to a region, investing in infrastructure, reinforcing a specific trade or transport corridor, or promoting technological developments. The relevance of a network is related to its connectivity. The more complex the network, the more valuable it becomes since the number of opportunities it creates can grow exponentially by connecting several locations at the same time.[60]

At present, there is no clear, deliberate approach to economic corridor development in IMT-GT. Economic corridor projects are typically national projects located in a corridor; and the mere collation of these projects would be considered as the development approach to the corridor. In a network perspective, this piecemeal approach would have to give way to a more comprehensive and coordinated spatial planning to maximize opportunities in economic corridor networks as they evolve. The factors to consider would include, among others: (i) the type of transport structures in the corridor in relation to the role of nodes and hubs; (ii) the network's ability to support flows based on speed, capacity, and safety; (iii) spatial proximity—some locations may be more central in one network but peripheral in another depending on the specialization and function of an area; and (iv) the density and intensity of economic activities and interconnectedness of cities and other urban areas.

The development of economic corridors as networks would have implications in developing value chains. The time, distance, and other costs of transportation will determine the optimal geographical organization of production, i.e., where raw materials are processed, where intermediate goods are produced, and where final goods are produced. Thus, mapping and planning for value chains cannot be delinked with planning for transport and economic corridor networks. There would be a need to map the entire value chain—from raw materials to export—and clearly identify how final prices (hence competitiveness) depend upon infrastructure investments. Once the value chains have been mapped, bottlenecks will have to be identified, and investments secured, to ensure that the goods reach international markets at competitive prices.[61]

Some of the interlink corridors that have emerged from the expansion of the existing corridors are illustrated in the following sections.

Interlink Corridors in Indonesia

The expanded EC3 covering eight provinces in Sumatera functions as an interlink corridor since the nodes in EC3 also connect to other corridors (ECs 4, 5, and 6) (Map 21). The main transport backbone of this interlink corridor is the existing Trans-Sumatera Highway and the ongoing Trans-Sumatera Toll Road that facilitates transport of commodities from the source areas to maritime gateways along Sumatera's eastern coast. The land connectors between Trans-Sumatera Highway/Trans-Sumatera Toll Road to the maritime gateway are as follows:

---

[60]   Metcalfe's law states that complex networks are exponentially more valuable than simple networks since they offer a large number of options in connecting locations. Thus, economic development is commonly associated with network complexity. Jean-Paul Rodrigue. 2020. *The Geography of Transport Systems*. Routledge, New York. https://transportgeography.org/.

[61]   ADB. 2014. Economic Corridor Development for Inclusive Asian Regional Integration: A Modeling Approach to Economic Corridors. Manila.

Map 21: Interlink Corridors in Indonesia

INDONESIA–MALAYSIA–THAILAND GROWTH TRIANGLE

▬▬	Economic Corridor 1
▬▬	Economic Corridor 1 Reconfiguration
▬▬	Economic Corridor 3
▬▬	Economic Corridor 3 Reconfiguration
▬▬	Economic Corridor 4
▬▬	Economic Corridor 4 Reconfiguration
▬▬	Economic Corridor 5
▬▬	Proposed Economic Corridor 6

⊛ National Capital
◉ Provincial/State Capital
• City/Town
▬▬ National Road
─── Other Road
···· Provincial Boundary
─·─· International Boundary
EC = economic corridor
Boundaries are not necessarily authoritative.

This map was produced by the cartography unit of the Asian Development Bank. The boundaries, colors, denominations, and any other information shown on this map do not imply, on the part of the Asian Development Bank, any judgment on the legal status of any territory, or any endorsement or acceptance of such boundaries, colors, denominations, or information.

Source: Asian Development Bank.

Medan (EC3) to Belawan (EC1) (Interlink Corridor A) – a 12 km toll road along the Belawan–Medan–Tanjung Morowa section. The toll road also connects to provinces in the northern part of Sumatera—Aceh, North Sumatera, West Sumatera, and the northern part of Riau. These provinces are the main sources for CPO, rubber, coffee, vegetables, cement, and other commodities that are exported to Malaysia through the maritime links between Belawan Port and Penang Port. Belawan is also connected to other areas in North Sumatera through rail transport.

Pekanbaru (EC3) to Dumai (EC4) (Interlink Corridor B) – a 131-km toll road consisting of six sections.[62] The toll road also connects with other cities in Sumatera that are part of the expanded EC3—Medan, Padang, and Jambi. Dumai connects to Malaysia through port-to-port maritime links. This interlink corridor supports the palm oil value chain as Dumai is the biggest maritime gateway for Indonesia's palm oil as well as other export commodities (e.g., vegetable products, animal and vegetable fats and oils, wood and articles of wood and cement).

Maritime link between Palembang (EC3) and Pangkalpinang (EC6) (Interlink corridor C). Palembang is connected to Pangkalpinang in Bangka Island via Ro-Ro ferry from Tanjung Api-Api Port to Tanjung Kalian Port. This interlink corridor supports the rubber industry. Raw materials coming from Muara Enim, Ogan Ilir, and other areas in EC3 are transported to Palembang as the center of the midstream rubber industry where it is processed to Standard Indonesia Rubber (SIR) 20. The Trans-Sumatera toll road (Palembang–Kayu Agung–Pematang Panggang–Terbanggi Besar–Bakauheni section) connects Palembang to Lampung, while the national road and partial toll road (Palembang–Simpang Indralaya section) connects Palembang with Bengkulu. These links facilitate the transport of export commodities from EC3 provinces to ports in Palembang (i.e., Boom Baru, Palembang–Kertapati, and Palembang–Plaju), which are gateways to Malaysia and other destinations. This interlink corridor also plays an important role in linking Pangkalpinang and its surrounding major gateways in Bangka Belitung Islands to Riau Islands.

Interlink Corridors in Malaysia

The maritime route that connects Langkawi (EC5) to Penang Port at George Town (EC1); Kuala Kedah, Kedah (EC1) and Kuala Perlis, Perlis (EC2) via ferry serves as an interlink corridor (Interlink Corridor A). Penang Port, Kuala Kedah, and Kuala Perlis are the tourist gateways to Langkawi Island with Kuah Jetty Terminal as the entrance point. Penang and Langkawi are positioned along the cruise liner routes in the Andaman Sea and Strait of Malacca. This interlink corridor generates synergies within the tourism industry.

The westward route in EC6 (EC6-MR2) functions as an interlink corridor (Interlink Corridor B). This interlink corridor traverses Kota Bahru, Kelantan (EC6), Penang Port at Butterworth (EC1/2), Padang Besar, Perlis (EC1/2) via the East–West Highway; and Port Klang (EC2) via North–South Expressway (E1/E2). Both Penang Port and Port Klang function as a maritime gateway for manufacturers in the E6, particularly in Kelantan.

The eastward route in EC6 (EC6-MR1) also functions as an interlink corridor (Interlink Corridor C). It connects Kota Bahru, Kelantan (EC6) with Port Klang, Selangor (EC2) and Johor Bharu, Johor (EC4) via the East Coast Expressway, Kuala Lumpur–Karak Highway, and North–South Expressway (E1/E2).

---

[62] The six sections of the Pekanbaru–Dumai toll road are Section I (Pekanbaru–Minas, 9.5 km); Section II (Minas–Petapahan, 24.1 km); Section III (Petapahan–North Kandis, 16.9 km); Section IV (North Kandis–South Duri, 26.25 km); South Duri–North Duri (29.4 km); and Section VI (North Duri–Dumai, 25.44 km). The Pekanbaru–Dumai toll road was opened in September 2020.

- The rail links—ECRL (which is under construction) and KTMB will connect Kuantan and Kemaman Ports in EC6 with Port Klang, Tanjung Pelepas Port, and Johor Port (EC2/EC4).

- The road link connects with Port Dickson (EC6), Negeri Sembilan (EC2), and Tanjung Bruas Port, Melaka (EC4).

Connectivity to the maritime gateways in the west coast will enable manufacturers in EC6 to have an alternative route for their shipments to Sumatera, South Asia, the Middle East, Africa and Europe.

The interlink corridors in Malaysia are shown in Map 22. The maritime route connecting ECs 1, 2, and 5 as interlink corridor A generates synergies within the tourism industry. Both interlink corridors B and C generate synergies in logistics, tourism, oil and gas manufacturing, and agriculture that are prevalent in ECs 1, 2, 4, 5, and 6. The synergies created in these corridors can help narrow the development gap between the less developed states in the east coast and the more developed states in the west coast through labor and resource mobility resulting from the development of growth nodes and conurbation areas.

Interlink Corridors in Thailand

The route connecting Chumphon (EC1) to Ranong (EC5) is an interlink corridor (Interlink Corridor A) that facilitates transport along AH2 from the central region via Highway No. 4 to Ranong Port. Ranong Port is designed to become a gateway trade to the Andaman seaports. Connecting EC1 to EC5 via Interlink Corridor A can increase trade at Ranong Port, as well as tourism activities between the Gulf of Thailand and the Andaman Sea downward to EC2.

The route from Surat Thani (EC1) to Phuket (EC5) via Highway No. 44 connects tourism destinations between the Gulf of Thailand and the Andaman Sea to create an inland tourism network between the east and west coasts of Thailand (Interlink Corridor B). Surat Thani along the Gulf of Thailand has many popular tourist destinations such as Samui Island, Tao Ko Island, and Nang Yuan Island (EC 1) with the tourist destinations in Phuket (Patong beach, Kata and Karon beach, Coral Island, Ko Khai Islands, Racha Islands, Ko Yao Islands) with those in Krabi (Phi Phi, Ko Poda, and Hong Island) (EC5).

EC1 links with EC2 via Highway No. 4 at Trang, whereas Kantang Port links with Thung Song Cargo Distribution Center via railways (57.6 km) in Nakhon Si Thammarat in EC1 or via Highway No. 403 (96.5 km) (Interlink Corridor C). This interlink will promote efficient transport of goods to the gateway in Penang Port that can help attract more trade and investments along the EC1 and EC2.

Route 4 connecting Trang (E2) to Songkhla (EC1) via Highway No. 406 (Interlink Corridor D) will allow greater link for trade and tourism between Gulf of Thailand and Andaman Sea. The interlink corridor will also support Trang and Langkawi to become a major gateway for trade and tourism along the corridor.

The addition of Phangnga and Krabi in EC5 enhances tourism potential through links with Satun in EC2 via Highway No.4, which can further connect with Langkawi and Penang through Tammalang Port as well as to Sabang. This opens the possibility of an integrated tourism corridor in the area between Thailand, Malaysia, and Sumatera Island in Indonesia. The integration of the EC5 with Phuket and Krabi will serve as the driving force to attract more tourists along the EC2 from Thailand to tourist destinations in Malaysia and Indonesia on a continuous basis and vice versa.

Map 22: Interlink Corridors in Malaysia

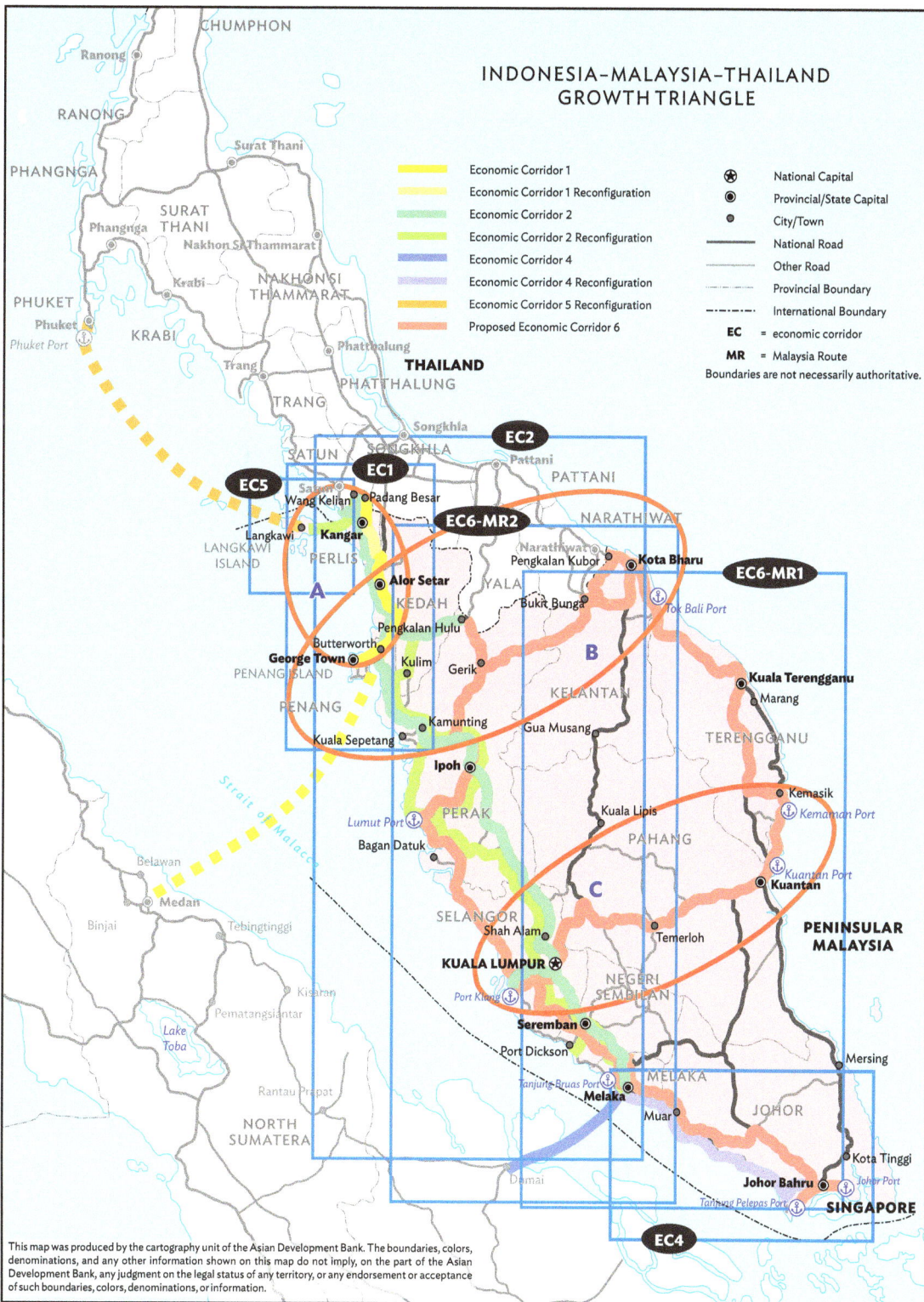

INDONESIA–MALAYSIA–THAILAND GROWTH TRIANGLE

Economic Corridor 1
Economic Corridor 1 Reconfiguration
Economic Corridor 2
Economic Corridor 2 Reconfiguration
Economic Corridor 4
Economic Corridor 4 Reconfiguration
Economic Corridor 5 Reconfiguration
Proposed Economic Corridor 6

National Capital
Provincial/State Capital
City/Town
National Road
Other Road
Provincial Boundary
International Boundary
EC = economic corridor
MR = Malaysia Route
Boundaries are not necessarily authoritative.

This map was produced by the cartography unit of the Asian Development Bank. The boundaries, colors, denominations, and any other information shown on this map do not imply, on the part of the Asian Development Bank, any judgment on the legal status of any territory, or any endorsement or acceptance of such boundaries, colors, denominations, or information.

Source: Asian Development Bank.

The value chain activities for rubber and halal industries take place in both EC1 and EC6 via Highway No. 406 where rubber plantations and livestock for halal food as well as processing industries can be found (Surat Thani, Nakhon Si Thammarat, Songkhla with Pattani, Yala, and Narathiwat). Route No. 406 also connects the production bases in the Southern Industrial Estate, Songkhla Special Economic Zone, and Narathiwat Special Economic Zone to the trade gateways along the Thai–Malaysian border at Padang Besa, Sadao, Ban Prakop, Betong, Buketa, Su-ngai Kolok, and Tak Bai Customs Checkpoints, as well as Songkhla Port.

The interlink corridors in Thailand are shown in Map 23.

Map 23: Interlink Corridors in Thailand

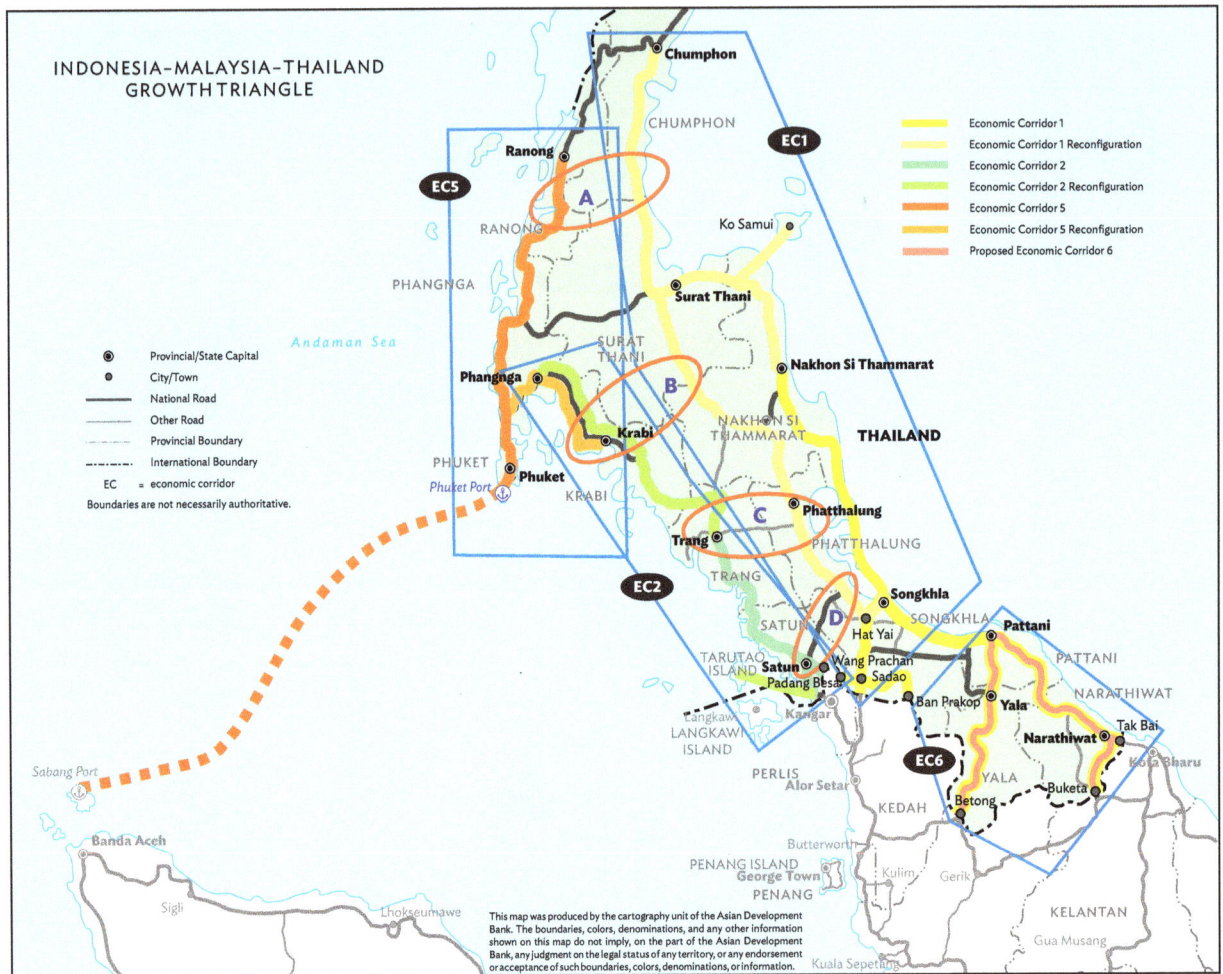

Source: Asian Development Bank.

ECONOMIC CORRIDORS FROM A VALUE CHAIN PERSPECTIVE

The Role of Economic Corridors in Value Chains

This chapter looks at the value chain[63] of three major products in IMT-GT—palm oil, rubber, and halal foods— to get a broad perspective on the geography of their production, processing, and distribution components. Because the development of value chain linkages is a key motivation for economic corridor development, it is useful to locate the geography of value chain components as a basis for determining the appropriate interventions to make the chain more efficient and their products more competitive.

Value chains can be facilitated by efficient physical infrastructure to facilitate movement of goods between production, processing, and distribution units. Value chains can also be shaped by the location of SEZs and industrial clusters, which are crucial for attracting investments, and creating the density required to enable logistics services to operate efficiently. Agglomeration in cities and urban centers provide the density required to realize economies of scale in production and marketing. Economic corridors can be better understood when seen as an integral part of the country or the region's value chain.

The study's terms of reference do not include the conduct of a value chain analysis. However, the study recommends that such an analysis be conducted from a spatial perspective. The proposed analysis can focus on leveraging the potential of the economic corridors to make value chains more efficient and competitive. This includes problems associated with infrastructure, intermodal transport and trade facilitation, and logistics services. Poor infrastructure could lead to high delivery costs, inefficient logistics can restrict the range and volume of products that can effectively reach export as well as domestic markets, and an unpredictable transport and trade facilitation regime can affect the overall performance competitiveness of products. In the context of IMT-GT's cross-border economic corridors, these factors become even more important because of the need to align policies and processes between the governments and to synchronize implementation at the provincial and state levels.

The sections that follow present an overview of three major value chains in IMT-GT from the perspective of economic corridors.

Palm Oil

Overview. The three IMT-GT countries combined produce about 90% of the world's palm oil. Indonesia is the largest producer, contributing 51% of global production in 2019, followed by Malaysia contributing around 35%; and Thailand, with around 4%. Indonesia and Malaysia are also the world's largest exporters of CPO, accounting for 57% and 33%, respectively, of total world CPO exports in 2018. Provinces and states in EC1, EC4, and EC6 are where the largest plantations and mills are located (Table 37). Most of the distribution points (BCPs and gateway ports) are also located in the economic corridors.

---

[63]   In this study, the distinction between the terms value chain and supply chain is not strictly applied. It is noted that a value chain is the process by which a company adds value to its raw materials to produce products eventually sold to consumers; while the supply chain represents all the steps required to get the product to the customer. https://www.investopedia.com/ask/answers/043015/what-difference-between-value-chain-and-supply-chain.asp#:~:text=The%20value%20chain%20is%20a,%20product%20to%20the%20customer.

Table 37: Key Provinces and States in the Palm Oil Value Chain

Indonesia		Malaysia		Thailand	
EC1	North Sumatera	EC2	Selangor	EC1	Surat Thani
EC4	Riau	EC4	Johor	EC1	Chumphon
EC4	West Sumatera	EC6	Perak	EC2	Krabi
EC6	South Sumatera	EC6	Pahang		

EC = economic corridor.
Source: Author.

The palm oil value chain consists of three basic phases. The upstream value chain involves the planting and cultivation of palm oil, as well as the production of fresh fruit bunches (FFBs), CPO, and CPKO. The midstream value chain involves refining, processing, by-products valorization, and biogas production. The downstream value chain comprises the manufacturing of end-products of palm oil matrixes, palm oil derivatives, and oleochemicals. The yield of palm oil matrixes can be divided into two, i.e., CPO derived from the fibrous mesocarp of FFBs, and CPKO derived from the palm kernel (the seed enclosed in a shell of the endocarp). The end-products of CPO and CPKO are mainly used for edible products, including cooking oil, margarine, confectionery, nondairy creamer, shortening, etc. On the other hand, the derived palm-based oleochemicals, which include fatty acids, fatty alcohols, fatty methyl esters, and glycerin are used as raw materials for cosmetics and personal care industries such as balms, lipsticks, soaps, detergents, cleaning products, and candles (Figure 11).

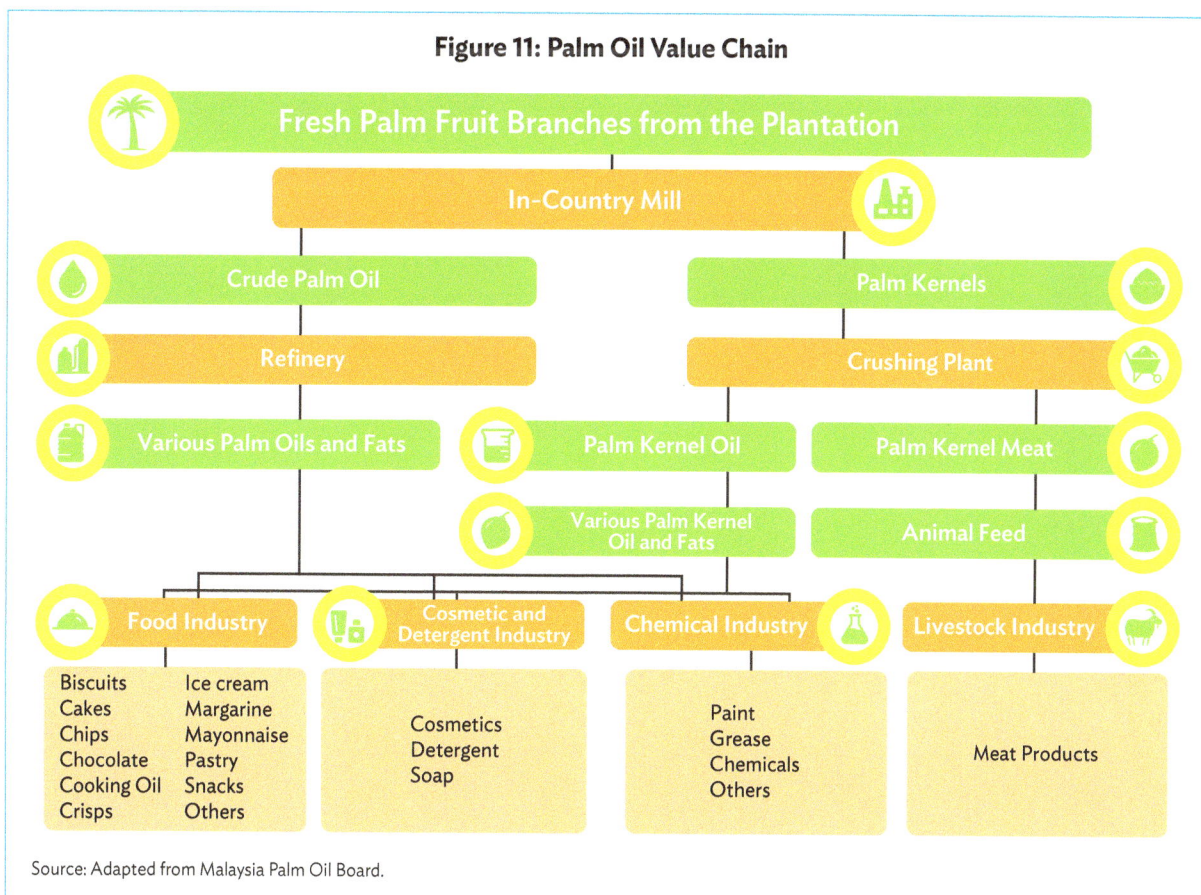

Figure 11: Palm Oil Value Chain

Source: Adapted from Malaysia Palm Oil Board.

The IMT-GT countries are in different phases of the value chain development for palm oil. Indonesia is mainly in the midstream industries, Malaysia is still basically in the upstream phase, and Thailand is in the downstream phase (Map 24). The expansion of the industry has been facilitated by government policies to encourage higher value-adding activities within the country in both upstream and downstream processing.

Indonesia

The palm oil value chain in Indonesia is dominated by three provinces in Sumatera—Riau, North Sumatera, and South Sumatera—where most production, milling, and processing activities take place. North Sumatera and Riau are centers for refineries and serve as transit points for the Sei Mangkei SEZ (North Sumatera) and the Pelintung, Lubuk Gaung, Pelindo Port industrial estates (Riau). The main distribution points are in North Sumatera (Belawan–Kuala Tanjung Port) and Riau Province (Dumai Port). South Sumatera and West Sumatera are transit points for CPO coming from other provinces. These provinces in Sumatera, which are all covered in EC3, are also part of other corridors: North Sumatera, EC1; Riau, EC4; West Sumatera, extended EC4; and South Sumatera, EC6.

Plantations. Indonesia's plantations are spread in 25 of its 34 provinces. Close to 60% of the hectares planted to palm oil trees are in Sumatera. Under the proposed reconfiguration of EC3, four provinces have been added to the existing four provinces, bringing the total number of provinces in the corridor to 8 out of the 10 Sumatera provinces. Riau, North Sumatera, and South Sumatera are the provinces with the largest palm oil plantations in Sumatera with a combined share of 38% to the national area planted (Table 38). The plantations in Sumatera are dominated by smallholders (58.9%), followed by big private estates (34.4%), and government estates (6.6%). Plantations in Sumatera have a higher productivity of 3.02 ton/hectare compared to the national average of 2.87 ton/hectare.

Production. North Sumatera, Riau, and South Sumatera are also the largest palm oil producers with a combined share of 43% to national palm oil production. Two-thirds of the mills are in these provinces. Overcapacity of mills in some provinces (e.g., North Sumatera) are met by buying FFBs from other provinces.

Map 24: Stylized Visualization of the Location of Palm Oil Value Chain Processes in the Indonesia–Malaysia–Thailand Growth Triangle

INDONESIA–MALAYSIA–THAILAND GROWTH TRIANGLE

Plantation
Mills
Refineries
Main Gateway Port
Border Crossing Point

National Capital
Provincial/State Capital
City/Town
National Road
Other Road
Provincial Boundary
International Boundary
Boundaries are not necessarily authoritative.

This map was produced by the cartography unit of the Asian Development Bank. The boundaries, colors, denominations, and any other information shown on this map do not imply, on the part of the Asian Development Bank, any judgment on the legal status of any territory, or any endorsement or acceptance of such boundaries, colors, denominations, or information.

Source: Asian Development Bank.

Table 38: Palm Oil Plantations and Production in Sumatera, 2018

Province	Plantations			Production		
	Total Area (hectares)	Share to Sumatera (%)	Share to Indonesia (%)	Total Production (tons)	Share to Sumatera (%)	Share to Indonesia (%)
Aceh	450,810	6.2	3.5	889,379	4.0	2.4
North Sumatera	1,476,354	20.2	11.6	5,445,831	24.7	14.9
West Sumatera	398,784	5.5	3.1	1,254,875	5.7	3.4
Riau	2,323,831	31.8	18.2	7,136,648	32.4	19.5
Jambi	772,843	10.6	6.0	1,988,248	9.0	5.4
South Sumatera	1,073,840	14.7	8.4	3,042,132	13.8	8.3
Bengkulu	340,749	4.7	2.7	900,349	4.1	2.5
Lampung	225,896	3.1	1.8	489,551	2.2	1.3
Bangka Belitung Islands	228,452	3.1	1.8	882,506	4.0	2.4
Riau Islands	10,460	0.1	0.1	31,104	0.1	0.1
Sumatera	**7,302,019**	**100.0**	**57.2**	**22,060,623**	**100.0**	**60.2**
INDONESIA	**12,761,586**		**100.00**	**36,594,813**		**100.00**

Note: Totals may not sum precisely because of rounding.
Source: BPS-Statistics Indonesia. 2019. *Indonesian Oil Palm Statistics 2018*. Jakarta: BPS-Statistics Indonesia.

Processing. The location of the refineries is more dispersed. Four provinces host refineries that serve as centers and transit points for other provinces. This underscores the importance of linking all provinces across Sumatera through EC3 via the existing Trans-Sumatera Highway and the ongoing Trans-Sumatera Toll Road. The four provinces where refineries are located and the provinces they serve are

- North Sumatera: Aceh, West Sumatera, Riau, and Bangka Belitung Islands

- Riau: North Sumatera, West Sumatera, Jambi, and Bangka Belitung Islands

- West Sumatera: North Sumatera, Jambi, and Bengkulu

- South Sumatera: Jambi and Bengkulu, as well as for Bangka Belitung Islands

Industrial estates, SEZs, and ports in North Sumatera (EC1/EC3) and Riau (EC3/EC4) play important roles in value chain processing and distribution. Refineries in Sei Mangkei SEZ in North Sumatera process CPO and CPKO for some of the big companies located in the zone.[64] The downstream products are shipped through Belawan Port (EC1), which is the second biggest maritime gateway port for palm oil exports.

Dumai City in Riau (EC4) has at least three industrial estates focusing on the palm oil industry (Pelintung, Lubuk Gaung, and Pelindo Port industrial estates) that produce palm kernel oil, cooking oil, biodiesel, and other palm oil-based products. These products are shipped through Dumai Port which is the biggest maritime gateway port for palm oil export in Indonesia.

West Sumatera along the west coast facing the Indian Ocean, as part of the extended EC4, will be able to expand the province's linkages with Riau in palm oil and rubber value chains, making it possible for the province to expand trade with Malaysia through Dumai Port along the Strait of Malacca. This will enhance

---

[64]   Two companies in Sei Mangkei SEZ that manufacture palm oil-based products are PT Unilever Oleochemical Indonesia which produces detergent, soap, and other downstream products and PT Industri Nabati Lestari, which produces olein, refined bleached palm oil, stearin, and fatty acid.

the province's economic status—being one of the provinces with the lowest GRDP in Sumatera. Refineries in West Sumatera that cater to Jambi and Bengkulu will also help expand value chain linkages of these provinces. Teluk Bayur and Padang Port in Padang City are the main export gateways of West Sumatera to India and the US, which are Indonesia's major markets for palm oil. Once completed, the Padang–Pekanbaru segment of the Trans-Sumatera Toll Road will enable faster and more efficient transport between the two cities.

Distribution. From the refineries, palm oil is either exported directly to other countries, or processed in downstream manufacture. In 2018, 28% of Indonesia's total palm oil production was consumed domestically; while 72% were exported to major markets, namely India (22%), the PRC (14%), Pakistan (8%), Bangladesh (5%), the Netherlands (4%), and Malaysia (4%).[65] Exports to Malaysia and Thailand, which are also major global producers, are small. Riau exports stearin to Malaysia and palm kernel expeller to Thailand via Dumai Port. Indonesia's palm oil exports of 43% are loaded in Dumai Port, followed by Belawan Port (12%). Other gateways for palm oil are Padang/Teluk Bayur (West Sumatera), Tarahan (Lampung), Kabil/Panau (Riau Islands), and Musi River (South Sumatera).

Midstream products (crude, refined, lauric oil) continue to dominate Indonesia's palm oil exports (92%) while downstream products (biodiesel and oleochemicals) account for only 8% (Figure 12). It has been estimated that a company's value-added in palm oil plantations is 72% while value-added in the processing stage is only 10 %,[66] thus providing little incentive for companies to shift to higher levels of the value chain.

Figure 12: Indonesia: Palm Oil Exports by Products, 2015–2019

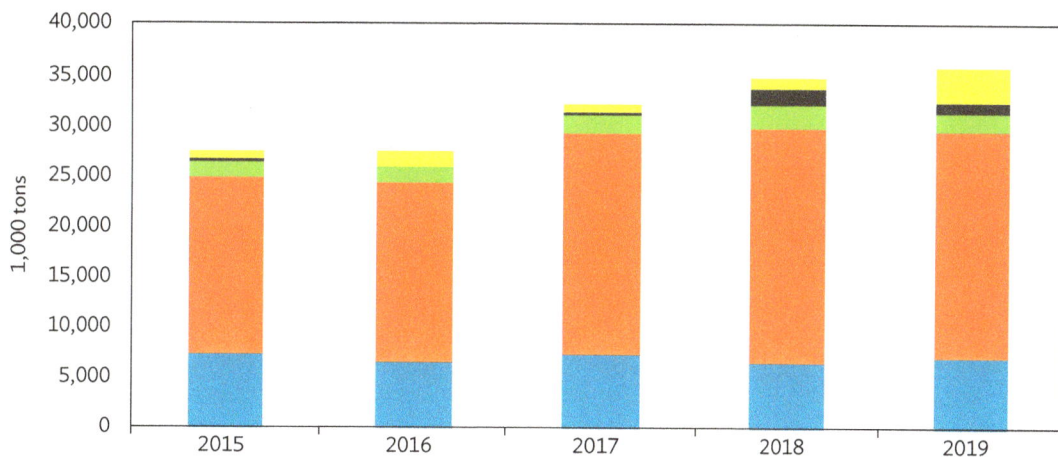

	2015	2016	2017	2018	2019
Oleochemicals	832	1,465	970	1,122	3,354
Biodiesel	206	4	164	1,560	1,148
Lauric	1,684	1,674	1,951	2,359	1,938
Refined	17,506	17,602	21,941	23,104	22,327
Crude	7,232	6,515	7,158	6,561	7,065

Source: Gabungan Pengsuhasa Kelapa Sawit Indonesia (GAPKI). 2021. Kenerja Industri Sawit 2021 dan Outlook 2022. https://gapki.id/KINERJA_SAWIT/KINERJA_INDUSTRI_SAWIT_INDONESIA_2021.pdf (accessed 2 August 2022).

---

65   BPS-Statistics Indonesia, 2019.

66   J. Hidayati and S. Hasibuan. 2019. Value Chain Analysis and Value Added Enhancement of Indonesia Crude Palm Oil Supply Chain. *International Journal of Advanced Science Engineering Information Technology*. 9(2): 397–404.

Since 2018, Indonesia's exports of oleochemicals and biodiesel have increased significantly. Oleochemical exports increased by 15.7% in 2018 and rose significantly by almost 200% in 2019. Biodiesel exports also recorded a dramatic increase of 851% in 2018. These trends augur well for the gradual movement of Indonesia's palm oil industry to downstream products. Other palm oil product exports (e.g. crude, refined, and lauric) have remained stagnant in the last 3 years.

Malaysia

Plantations and production. The dominant players in the palm oil industry in Malaysia are Johor, Pahang, Perak, Sabah, and Sarawak. Sabah and Sarawak are non-IMT-GT states located in the island of Borneo and account for 26% and 27%, respectively, of the country's total plantation area. Johor, Pahang, and Perak are IMT-GT participating states and are all part of economic corridors. The areas planted to palm oil are largest in these three states, with Pahang and Johor contributing 13% each, and Perak contributing 7%, to total national area planted. Forty-four percent of the plantations are owned by private estates, 29% by independent smallholders, and the remaining 27% by state-owned enterprises (Table 39).

Among the EC states in the peninsula, Johor is the largest producer of FFBs (16%) as well as CPO (16%). Pahang, a state proposed for EC6, is the second most important state contributing 14% to the country's CPO production, followed by Perak (EC2) with 10%. Of the 451 mills in Malaysia, around 50% are in the EC states. Those with the most number of mills are Pahang (70), Johor (61), and Perak (45). Among the non-EC states, Sabah (128) and Sarawak (81) have the most number of mills.

Processing. For midstream activities, around 60% of palm crusher plants are located in EC states. These plants produce palm kernel oils and palm kernel cakes. Among the EC states, Selangor (EC2) was the largest producer of palm kernel oil (24%) and palm kernel cake (23%) in 2018, followed by Johor with a 19% share for each product.

There are 50 refineries in Malaysia for downstream activities. Johor and Selangor, each has 13 refinery plants. The refineries process CPO into various palm oils and fats—refined, bleached, and deodorized (RBD) palm oil, RBD palm olein, RBD palm stearin, cooking oil, crude palm olein, palm fatty acid distillate, and crude palm stearin—for the use especially in the food industry, cosmetics, and detergents, chemical industry, and livestock industry. Among the processed products, RBD palm oil accounted for 42%, and RBD palm olein accounted for 30% of the production of processed palm oil products in 2018.[67] The size of industries utilizing palm oil-based products is relatively small, accounting for only 4% of the total sales of manufactured products in 2018.

---

[67] RBD palm oil is now the most widely used vegetable oil in the world, a key component of foods ranging from baked goods to salad dressings to ice cream. RBD palm olein is also used as cooking oil as well as frying oil for the food industries such as salad and cooking oils in households, industrial frying fat of instant noodles, potato chips, donuts, condensed milk, snack food and ready-to-eat food. It is also used as a raw material for margarine and shortening.

Table 39: Palm Oil Plantations and Production in Malaysia, 2018

State	Area Planted '000 hectares	Share (%)	FFBs received by Mills '000 tonnes	Share (%)	No. of FBB mills	Crude Palm Oil '000 tonnes	Share (%)	Palm Kernel '000 tonnes	Share (%)
EC States									
Pahang (EC6)	756	13	14,079	14	70	2,754	14	729	15
Johor (EC4)	748	13	15,858	16	61	3,113	16	877	18
Perak (EC2)	413	7	9,725	10	45	1,861	10	528	11
Negeri Sembilan (EC2)	187	3	3,530	4	16	679	3	191	4
Terengganu (EC6)	169	3	2,436	2	13	486	2	124	3
Kelantan (EC6)	155	3	1,428	1	10	295	2	73	2
Selangor (EC2)	136	2	2,742	3	16	520	3	149	3
Kedah (EC1/2)	90	2	1,331	1	6	266	1	71	1
Melaka(EC2/EC4)	57	1	–	–	–	–	–	–	–
Penang (EC1/EC2)	15	0*	–	–	–	–	–	–	–
Perlis (EC1/EC2)	1	0*	–	–	–	–	–	–	–
Subtotal	2727	47	51,129	51	237	9,974	51	2742	57
Non-IMT-GT States									
Sabah	1,549	26	25,044	25	128	5,139	26	1,180	24
Sarawak	1,572	27	21,111	21	81	4,179	21	875	18
Subtotal	3,121	53	46,155	46	209	9,318	47	2,055	42
Total (Malaysia)	**5,849**	**100**	**98,410**	**100**	**451**	**19,516**	**100**	**4,859**	**100**

* = very negligible, – = not available, EC = economic corridor, FBB = fresh fruit bunch, IMT-GT = Indonesia–Malaysia–Thailand Growth Triangle.
Note: The total for Malaysia may be bigger than the sum of EC and non-EC states because the data for Melaka, Penang, and Perlis are not reflected in the table.
Sources: Department of Agriculture Malaysia. 2019. *Industrial Crop Statistics Malaysia 2018*. Putrajaya: DOA Malaysia. Malaysian Palm Oil Board (MPOB). 2019. *Malaysian Oil Palm Statistics 2018*. Bangi: MPOB. Ministry of Plantation Industries and Commodities.

Distribution. In terms of production to export ratio, Malaysia exports 84% of its total CPO. The bulk of these exports are upstream products. In 2018, processed palm oil accounted for 51% of total exports followed by oleochemicals (22%) and CPO (12%). The main markets for palm oil and palm kernel oil products in 2018 were India, the European Union (EU), the PRC, Pakistan, and the Philippines. These countries together, accounted for 49% of palm oil and 70% of palm kernel oil exports. For palm oil-based oleochemicals and biodiesel, the top five export markets in 2018 were the PRC, the EU, the US, Japan, and India. Although Malaysia is one of the world's leading producers of palm oil, it still imports from Thailand and Indonesia to meet the demand of local industries. Malaysia imported 1.0 million tons of palm oil from Indonesia, accounting for 89% of the country's total imports, followed by Thailand, with 9%, in 2019.

Johor Port (Pasir Gudang) and Tanjung Pelepas Port (Stulang) accounted for 24% of the volume of palm oil exports in 2018, followed by Port Klang with 23%. Johor Port in Pasir Gudang has the largest palm oil terminal in the world. Johor, which has been proposed to be part of EC4 and EC6 will play a pivotal role in enhancing value chain linkages in the economic corridors for CPO and related products.

Thailand

Plantations and mills. Thailand is the third largest palm oil producer in the world, but it accounts for only 3.9% of global production after Indonesia and Malaysia. Ninety percent of palm oil plantations and their processing facilities are in the south, with the provinces of Surat Thani (23.4%), Krabi (21.8%) and Chumphon (20.5%) accounting for 65% of the country's palm oil plantations. The remaining 10% of palm oil plantations is found in the center, north, and northeast regions of Thailand. Palm oil mills are located mostly in Chumphon (48%), Krabi (42%), and Surat Thani (34%), which serve as collection areas of fresh palm oil in the southern provinces. Fresh palm oil is transported to palm oil mills and refineries in the central plains of Thailand. There are 170 mills in Thailand with an estimated production capacity of 2.8 million tons of CPO per year (Table 40).

Table 40: Palm Oil Plantations and Production in Thailand, 2018

Provinces/Economic Corridor	Palm Fruit Plantations			Processing
	Area (hectares)	Production (tons)	Share (%)	Number of Palm Oil Mills
Surat Thani (EC1)	188,713	3,640,097	23.4	34[a]
Krabi (EC2)	173,790	3,383,122	21.8	42
Chumphon (EC1)	158,015	3,237,336	20.5	48[b]
Nakhon Si Thammarat (EC1)	84,809	1,553,088	10.0	9
Phangnga (EC5)	41,866	701,746	4.5	6
Trang (EC2)	30,718	556,291	3.6	7
Ranong (EC5)	19,048	366,956	2.4	3
Satun (EC2)	17,322	276,557	1.8	7
Phatthalung (EC1)	11,591	148,996	1.2	3
Songkhla (EC1)	10,004	156,546	1.0	9
Narathiwat (EC6)	8,570	108,426	0.7	1
Pattani (EC6)	2,923	45,772	0.3	1
Yala (EC6)	1,168	10,574	0.1	–
Phuket (EC5)	325	4,593	0.03	–
All ECs		**Total**	**90.3**	**170**
Others			**9.7**	
All Thailand			**100.0**	

– = not available, EC = economic corridor.
[a] One refinery and one biodiesel plant.
[b] One refinery and one power plant.
Sources: Compiled by the author from: Office of Agricultural Economics, 2018. http://www.oae.go.th/assets/portals/1/fileups/prcaidata/files/oilpalm%2061.pdf; http://www.oae.go.th/assets/portals/1/files/ebook/2562/tradestat61.pdf; https://www.set.or.th/dat/news/201902/19015402.pdf.

Processing. From the mills, the CPO is processed by 19 palm oil refineries throughout the country into refined palm oil (RPO, 38%), biodiesel (37%), CPO for export (11%), and CPO for stock (14%). Currently, the domestic palm oil refining capacity (estimated at 2.5 million tons)[68] is insufficient to absorb the country's CPO supply, so mills depend on several other industries to take up the balance. They include biodiesel (B100), electricity and steam generation, biogas industries, and oil storage facilities. Seventy-five percent of CPO is used for the processing of downstream products (e.g., edible oil, starch, and biodiesel, among others) (Figure 13).

---

[68] Estimated by the Office of Industrial Economies.

Figure 13: Value Chain of Thailand Palm Oil Industry (2018)

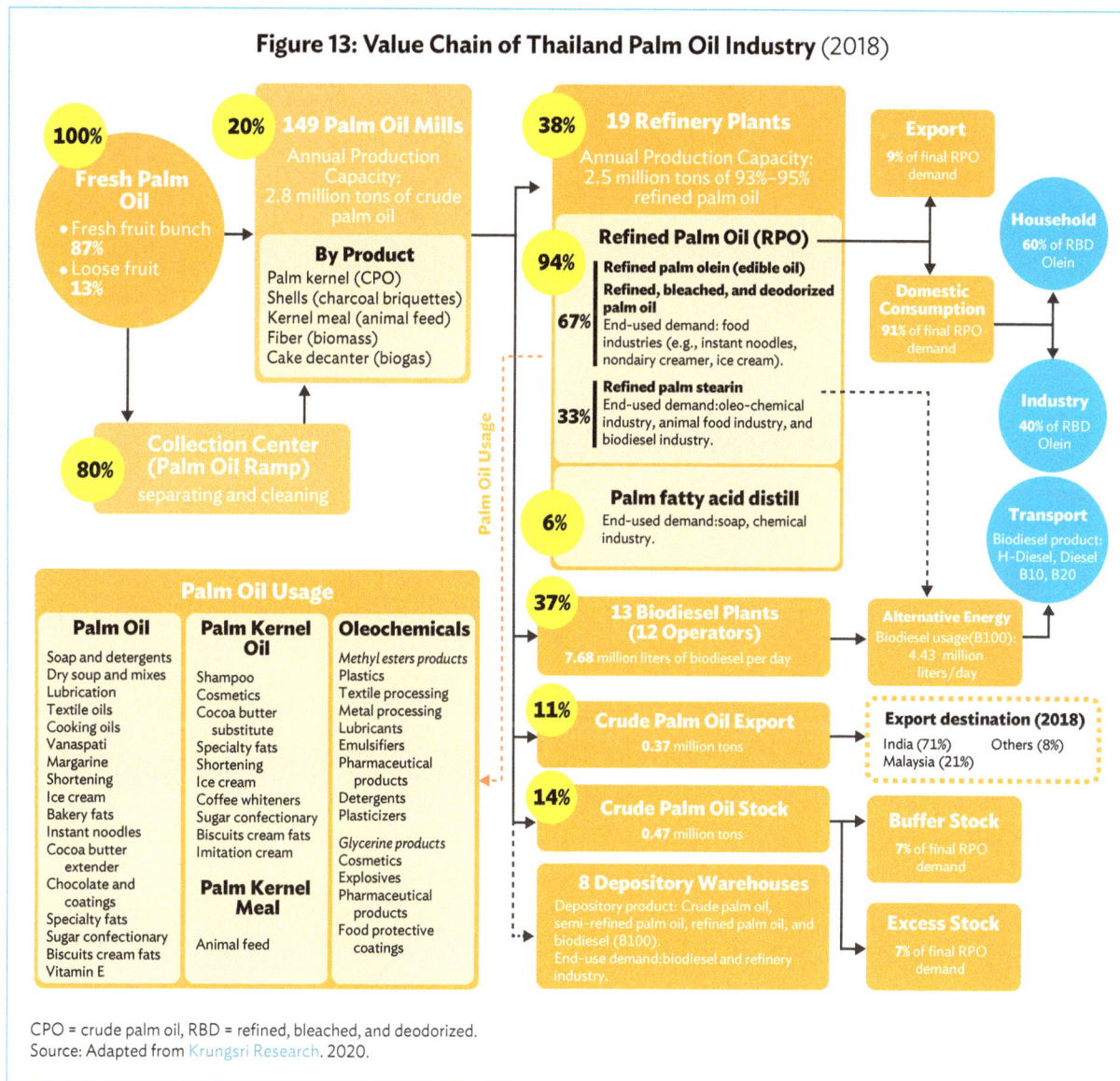

100%

Fresh Palm Oil
- Fresh fruit bunch 87%
- Loose fruit 13%

80%

Collection Center (Palm Oil Ramp)
separating and cleaning

20%

149 Palm Oil Mills
Annual Production Capacity: 2.8 million tons of crude palm oil

By Product
Palm kernel (CPO)
Shells (charcoal briquettes)
Kernel meal (animal feed)
Fiber (biomass)
Cake decanter (biogas)

Palm Oil Usage

38%

19 Refinery Plants
Annual Production Capacity: 2.5 million tons of 93%–95% refined palm oil

Refined Palm Oil (RPO)

94%
67% Refined palm olein (edible oil)
Refined, bleached, and deodorized palm oil
End-used demand: food industries (e.g., instant noodles, nondairy creamer, ice cream).

33% Refined palm stearin
End-used demand: oleo-chemical industry, animal food industry, and biodiesel industry.

6% **Palm fatty acid distill**
End-used demand: soap, chemical industry.

37% **13 Biodiesel Plants (12 Operators)**
7.68 million liters of biodiesel per day

11% **Crude Palm Oil Export**
0.37 million tons

14% **Crude Palm Oil Stock**
0.47 million tons

8 Depository Warehouses
Depository product: Crude palm oil, semi-refined palm oil, refined palm oil, and biodiesel (B100).
End-use demand: biodiesel and refinery industry.

Export
9% of final RPO demand

Domestic Consumption
91% of final RPO demand

Household
60% of RBD Olein

Industry
40% of RBD Olein

Transport
Biodiesel product: H-Diesel, Diesel B10, B20

Alternative Energy
Biodiesel usage(B100): 4.43 million liters/day

Export destination (2018)
India (71%)   Others (8%)
Malaysia (21%)

Buffer Stock
7% of final RPO demand

Excess Stock
7% of final RPO demand

Palm Oil Usage

Palm Oil	Palm Kernel Oil	Oleochemicals
Soap and detergents	Shampoo	*Methyl esters products*
Dry soup and mixes	Cosmetics	Plastics
Lubrication	Cocoa butter substitute	Textile processing
Textile oils	Specialty fats	Metal processing
Cooking oils	Shortening	Lubricants
Vanaspati	Ice cream	Emulsifiers
Margarine	Coffee whiteners	Pharmaceutical products
Shortening	Sugar confectionary	Detergents
Ice cream	Biscuits cream fats	Plasticizers
Bakery fats	Imitation cream	*Glycerine products*
Instant noodles		Cosmetics
Cocoa butter extender	**Palm Kernel Meal**	Explosives
Chocolate and coatings		Pharmaceutical products
Specialty fats	Animal feed	Food protective coatings
Sugar confectionary		
Biscuits cream fats		
Vitamin E		

CPO = crude palm oil, RBD = refined, bleached, and deodorized.
Source: Adapted from Krungsri Research. 2020.

Distribution. About 91% of the RPO produced by the refineries are distributed for domestic consumption and 9% are exported to meet final demand. The CPO export markets are India (71%), Malaysia (21%), and smaller markets (e.g., Germany, Singapore, and the Lao PDR) with a combined share of 8%. At present, CPO from the EC1 and EC2 are transported by trucks to Laem Chabang deep-seaport to be shipped via Singapore Port onwards to India and other destinations. The development of Ranong deep-seaport will provide a more efficient route for palm oil exports to India as transport costs are reduced and Thailand's competitiveness improves.

Findings and Recommendations

Indonesia

The Government of Indonesia has begun to shift its priorities to downstream industries for palm oil. This policy is supported by several government initiatives including infrastructure and related improvements in economic corridors in Sumatera.

(i)   The ongoing development of Sei Mangkei SEZ is an important priority and its timely completion, together with the completion of Tebingtinggi–Kisaran toll road segment, will greatly improve the efficiency of transporting palm oil produce from plantations to mills to refineries in Sei Mangkei where some of the big companies processing CPO and CPKO are located.

(ii) To complement road improvements in the Trans-Sumatera Toll Road, the Trans-Sumatera railway project may need to be reactivated, especially the development of Sei Mangkei–Kuala Tanjung segment, which will facilitate the transport of palm oil downstream products to the designated international hub port of Kuala Tanjung.

(iii) The development of the toll road segment connecting South Sumatera–Jambi–Riau–North Sumatera should be prioritized to facilitate the transport of palm fruit bunches from these four provinces where the largest plantations and mills are located to the midstream–downstream processing centers and transit points in Dumai and Belawan.

(iv) The availability of sufficient and quality feeder roads from peripheral plantation areas to the toll roads and national highways should also be put in the agenda of regional development plan of each related province, in collaboration with palm oil companies. Where feasible, feeder roads for palm oil should be separated from public roads.

(v)   The proposed route for EC6 would support the palm oil downstreaming policy by using a business-friendly environment in Batam, Bintan, Karimun as the free trade zone and free port to support palm oil refinery and manufacturing industries. The aim is to reduce the large portion of palm oil exports in the form of CPO and CPKO.

(vi) To accommodate big export markets across the Indian Ocean (India, Pakistan, and Bangladesh), refineries in the western part of Sumatera (i.e., Padang, West Sumatera Province) should be given support in terms of road-to-port infrastructure improvements. The proposed expansion of EC3 and EC4 to include West Sumatera is an important step in this direction. West Sumatera's proposed inclusion in the extended EC4 will enable the province to link with Dumai Port for its exports of palm oil to Malaysia and other destinations. Panjang Port in Padang has the potential to become a major export gateway for both West Sumatera and Bengkulu Provinces, even though this area is prone to earthquakes. To further explore this idea, a feasibility study may be needed.

Malaysia

ECs 1, 2, 4, and 6 have a comparative advantage in the palm oil industry, with the state of Johor as the largest producer of palm oil in the peninsula. Most of the palm oil plantations are in the hinterland areas while the processing industries for palm oil, especially downstream activities, are mostly concentrated in industrial estates.

Road and rail networks facilitate the palm oil value chain in their respective corridors and also between ECs 1, 2, 4, and 6. Ports in these corridors, namely Port Klang, Penang Port, Lumut Port, Tanjung Pelepas Port, Johor Port, and Kuantan Port are accessible by road and rail.

To support palm oil value chain development, planning for economic corridors should focus not only on the main transport backbone, but also on transport links that enhance the efficiency of logistics services, which is crucial for value chains. The following are important factors to consider:

(i)   Last mile connectivity—both gateway-based and hinterland-based—could help facilitate transport and bring down logistics costs at various stages of the value chain.

(ii) Improved connectivity from industrial estates to seaports will facilitate exports of products to international markets and can contribute to the competitiveness of the products.

(iii) Railway spur lines should be built for ports that do not have direct rail links with major economic centers. The proposed railway spur lines are from Bukit Kayu Hitam (Kedah) to Arau (Perlis) (EC1 and EC2)[69] and Ipoh Cargo Terminal to Lumut Port (Perak) (EC2).[70] This will improve transport connectivity and support value chain development in palm oil.

(iv) The role of inland ports in the ECs needs to be further enhanced. The existing inland ports in the ECs are Ipoh Cargo Terminal (Perak), Nilai Inland Port (Negeri Sembilan), Segamat Inland Port (Johor), and Batu Pahat Container Terminal (Johor). Inland ports will allow many supply chain functions to take place further inland and offer better access to inland markets.[71]

The EC6 states—Kelantan, Terengganu, and Pahang—are among the major producers of palm oil. The ECRL route from Kota Bahru to Port Klang and the East Coast Highway from Tumpat to Kuala Lumpur will develop a road–rail–ports intermodal link particularly to Kemaman Port and Kuantan Port that will support the development of value chains in the region. Both ports in the EC6 serve as trade gateways for manufacturers to export their products to East Asia. Manufacturers in the EC6 can also use this overland route as a land bridge to export their products by using ports on the west coast, such as Port Klang and Tanjung Bruas Port.

Industry clusters for palm oil should be promoted. An industry cluster represents the entire value chain of a broadly defined industry from suppliers to end-products, including supporting services and specialized infrastructure. Industry clusters are geographically concentrated and interconnected by the flow of goods and services, which is stronger than the flow linking them to the rest of the economy. While the concept of industrial clusters differs from that of industrial estates, industrial clusters can be developed alongside, or in proximity to, industrial estates. In Malaysia, Johor in EC4 has a dedicated industrial estate to support palm oil value chain activities with the development of the Tanjung Langsat Palm Oil Industrial Cluster. This economic zone is connected to Johor Port (Pasir Gudang) and Tanjung Pelepas Port (Gelang Patah) by road.

Thailand

The Thai government has planned to develop Southern Thailand into a rubber and palm oil hub within the subregion. Currently, most CPO exports from EC1 and EC2 provinces are transported by trucks to Laem Chabang deep-seaport to be shipped via Singapore Port, to India and other destinations. However, there is

---

69   R. Agustin. 2019. Rail Link Better than ECRL to Boost Trade. *Free Malaysia Today.* 9 January.

70   *Perak Today.* 2010. Railway Link to Lumut. 21 September.

71   J.P. Rodrigue, J. Debrie, A. Fremont, and E. Gouvernal. 2010. Functions and Actors of Inland Ports: European and North American Dynamics. *Journal of Transport Geography.* 18(4): July. pp. 519–529.

a great potential to transport CPO from EC1 and EC2 through EC5 via the Ranong deep-seaport. If Ranong Port is utilized and developed to efficiently accommodate additional cargo volume, CPO from Ranong can be directly exported to India, Pakistan, Sri Lanka, and other destinations in South Asia and Europe. Transport costs and time will be significantly reduced and product competitiveness improved.

Highways leading to gateway ports in EC5 must be upgraded to facilitate the transport of palm oil products across the corridor. More specifically, the following improvements could be undertaken:

(i)   Upgrade Highway No. 4 to four lanes from Ranong (EC5) to Krabi (EC2);

(ii) Upgrade Highway No. 4 to four lanes from Chumphon (EC1) to Ranong (EC5), connecting AH2 from central region via Highway No. 4 to Ranong Port;

(iii) Upgrade Ranong Port by investing in port equipment to facilitate goods handling and transport of CPO and other products from the economic corridors to India, Sri Lanka, and Pakistan or transshipment via India seaports to Africa, Middle East, and Europe respectively;

(iv) Link Ranong Port with BIMSTEC subregion by implementing the MOU between Ranong Port and Navayuga Container Terminal and Krishna Patnam Port, India.

Moreover, 75% of Thailand's palm oil industry consists of downstream activities. Thai investments in midstream and downstream industries in Sumatera will contribute to strengthening the palm oil industry value chain for Indonesia.

Rubber

Overview. Thailand, Indonesia, and Malaysia are among the world's leading producers and exporters of natural rubber. Thailand is the world's major rubber producer. In 2017, Thailand produced 4.42 million tons of natural rubber or 36% of global production. Indonesia is the second largest producer with a share of 26%, followed by Viet Nam (8.6%), the PRC (8%), and Malaysia (5.5%). Most of the provinces involved in the rubber value chain in IMT-GT are in EC1 and EC6 (Table 41).

Table 41: Key Provinces and States in the Rubber Value Chain

EC	Indonesia	EC	Malaysia	EC	Thailand
EC1	North Sumatera	EC1	Kedah	EC1	Surat Thani
EC3	Jambi		Perlis		Nakhon Si Thammarat
EC4	Riau	EC4	Johor		Songkhla
EC6	South Sumatera		Kelantan		Chumphon
		EC6	Terengganu		
			Pahang		

EC = economic corridor.
Source: Study team.

About 75% of the plantation and production facilities in Thailand are located in EC1, with distribution points by land along the coasts in Surat Thani and the borders with Malaysia, and by sea transport via Kantang Port and Songkhla Port. In Indonesia, North Sumatera, Jambi, Riau, and South Sumatera are the main provinces with the biggest stakes in the rubber industry with Tanjung Priok Port (Jakarta) and Belawan Port as the main gateways. In Malaysia, all of the rubber production takes place in the ECs1, 4, and 6 , with Penang Port and Port Klang as the main distribution points (Map 25).

Map 25: Stylized Visualization of the Location of Rubber Value Chain Processes in Indonesia–Malaysia–Thailand Growth Triangle

Source: Asian Development Bank.

Indonesia's strategy is to increase the production of natural rubber, especially in Sumatera where most processing plants are located and develop its processing industries. Indonesia allows foreign investors to invest in rubber plantations and rubber processing business, including automobile manufacturing. Malaysia's strategy is to enhance its downstream capacities to become the leading producer of rubber products and become a "Global Center of Excellence for Rubber." It aims to increase its global market share of rubber gloves and tires. Thailand is presently focused on shifting from upstream–midstream activities to developing downstream products. Thailand is actively promoting foreign direct investments in the rubber industry to promote rubber innovation and development in concentrated latex, compound rubber, and related industries. It is also collaborating with trading partners in the international rubber, market to make Thailand an original equipment manufacturer (OEM) for rubber which can ultimately impact on the stability of domestic rubber prices.

Collaboration among the three countries in rubber is well-advanced and exemplified in the Rubber Cities Cooperation Project. The main agenda for this collaboration is to create the desired regional ecosystem to promote downstream activities in the rubber value chain to boost rubber consumption. The project's desired outcome is to transform IMT-GT from a major natural rubber producer into a regional and ultimately global player in rubber products manufacturing. There are four dedicated sites for the project located in Kedah in Malaysia, Songkhla in Thailand, and Tanjung Api-Api SEZ, and Sei Mangkei SEZ in Indonesia. The Kedah Rubber CIty (KRC), for example, which is both a national and regional project will focus on four core rubber sub-industries: catalytic anchor tenants; specialized latex and rubber products; precision-engineered rubber products; and "green" rubber products, which will produce high value-added downstream products from both natural and synthetic rubber.

The rubber value chain. The rubber value chain consists of the production of primary or raw materials, intermediate products, and final products. From the rubber plantations, fresh latex is processed into field latex, unsmoked sheet, and cup lump (upstream products) and collected by middlemen and brokers at multiple levels of the village, where rubber factories are usually located. These products are processed by factories into intermediate products (midstream) such as latex concentrate, ribbed-smoked sheets, and block rubber. These are then processed by the factories into downstream products such as rubber gloves, re-milled rubber and rubber latex, rubber tires for vehicles, and rubber footwear (including leather footwear) (Figure 14).

Figure 14: Rubber Value Chain

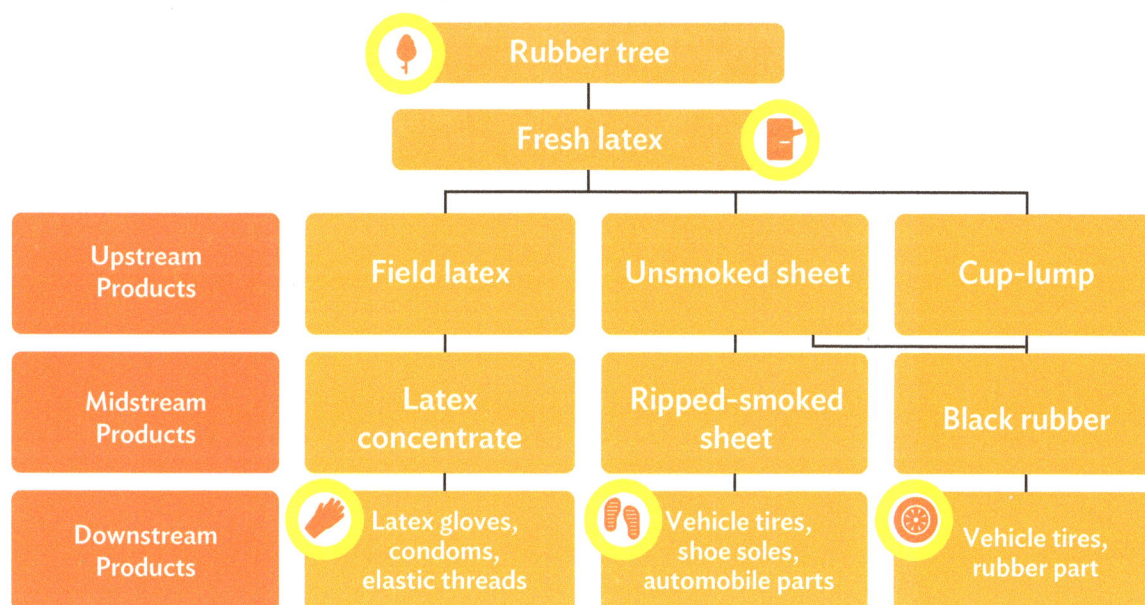

Source: Adapted from J. Chanchaichujit, J. F. Saavedra-Rosas. 2018. The Elements of the Natural Rubber Industry Supply Chain. In: *Using Simulation Tools to Model Renewable Resources*. Palgrave Macmillan, Cham.

Indonesia

Indonesia is the second biggest natural rubber producer in the world, next to Thailand. Indonesian rubber is the only commercial source of natural rubber produced with a unique mechanical characteristic (i.e., tear resistant), which constitutes half of the world's total production.

Plantations. Rubber plantation areas in Indonesia are spread in 26 of 34 provinces. Sumatera has the largest rubber plantation area contributing 70% to the total national area planted to rubber. South Sumatera (22.8%), North Sumatera (12.3%), and Jambi (10.3%) are the three provinces with the largest rubber plantation areas in Indonesia. The whole Sumatera is also the largest natural rubber producer, contributing 76% to Indonesia's natural rubber production (Table 42).

The productivity of Sumatera's plantations is 1.06 tons/ha which is higher than the national average of 0.99 ton/ha. Indonesia's productivity however is low compared to Thailand where productivity could reach 1.80 tons/ha. Productivity of other major producers are also higher: Viet Nam, 1.72 tons/hectare and Malaysia, 1.52 tons/hectare. Aging trees and the low investment capability of smallholder farmers (86.38% of plantation owners) to invest in new trees is a key factor accounting for low productivity. It has been difficult to encourage smallholder farmers to regenerate their rubber trees due to the high cost and potential loss of income during the replantation period.

Table 42: Rubber Plantations and Production in Sumatera, 2018

Province	Plantations			Production		
	Total Area (hectares)	Share to Sumatera (%)	Share to Indonesia (%)	Total Production (tons)	Share to Sumatera (%)	Share to Indonesia (%)
South Sumatera (EC3)	838,636	32.3	22.8	982,423	35.7	27.1
North Sumatera (EC1)	450,329	17.4	12.3	461,190	16.8	12.7
Jambi (EC3)	378,695	14.6	10.3	315,724	11.5	8.7
Riau (EC4)	350,205	13.5	9.5	368,904	13.4	10.2
Lampung (EC3)	157,682	6.2	4.3	160,022	5.8	4.4
West Sumatera (EC4)	130,331	5.0	3.6	152,508	5.5	4.2
Bengkulu (EC3)	99,015	3.8	2.7	122,522	4.5	3.4
Aceh (EC5)	97,951	3.8	2.7	98,380	3.6	2.7
Bangka Belitung Islands (EC6)	47,286	1.8	1.3	59,478	2.2	1.6
Riau Islands (EC6)	25,185	1.0	0.7	30,186	1.1	0.8
Sumatera	**2,575,315**	**100.0**	**70.2**	**2,751,337**	**100.0**	**75.8**
INDONESIA	**3,671,302**		**100.0**	**3,630,268**		**100.0**

Source: Ministry of Agriculture-Republic of Indonesia. 2018. *Tree Crops Estate Statistics of Indonesia 2017–2019*. Jakarta: Directorate General of Estate Crops-Ministry of Agriculture-Republic of Indonesia.

Processing. The rubber latex produced by farmers in the rural areas are collected by middlemen and brokers at multiple levels of the village, subdistrict, and urban areas where rubber factories are usually located. These factories may be classified into upstream and downstream factories. The upstream industry usually produces Standard Indonesian Rubber/Technically Specified Rubber, or commonly known as block rubber, ribbed smoked sheet, and concentrated latex. The downstream industry products include gloves, thread, footwear, retread tires, medical gloves, carpets, and other tools, among others.

Sumatera has 56 factories: 33 for upstream processing and 23 for downstream products. Thirty-nine or 70% of these factories are in North Sumatera (29) and South Sumatera (10). Although South Sumatera has the largest plantation area and the biggest production of natural rubber, the number of factories in the province is significantly smaller than in North Sumatera (29). The 10 factories in South Sumatera produce upstream products such as Standard Indonesian Rubber and ribbed smoked sheet, and brown crepe. The development of the Tanjung Api-Api SEZ is envisaged to address the situation with its designation as one of the four rubber cities in IMT-GT.

Most rubber factories in North Sumatera are engaged in downstream products such as gloves, footwear, toys, and tires. The large number of factories in North Sumatera can accommodate rubber latex for processing from other provinces including South Sumatera. Processing capacity is also being developed through the Sei Mangkei SEZ, which is also one of the designated rubber cities. Sei Mangkei SEZ's participation in the rubber city initiative will enhance its role in processing raw rubber from South Sumatera, Jambi, Riau, and other provinces in Sumatera. Belawan Port in North Sumatera, which currently handles about 19% of rubber product exports will be supplemented by Kuala Tanjung Port, which is being developed as an international hub port.

Distribution. Based on Indonesia's Investment Data of 2018, around 85% of natural rubber production was exported and 15% was absorbed domestically mainly by the automotive industry. The rubber-based manufacturers are concentrated in North Sumatera, Banten, and West Java. The last two provinces are located on Java Island.

The biggest maritime gateway port for rubber-based products was Tanjung Priok Port in Jakarta which accounted for 46.5% of export value in 2018, followed by Belawan Port with a contribution of 19% in terms of both volume and value. Belawan Port, which is an interlink node in EC1 and EC3, is a loading port for trade with Malaysia and Thailand (Table 43).

Table 43: Rubber Exports by Port of Loading in Indonesia, 2018

No	Port of Loading	Rubber and Articles Thereof			
		Volume (million tons)	Share to Indonesia (%)	Value ($ million)	Share to Indonesia (%)
Sumatera					
1	Belawan	0.7	19.0	1,181.3	18.5
2	Musi River	0.7	19.0	949.1	14.9
3	Jambi	0.3	7.6	379.7	6.0
4	Padang/Teluk Bayur (West Sumatera)	0.2	5.7	290.4	4.6
5	Panjang	0.07	1.8	91.2	1.4
6	Batu Ampar (Batam)	0.00	0.07	22.8	0.4
7	Palembang–Plaju	0.00	0.06	3.3	0.05
Java					
1	Tanjung Priok	1.4	38.1	2,965.3	46.5
2	Tanjung Perak	0.22	6.2	320.3	5.0
3	Tanjung Emas	0.24	6.6	35.6	0.6
	Total Indonesia	**3.6**	**100.0**	**6,380.1**	**100.0**

The export data includes natural and synthetic rubber.
Source: BPS-Statistics Indonesia, 2020.

The three major markets for Indonesia's rubber exports are the US (23%), Japan (15%), and the PRC (11%). Rubber blocks comprised 85.4% of exports, followed by mixtures of natural rubber (5.5%). Indonesia's rubber exports are mostly midstream products. Indonesia's exports to Thailand and Malaysia are small—contributing around 1% each to Indonesia's total exports in 2018. Indonesia's imports from the two countries were higher and consisted mostly of natural rubber latex-centrifuge concentrate and synthetic rubber of other polybutadiene-styrene rubber and XSBR2 and nitrile-butadiene rubber.

Malaysia

Plantations. Malaysia ranked fifth among the largest natural rubber producers in the world in 2018, contributing 4% to world natural rubber production. Thailand was the largest natural rubber producer, followed by Indonesia. The States of Kedah and Perlis (EC1 and EC2) account for 24% of the total area planted to rubber in Malaysia; followed by Kelantan and Terengganu (EC6) with 17%. The EC states are also major producers of natural rubber, accounting for 60% of total national production (Table 44).

Table 44: Rubber Plantations and Production in Malaysia

State	Plantations		Production		Rubber Product Manufacturers (Number of plants)
	Area (hectare)	Share (%)	Natural Rubber Production (Tons)	Share (%)	
IMT-GT/EC States					
Kedah and Perlis (EC1 and EC2)	18,567	24	14,285	27	39 (Kedah-35 Perlis-4)
Kelantan** and Terengganu (EC6)	12,850	17	8,252	16	1 (Kelantan-1 Terengganu-0)
Perak (EC2)	7,447	10	5,344	10	67
Negeri Sembilan (EC2)	7,009	9	8,302	16	20
Selangor (EC2)	4,915	6	2,684	5	187
Melaka (EC4)	707	1	804	2	19
Penang* (EC2)	–	–	–	–	35
Johor (EC4)	7,243	9	6,762	13	45
Pahang (EC6)	6,345	8	6,548	12	3
Subtotal	65,083	60	38,696	100	416
Non-IMT-GT States					
Sabah and Sarawak	12,322	16	56	0	3 (Sabah-1 Sarawak-2)
Kuala Lumpur	–	–	–	–	9
Total (Malaysia)	**77,405**	**100**	**53,037**	**100**	**428**

– = not available, EC = economic corridor, IMT-GT = Indonesia–Malaysia–Thailand Growth Triangle.
Notes:
* No estates were recorded in Penang.
** Kelantan is existing IMT-GT State.
Numbers may not add up to the total for Malaysia because of nonavailability of data for some states.
Sources: Department of Statistics. 2017. Annual Rubber Statistics 2016. Putrajaya: DOS Malaysia, [1] Ministry of Plantation Industries and Commodities. Directory of Rubber Product Manufacturers. Retrieved from https://www.mpic.gov.my/mpi/en/data-terbuka.

Processing. There are 428 rubber manufacturing plants in Malaysia of which 97% (416 plants) are in economic corridor states. Selangor, which is close to Port Klang, accounts for 44%, while Kedah, Perlis, Penang, and Perak (north), which are close to Penang Port, account for 32%. These plants operate in industrial parks supported by the government where manufacturing enterprises are entitled to fiscal incentives. The states in the EC1, EC2, and EC6 are among the major natural rubber producers in the country.

Distribution. Malaysia's rubber product exports include rubber gloves; surgical gloves; new tires; tubes, pipes and hoses; and latex thread. Rubber gloves is a major export product valued at $4 billion or 74% of total rubber products exports in 2018. The main export markets in 2018 are the US (22%) and the PRC (19%). Malaysia also exports rubber products to Thailand and Indonesia although the volume is relatively small (3% share for Thailand exports and 2% share for Indonesia exports). This reflects the existence of intra-industry trade between the world's leading producers of natural rubber.

Malaysia trades with Indonesia and Thailand in rubber products to meet the demand in domestic supply. In 2018, rubber imports (two-thirds of which is natural rubber) from Thailand accounted for 30% of the country's total rubber and rubber product imports. Malaysia's exports consisted mostly of rubber tires.

The balance of trade in rubber and rubber products was in Thailand's favor by $929 million. Malaysia's rubber trade with Indonesia was significantly lower at $198 million. The major import was rubber tires, while the major export was synthetic rubber. Trade among the three countries indicates Malaysia's dependence on Thailand for the supply of natural rubber (upstream) and Indonesia for synthetic rubber (midstream) (Table 45).

Table 45: Malaysia's Trade with Thailand and Indonesia: Rubber and Rubber Products, 2018

SITC	Product	$ million			
		Import	Export	Total Trade	Balance of Trade
THAILAND					
231	Natural Rubber, Natural Gums, In Primary Forms	710	2	713	(708)
232	Synthetic Rubber; Reclaimed Rubber, Waste, Parings and Scrap of Unhardened Rubber	64	78	142	14
621	Materials of Rubber	13	10	23	(3)
625	Rubber Tires, Interchangeable Tire Treads, Inner Tubes and Tire Flabs	256	51	307	(205)
629	Articles of Rubber, nes	48	22	70	(27)
	Subtotal	**1,092**	**163**	**1,255**	**(929)**
	Share of Thailand in Total Rubber and Rubber Products (%)	**30**	**5**	**19**	
	Share of Thailand in All Commodities (%)	**0.5**	**0.1**	**0.3**	
INDONESIA					
231	Natural Rubber, Natural Gums, In Primary Forms	6	0	6	(6)
232	Synthetic Rubber; Reclaimed Rubber, Waste, Parings and Scrap of Unhardened Rubber	6	41	46	35
621	Materials of Rubber	5	22	27	16
625	Rubber Tires, Interchangeable Tire Treads, Inner Tubes and Tire Flaps	79	16	95	(64)
629	Articles of Rubber, nes	13	11	24	(2)
	Subtotal	**109**	**89**	**198**	**(20)**
	Share of Indonesia in Total Rubber and Rubber Products (%)	**3.0**	**2.9**	**2.9**	
	Share of Indonesia in All Commodities (%)	**0.1**	**0.04**	**0.04**	

() = negative, nes = not elsewhere specified, SITC = Standard International Trade Classification.
Source: Department of Statistics. Retrieved at https://metsonline.dosm.gov.my/.

Penang Port and Port Klang are the main trade gateways for rubber. In 2018, rubber latex exports accounted for 21% of total commodities shipped via Penang Port. Rubber and rubber goods shipped via Port Klang are much less, accounting for about 1% of all commodities shipped via the port. For land borders, Bukit Kayu Hitam and Padang Besar are the main gateways for rubber trade between Malaysia and Thailand.

Thailand

Plantations and production. Thailand has the second largest rubber plantation area in the world after Indonesia. Plantations in EC provinces comprise 60% of total national area planted to rubber. The provinces with the largest rubber plantation areas are Surat Thani (11.3%), Songkhla (8.5%), and Nakhon Si Thammarat (6.6%) (Table 46). These three provinces, which are all in EC1, account for 26% of the total area planted to rubber. Rubber plantation areas in EC6—Pattani, Yala, and Narathiwat—constitute another 11.6%. EC1 and EC6 play an important role in the development of the rubber value chain in Thailand. The south is situated in a tropical zone which is suitable for rubber cultivation compared to other regions. The rubber plantations in the southern region located in economic corridors constitute 54% of the rubber plantation areas nationwide.

Table 46: Rubber Plantations and Production in Thailand, 2018

	Plantations		Production	
	Area (hectares)	Share (%)	Production of Tapped Rubber (tons)	Share (%)
Surat Thani (EC1)	407,113	11.2	547,211	11.4
Songkhla (EC1)	316,599	8.7	410,402	8.5
Nakhon Si Thammarat (EC1)	240,052	6.6	389,280	8.1
Trang (EC2)	233,154	6.4	328,897	6.8
Yala (EC6)	199,718	5.5	261,043	5.4
Narathiwat (EC6)	161,141	4.5	197,937	4.1
Phatthalung (EC1)	142,291	3.9	210,694	4.4
Phangnga (EC2)	99,624	2.8	146,367	3.0
Krabi (EC2)	89,445	2.5	131,669	2.7
Chumphon (EC1)	83,895	2.3	123,081	2.6
Satun (EC2)	67,449	1.9	89,933	1.9
Pattani (EC6)	59,192	1.6	84,238	1.8
Ranong (EC5)	49,856	1.4	65,982	1.4
Phuket (EC5)	10,738	0.3	12,726	0.3
All ECs	**2,160,267**	**59.7**	**2,999,460**	**62.3**
Other Thailand	**1,459,937**	**40.3**	**1,814,067**	**37.7**
All Thailand	**3,620,204**	**100.0**	**4,813,527**	**100.00**

EC = economic corridor.
Sources: Office of Agriculture Economic, Ministry of Agriculture. 2019. Agriculture Economic Data. Bangkok, Government of Thailand. 2018. Thailand Foreign Agricultural Trade Statistics. Bangkok, United Palm Oil Industry Public Company Limited. 2019. Palm Industry Overview.Bangkok.

Thailand is also the world's major producer and exporter of natural rubber. In 2017, Thailand produced 4.42 million tons of natural rubber (36% of global production) of which 83% were exported. In terms of intermediate processed rubber, Thailand produces most of technically specified rubber, followed by concentrated latex, mixture, ribbed smoked sheet, and other types of rubber such as compound rubber.

Processing. The upstream industry involves rubber farmers and rubber tappers. Farmers, farmer groups or organizations, cooperatives and small retailers or rubber shops collect natural rubber from plantations and transport these to factories to be used as raw materials in the processing of primary products or semi-finished products. Some farmers are also involved in rubber processing to add value to their primary production.

Tapped rubber, which is the primary upstream product, is processed into three products namely: (i) latex, (ii) raw rubber sheets, and (iii) cup lump or rubber crumb. Semi-finished products include ribbed smoked sheet, technically specified rubber/standard Thai rubber (TSR/STR), concentrated latex, compound rubber, and skim rubber. These products are manufactured according to standard qualifications for domestic and international downstream producers (Figure 15).

Figure 15: Thailand's Rubber Products Value Chain

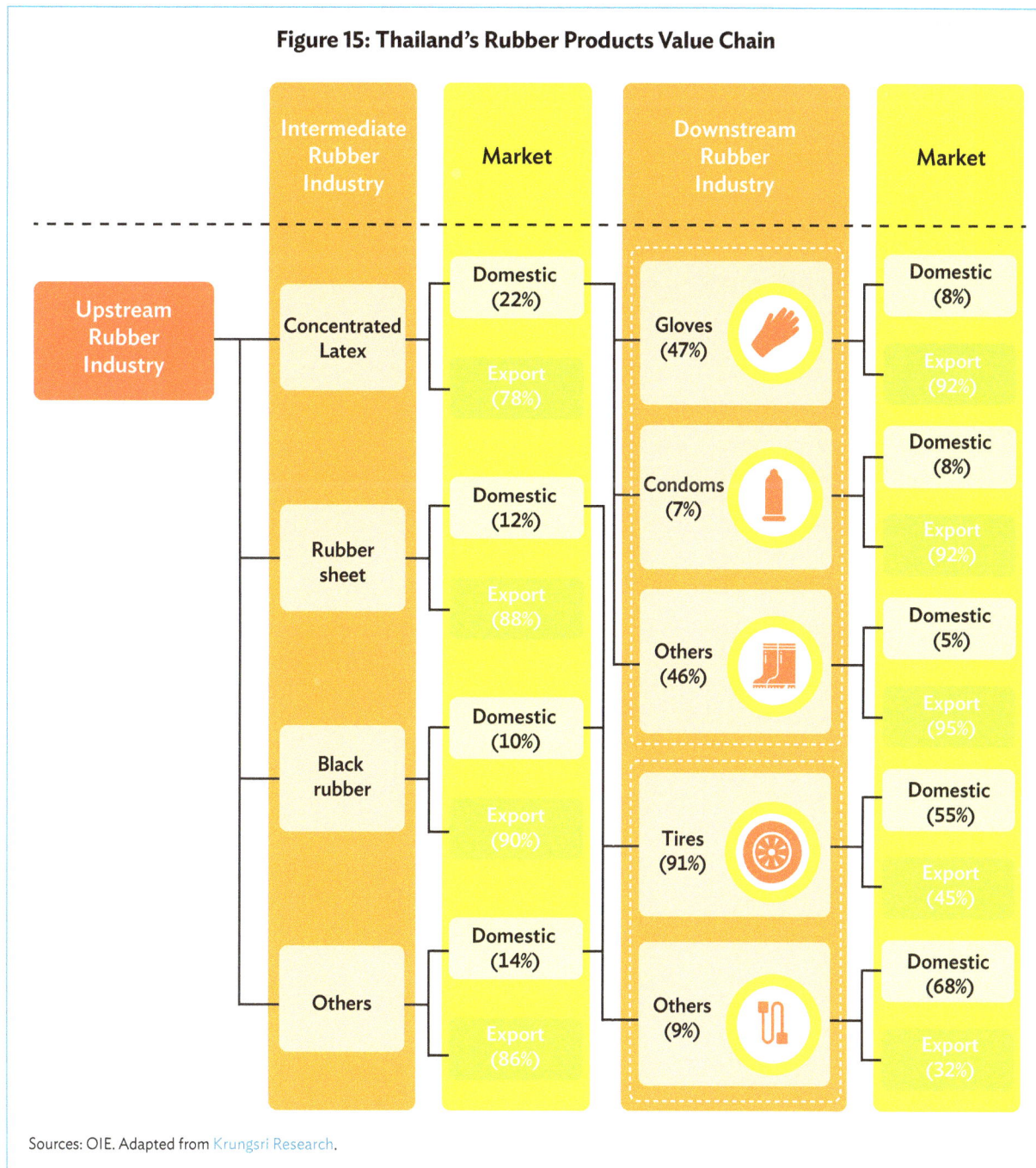

Sources: OIE. Adapted from Krungsri Research.

The downstream industry processes raw materials from intermediate industries into final products for consumers. Final products include pillows, latex mattresses, rubber gloves, condoms, rubber roads, auto tires, motorcycle tires, aircraft tires, rubber bands, conveyor belts, athletic shoes, waterproof strips, and many others. In some cases, synthetic rubber, which is developed from the petrochemical sector, is produced as an alternative to natural rubber or mixed with natural rubber to enhance qualifications for various purposes.

Distribution. Thailand's rubber latex exports contribute around 78% to total rubber exports; the remaining 12% is for domestic production. The major markets for rubber latex are the PRC (56%), Malaysia (14%), the EU (7%), Japan and the US (5%), and the Republic of Korea (3%). The key distribution points for rubber products by land are: (i) along the coastal route in Surat Thani to Laem Chabang Port (34%) for export to other countries, (ii) Padang Besa BCP (33%) to Penang Port and Singapore Port for export to other countries, and (iii) Sadao BCP (14%) to Malaysia. Distribution via sea transport is via Kantang Port (3%) and Songkhla Port (3%) from where rubber goods are shipped to Penang Port and Singapore for export to other countries. Phuket Port is also a distribution point from where rubber products are shipped directly to other destinations.

Thailand promotes foreign direct investments in the rubber industry by providing incentives according to the criteria of the Board of Investment of Thailand and the Rubber City in Songkhla, which provides opportunities for investments in rubber innovation, concentrated latex, compound rubber, and related industries. Thailand is active in searching for, and cooperating with, trading partners in the international rubber market to make Thailand an OEM. Thailand's wide-ranging potential makes it equipped to become an OEM center for rubber, which ultimately impacts on the stability of domestic rubber prices.

Findings and Recommendations

Indonesia

Belawan Port, which is both in EC1 and EC3 currently serves as a strategic gateway for Sumatera's rubber exports and imports. With Sei Mangkei SEZ having been positioned to promote downstream activities for rubber and palm oil, the development of Kuala Tanjung Port which is closer to Sei Mangkei, would give further boost to the rubber industry by easing logistics, infrastructure, and permit issuances needed for the SEZ to flourish. Considering that Sei Mangkei has been designated as a Rubber City under the IMT-GT, the government will need to address the outstanding issues in the development of the Sei Mangkei SEZ (e.g., land procurement, reliability of electricity, affordability of gas) to provide a conducive environment for investors, especially in downstream activities.

Kuala Tanjung Port will give North Sumatera, which has the greatest number of rubber factories, direct access to world markets for the first time. Kuala Tanjung Port has already developed direct maritime links to several ports in Malaysia across the Strait of Malacca. The ongoing development of Kuala Tanjung Port will have to focus on its increasing role in global supply chain management and logistics networks given the emerging competition among hub ports in the region.

The large quantity of rubber latex produced in South Sumatera—the biggest natural rubber producer in Sumatera region—is not supported by an adequate number of midstream and downstream manufacturers in the province at present. It is envisaged that Tanjung Api-Api SEZ in South Sumatera, which started operations in 2018, will address this gap through large scale investments in the rubber downstream industry as well as CPO and petrochemicals. At present however, progress in the development of the Tanjung Api-Api SEZ has met with several issues regarding land use and the risk of land subsidence, the safety of the port basin for big ships, and the construction of the planned toll road from Palembang to Tanjung Api-Api, which has been held in abeyance pending the construction of the seaport in the SEZ. The resolution of these issues are critical to the further development of the rubber value chain considering that Tanjung Api-Api has also been designated as a Rubber City for Indonesia under the IMT-GT framework.

Malaysia

ECs 1, 2, 4, and 6 have comparative advantages in the rubber and rubber products, where a large part of the plantations are in the hinterlands. Kedah is the major producer of natural rubber in the peninsula, with most processing facilities, especially for downstream activities, are mostly concentrated in industrial estates.

The road and rail networks in ECs facilitate the transport of rubber and rubber products along the value chain. International gateway ports in the ECs are accessible by road and train. Bukit Kayu Hitam BCP and Padang Besar BCP in EC1 are the main border trade gateways for rubber and rubber products to Thailand. Thai traders in Southern Thailand also use the border trade gateways to export rubber products to the peninsula and the international market via Penang Port.

Transport links that enhance the efficiency of logistics services are crucial for value chains. Last mile connectivity—both gateway-based and hinterland-based—could help facilitate transport and bring down logistics costs at various stages of the value chain. Improved connectivity from industrial estates to seaports will facilitate export of products to international markets and can contribute to the competitiveness of the products.

The role of existing inland ports in the ECs needs to be further enhanced as they allow many value chain functions to take place further inland and offer better access to inland markets. The related inland ports in the ECs are Ipoh Cargo Terminal (Perak), Nilai Inland Port (Negeri Sembilan), Segamat Inland Port (Johor), and Batu Pahat Container Terminal (Johor).

Railway spur lines are planned to be built in the ECs for ports that have no direct rail links with major economic centers. Railway spur lines that are being proposed in the ECs are Bukit Kayu Hitam (Kedah) to Arau (Perlis) (EC1 and EC2) (footnote 68), Ipoh Cargo Terminal to Lumut Port in Perak (EC2) (footnote 69), and Pulau Sebang/Tampin to Tanjung Bruas Port (Melaka) (EC4).[72] There is also a proposal to revive Seremban Railway Station to Port Dickson. The Seremban–Pork Dickson line was closed in 2008 following the derailment of a freight train in Port Dickson to Ipoh.[73]

Kelantan, Terengganu, and Pahang in EC6 are among the major producers of natural rubber. The ECRL route from Kota Bharu to Port Klang and the East Coast Highway from Tumpat to Kuala Lumpur will develop a road–rail–ports intermodal link particularly to Kemaman Port and Kuantan Port that will support the development of value chains in the region. Both ports in the EC6 serve as trade gateways for manufacturers to export their products to East Asia. Manufacturers in the EC6 can also use this overland route as a land bridge to export their products by using ports in the west coast, such as Port Klang and Tanjung Bruas Port.

---

[72] Under the Melaka's State Structure Plan 2015–2035 (Melaka 2035), a proposal was made to build a railway connecting Tg. Bruas Port with the Inland Port to be developed in Taboh Naning (Alor Gajah, Melaka). The Taboh Naning Inland Port will be built by the State Government in collaboration with the Federal Government. This Inland Port will be connected to Pulau Sebang/Tampin Station. However, the proposal to build the Inland Port Taboh Naning, in Alor Gajah (Melaka) and the railway is still in the planning phase.

[73] *The Star.* 2016. Seremban-PD Rail Link to be Revived. 24 November.

Industrial clusters for rubber and rubber products should be promoted. The KRC in EC1 is an example of a rubber and rubber product industry cluster and is currently an IMT-GT project with the participation from Thailand and Indonesia. The implementation of the KRC project needs to be accelerated as a model for developing and advancing the rubber city concept in other ECs.

Thailand

The Government of Thailand is promoting the southern region to become a rubber industry hub by establishing the IMT-GT Rubber City in Songkhla. Investments in the Rubber City will enjoy privileges especially, those that are geared toward downstream products.

Indonesia, Malaysia, and Thailand can upgrade and integrate the value chain of rubber by focusing on research and development and sharing innovations across the different sectors in the industry involved in upstream, intermediate, and downstream industries. The objective is long-term value creation and employment generation, benefiting the development of IMT-GT economic corridors.

The reconfigured EC1, EC5, and the proposed EC6 route will cover a wider area of rubber supply chain activities in IMT-GT. The new EC6 will support cross-border supply chains along the border in the eastern region of Thailand and Malaysia where rubber production and rubber products manufacturing are mostly concentrated. Moreover, EC6 will connect multimodal logistics systems (road, rail, and waterway) that will promote greater industrial efficiency and viability that can lead to job creation and income generation for the local community.

EC1 currently serves as a strategic gateway for transporting rubber and EC6 has great potential to become a major gateway as well. IMT-GT has prioritized a number of physical connectivity projects to promote multimodal connectivity in these two corridors covering road, rail, seaports, airports, CIQs, SEZs, ICDs, and relevant logistics facilities:

(i)   Constructing: (a) the second bridge across Kolok River at Su-ngai Kolok – Rantau Panjang; (b) the bridge over Kolok River at Tak Bai–Pengkalan Kubur; and (c) upgrading the Thailand–Malaysia Friendship Bridge across Kolok River at Buketa–Bukit Bunga to facilitate the transport of rubber and other cargoes to Kelantan, Kuantan, and Penang Ports in Malaysia.

(ii) Connecting the railway route from Su-ngai Kolok Railway Station to Pasir Mas Railway Station in Kelantan Malaysia covering 20 km (2 km in Thailand and 18 km in Malaysia) to create an alternative rubber product transport route via Kuantan Port to the PRC (Kuantan Port has been designated as the BRI Port connecting to the PRC).

(iii) Stimulating the establishment of Narathiwat SEZ to promote and attract investors in processed rubber, rubber wood, and halal food industries that can create jobs and generate incomes in EC6.

(iv) Connecting the new Sadao border crossing with new Padang Besar border crossing to increase capacity for large-scale movement of passengers and cargoes.

(v)   Utilizing railway transportation at Padang Besa/Padang Besar BCP and establishing a large customs-controlled area to facilitate container shipments to Penang Port.

Halal Food

Overview. Halal products and services is an important area of cooperation in IMT-GT because of the subregion's large Muslim population and its huge potential to supply a huge global demand for halal products. There are approximately 1.9 billion Muslims globally, of which 60% (1.14 million) live in Asia, with a concentrations in Southeast Asia and the Middle East. The Muslim population is projected to increase by 35%, reaching 2.2 billion by 2030.[74] In IMT-GT, the Muslim population is estimated at 248 million or 13% of the global Muslim population.

Strong complementarities among the IMT-GT provinces and states augur well for the development of the halal industry in the subregion. Indonesia and Thailand have a rich agricultural base that can supply the raw materials for halal food and beverage. Malaysia has developed a halal ecosystem and a strong halal brand due to highly developed standards and an advanced certification process, while Thailand has made noteworthy progress in halal science and technology. Indonesia has also taken steps to implement a certification system consistent with international standards supported by halal science.[75] The IMT-GT Blueprint 2017–2021 advocates member countries to build on one another's strengths to tap into the burgeoning halal markets through sharing of knowledge, developing cross-border value chains, and development of standards and certification for halal.

From an economic corridor perspective, the linkages between Southern Thailand and northern Malaysia are quite well-developed and the transport networks that link both countries can be considered as a logistics corridor supporting the value chains including halal. Logistics plays a key role in protecting the halal integrity of halal food through proper transportation, storage, and handling along the supply chain until it reaches its destination. Trade facilitation at the borders must be improved to be responsive to the requirements for halal logistics to avoid contamination in transporting the goods and multiple loading and unloading of goods.

The lack of halal logistics service providers (LSPs) is one of the key challenges faced by halal enterprises and is one area where closer collaboration would be needed. The areas of collaboration may include certification standards for LSPs, exchange of information about the causes of contamination and practices to avoid, and capacity development to increase the pool of experts in the region for halal logistics. The need for halal-dedicated infrastructure such as warehouses, storage units, and transport fleets must also be addressed. These infrastructure units will require substantial investments which LSPs, mostly SMEs, may not be able to afford.

It may also increase logistics cost which could ultimately impinge on the competitiveness of the halal product. IMT-GT countries have taken steps to motivate logistics companies to adopt halal practices.[76] Malaysia has taken a leadership role in this area and has put in place two locally developed standards that are used by halal-certified LSPs.[77] However, as LSPs move across the economic corridors along the value chain, standards for LSP certification would need to be aligned to avoid extended lead times, long and unreliable transit time, multiple consolidations, multiple freight modes and cost options. Trade facilitation initiatives in the IMT-GT should incorporate the specific requirements of halal logistics to motivate LSPs to adapt halal practices.

---

[74] Pew Research Center's Forum on Religion & Public Life. Accessed 28 September 2020.

[75] IMT-GT Implementation Blueprint 2012–2016.

[76] Suhaiza Zailani, Mohammad Iranmanesh, Azmin Azliza Aziz, and Kanagi Kanapathy. 2017. Halal Logistics Opportunities and Challenges. *Journal of Islamic Marketing*. 8(1). pp. 127–139.

[77] MS 1900:2014 and the MS 2400:2010. The MS 1900:2014," Quality management-system-requirements from the Islamic perspective" is an extension of ISO 9001. The MS 2400:2010 "Halalan-Toyyiban Assurance Pipeline Standard covers transportation, warehousing and retail.

Within the IMT-GT countries, Thailand in particular has a logistical advantage over neighboring countries because of shared borders with the Lao PDR, Cambodia, Malaysia, Myanmar, and the PRC provinces. Halal products can be shipped from the Gulf of Thailand and the Andaman Sea to the Middle East and Europe. For exports of halal products to Indonesia, Thailand exporters will have to go through Penang Port and Pakbara Port in the Andaman Sea coast in Satun when it is developed. Pakbara Port, as well as the planned second Songkhla deep-seaport in the Andaman Sea coast are envisaged to become a major gateway for imports and exports between Thailand and BIMSTEC countries (including India) and the Middle East.

Indonesia needs to step up with its halal certification standards. Despite Sumatera's abundant agricultural resources to supply the inputs for halal processing, its halal export is relatively small because the country's halal product certification is still not widely recognized in the global market

Halal food supply chain. The production of halal food starts from the ordering of raw materials from suppliers who can present evidence of compliance with safety standards and certifications with halal marks and traceability. These include documents certifying that the storage and transport of the raw materials have not been contaminated with non-halal elements. The process of certification is important in the production of halal food from the production, storage, transport, processing, packaging, and distribution stages to ensure safety for consumers and product quality (Figure 16).

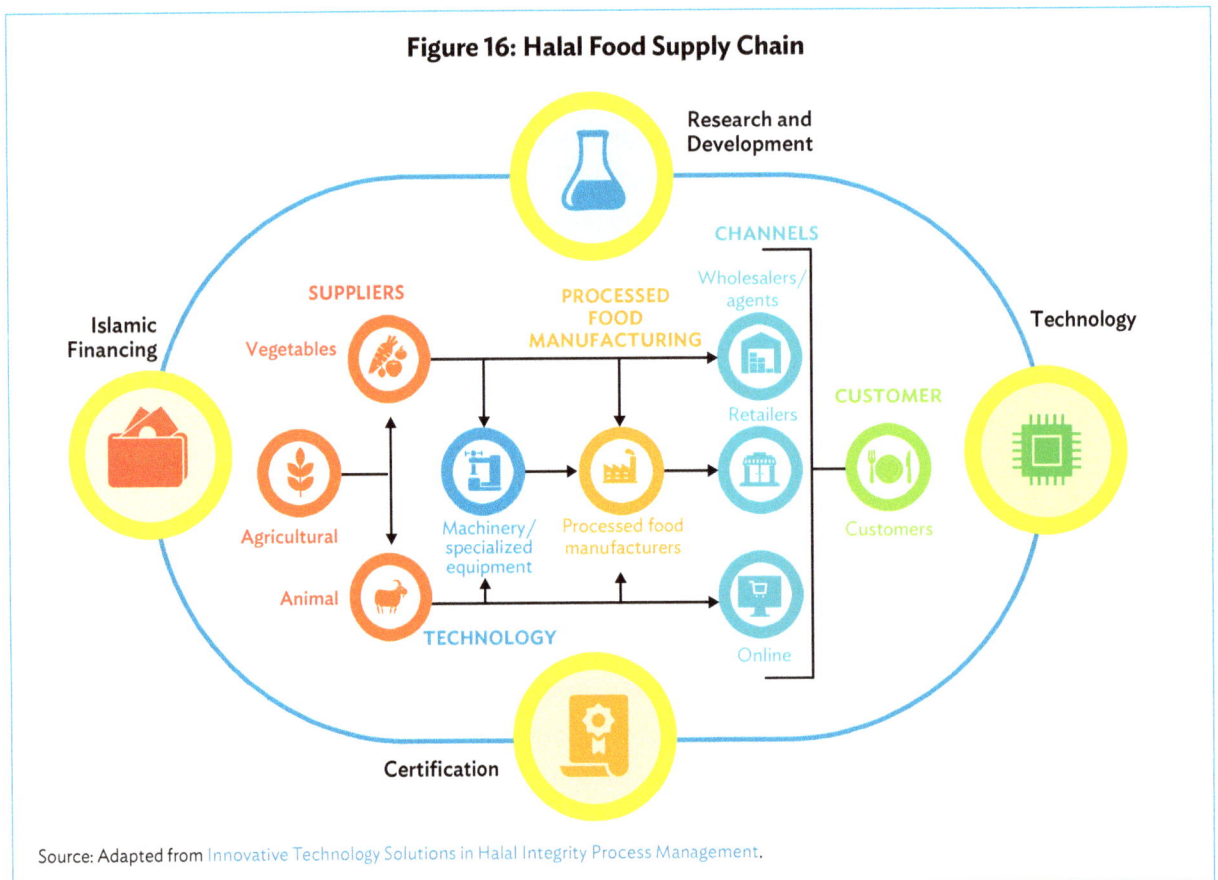

Figure 16: Halal Food Supply Chain

Source: Adapted from Innovative Technology Solutions in Halal Integrity Process Management.

The halal market is not limited to food items alone; it covers a wide range of products including pharmaceuticals, cosmetics, fashion, and other non-consumables. It also covers services such as health care, tourism, finance, logistics, branding, and marketing. The following section describes the value chain for halal food and beverages focusing on fisheries and horticulture subsectors as inputs to the finished halal product.

Indonesia

The Indonesia Islamic Economic Masterplan 2019–2024 focuses on six halal-related industries, namely (i) halal food and beverages, (ii) halal tourism, (iii) Muslim fashion, (iv) halal media and recreation, (v) halal pharmaceutical and cosmetics, and (vi) renewable energy. In terms of the value chain, the halal food and beverage industry is important because it draws on the agriculture sector for the supply of raw materials in the manufacture of the final products that cater to a wide range of consumer needs.[78]

Indonesia as a supplier of agricultural products. Sumatera plays a major role in the halal food value chain as a major producer of capture fisheries and horticulture products. In 2017, Sumatera's share of national production of these commodities were 30.3% for capture fisheries, 19.8% for vegetables, and 27.5% for fruits. Within Sumatera, North Sumatera (EC1) was the largest producer of capture fisheries (37.2%) and vegetables (31.2%), while Lampung (EC3) was the largest producer of fruits (44.2%). Food crops and livestock are also important subsectors in the halal food and beverage industry, but Sumatera's production of these commodities is far behind Java.

Certification process. Halal food and beverages undergo an official halal certification process to obtain a halal logo that signifies that the product is permissible to be consumed by Muslims. For non-Muslims, the logo can represent a symbol of cleanliness, quality, purity, and security. The certifying authority is the Organizing Agency for Halal Product Assurance (*Badan Penyelenggara Jaminan Produk Halal* [BPJPH]) under the Ministry of Religious Affairs. The agency conducts inspection through all stages of the value chain from purchasing materials, receiving, storage, processing, packaging, and distribution. The number of products getting the halal certification has been increasing from year to year from about 20,000 in 2012 to about 53,000 l in 2017.[79]

The number of food and beverage factories in Sumatera recorded by the Ministry of Industry is only about 10% of the factories in Indonesia. This number is small relative to the large volume of agricultural materials produced in Sumatera, implying a significant room for expanding halal food production especially in North Sumatera (EC1), Lampung (proposed for EC3), Riau and West Sumatera (extended EC4), and South Sumatera (proposed EC6).

Halal market. As the country with the biggest Muslim population in the world, Indonesia is also the biggest halal food market. Based on the State of Islamic Economy Report 2018/2019, Indonesia recorded the highest halal food expenditure in 2017 amounting to $170 billion or 13.04% of total global halal food market spending ($1,303 billion). However, in terms of halal food development, including for export, Indonesia ranked only in the 11th position together with Saudi Arabia, trailing behind the United Arab Emirates and Malaysia in the first and second place, respectively.[80] Indonesia's weak standing may be accounted for by the fact that the country's

---

[78]   Indonesian Ministry of National Development Planning. 2018. *Indonesia Islamic Economic Masterplan 2019–2024.* Jakarta: Indonesian Ministry of National Development Planning. p. 51.

[79]   Lembaga Pengkajian Pangan, Obat-obatan, dan Kosmetika Majelis Ulama Indonesia (LPPOM MUI), quoted from Indonesia Islamic Economi Masterplan 2019–2024.

[80]   Dubai International Financial Centre, Thomson Reuters, & DinarStandard. 2018. State of the Islamic Economy Report 2018/19.

halal product certification is still not widely recognized in the global market.[81] Based on the data from LPPOM-MUI, Indonesia was the fourth largest food importing country in the world in 2017.

Trade. Exports of fisheries and livestock-related products from Sumatera were relatively small compared to Indonesia's total export. For fisheries, there were only two ports in Sumatera that recorded cumulative significant values of around 12.3% in 2017; these are Belawan Port in North Sumatera (8.2%), and Panjang Port in Lampung (4.1%). Both ports were far behind ports in Java, especially Tanjung Perak in East Java (39.2%) and Tanjung Priok in Jakarta (32.6%) (Table 47). Moreover, Sumatera's contribution to the national export was smaller than its contribution to the national production of this subsector (30.3%), signifying that a significant share of production was consumed in the domestic market. Exports of raw materials (unprocessed product exports) were also significantly higher (77%) than processed or downstream products at 23%. This implies that the halal value chain in Sumatera could be expanded extensively especially in North Sumatera and Lampung.

Table 47: Ports of Loading for Exports of Fisheries and Fruits and Vegetables, 2017
(Share of total exports of the commodity)

Port	Fisheries (%)	Port	Fruits and Vegetables* (%)
Sumatera	**23.6**	**Sumatera**	**64.7**
Belawan	8.2	Belawan	19.6
Panjang	4.2	Panjang	19.1
Tanjung Balai Asahan	0.1	Jambi	6.5
Batu Ampar (Batam)	0.04	Sungai Guntung, Riau	3.2
Other ports with less than 0.04% share each	11.1	Other ports with less than 1% share each	16.3
Java	**76.4**	**Java**	**35.3**
Tanjung Perak	39.2	Tanjung Perak	18.7
Tanjung Priok	32.6	Tanjung Priok	14.9
Tanjung Emas	4.6	Tanjung Emas	1.7
Total Indonesia	**100**		**100**

* Share to total exports of the commodities in all ports.
Source: BPS-Statistics Indonesia, 2020.

For vegetables and fruits, Sumatera played an important role as the biggest contributor to Indonesia's total exports in these subsectors (around 65%) in 2017. Upstream products however dominated exports with a 78% share to total exports, compared to only 22% in the downstream category. The major ports of loading are Belawan Port in North Sumatera and Panjang Port in Lampung, each with a share of 19% each to total exports, higher than the share of ports in Java. There is scope for further development of the downstream value chain of halal food from vegetables and fruits, especially in North Sumatera (EC1), Lampung, and Jambi (EC3), as well as Riau (EC4).

As for trade with Malaysia, Sumatera generated a trade deficit in meat and fish preparations, and a slight surplus in vegetables and fruit preparations in 2017. For Thailand, exports of meat and fish preparations far exceeded imports; however, for vegetable and fruits preparations, imports were significantly higher (Table 48).

---

[81] Indonesian Ministry of National Development Planning. 2018. *Indonesia Islamic Economic Masterplan 2019–2024*. Jakarta: Indonesian Ministry of National Development Planning. p. 59.

**Table 48: Indonesia's Trade with Malaysia and Thailand on Meat and Fish Preparations
and Vegetables and Fruits, 2017** ($ million)

Port of Loading	Meat and Fish Preparations (HS16)*				Vegetables and Fruits Preparations (HS 20)**			
	Malaysia		Thailand		Malaysia		Thailand	
	Export	Import	Export	Import	Export	Import	Export	Import
Panjang	–	–	–	1.4	433.5	–	–	1.5
Belawan	866.4	21.1	15,058.7	–	995.1	607.4	42.1	2,690.7
Sungai Guntung	–	–	–	–	80.0	–	–	–
Batu Ampar	–	678.8	–	28.9	1.5	465.5	–	192.0
Sekupang	–	5,406.3	–	32.5	–	41.9	–	358.0
Total	**866.4**	**6,106.1**	**15,058.7**	**62.7**	**1,510.1**	**1,114.7**	**42.1**	**3,242.2**

– = not available, HS = Harmonized System.
Notes:
Totals may not sum precisely because of rounding
*HS code 16: Preparations of meat, of fish or of crustaceans, mollusks, or other aquatic invertebrates.
**HS code 20: Preparations of vegetables, fruit, nuts, or other parts of plants.
Source: BPS-Statistics Indonesia, 2020.

Malaysia

Accreditation process. Malaysia's strategic location has made the country an ideal halal investment destination. Malaysia has 14 strategic locations of Halal Malaysia (HALMAS) industrial parks designated by the Halal Development Corporation (HDC) encompassing 200,000 acres of land for investors and industry players to tap into the growing opportunities for halal. Malaysia's concept of a halal industrial park is a community of manufacturing and service businesses located on a common property with the aim of preserving the integrity of halal products. The HALMAS is an accreditation given to halal park operators that meet the requirements stipulated under the HDC-designated halal park development. A HALMAS status entitles industry players and investors to enjoy incentives facilitated by HDC. The development of halal products has been further stimulated by the designation of halal hubs in each state in Malaysia.[82]

Halal food industry. Driven by halal product global demand, Malaysia is actively promoting investment in the halal food and beverages sector.[83] The vegetable and animal oils, fats and food processing industry, and the beverage industry are discussed to illustrate the halal food supply chain in Malaysia.[84]

Input suppliers for the food and beverage industry include (i) fruit crops, (ii) cash crops, (iii) industrial crops, (iv) rice, and (v) CPO sectors. These types of crops are grown by individual private farmers, smallholders, and estates. Crops are processed by local food processing factories into vegetable and animal oils and fats, and food and beverages products. Factories apply for halal certification and status from the government to be recognized as halal establishments.

[82] Emi Normalina Omar and Harlina Suzana Jaafar. 2011. Halal Supply Chain in the Food Industry - A Conceptual Model. Paper presented at IEEE Symposium on Business, Engineering and Industrial Applications (ISBEIA), Langkawi, Malaysia, September.

[83] Halal Development Corporation Berhad. https://www.hdcglobal.com/promoted-sectors/.

[84] Most of the statistics published on the halal food industry are at the national level. Information published according to the breakdown by state are also available, however, only at the production stage. The latest statistics for the halal food industry published by the Department of Statistics Malaysia was in 2016; Economic Census 2016; *Halal Statistics*. Accordingly, data from 2015 was used to describe the halal food supply chain.

In 2015, there were 2,151 halal-certified establishments, 84% (1,800) of which are located in EC states (Table 49). Of these 2,151 establishments, 115 are in the vegetable, animal oils and fats, and food processing industry with output valued at $20 billion, and 1,737 are in the beverage industry with halal output valued at $13 billion. Some halal establishments operate in halal parks operated by the state government, the private sector and other government agencies.

Table 49: Halal Establishments in the Manufacturing Sector based on Halal Certification, 2015

Economic Corridor	State	Establishments
EC1	Penang	230
	Kedah	126
	Perlis	6
EC2	Perak	233
	Selangor	549
EC4	Melaka	94
	Johor	398
EC6	Kelantan	64
	Terengganu	35
	Pahang	65
All ECs		**1,800**
	Sabah	83
	Sarawak	85
	Negeri Sembilan	78
Non-ECs		246
	FT Kuala Lumpur	102
	FT Labuan	3
Malaysia		**2,151**

EC = economic corridor, FT=federal territory.
Source: Department of Statistics. 2016. *Economic Census 2016:* Halal Statistic Malaysia.

Distribution. Halal food products are distributed to a network of wholesalers and retailers in the local market, as well as exporters. The value of the country's halal exports in 2015 was $10 billion or 5% of the country's total exports. Among Indonesia's top 10 export markets, the countries with the largest share of halal food exports were the Philippines (12.5%), the US (9.4%), the Netherlands (6.2%), and Australia (6.0%). The share of halal exports to Thailand and Indonesia is 4.2% and 3.2%, respectively (Table 50). The main halal products exported to these markets are (i) food products, (ii) beverages, (iii) processed animals or vegetable oils and fats, and (iv) wax of animal or vegetable origin.

**Table 50: Malaysia Halal Product Exports by Destination, Ranked According to
Share of Halal Exports, 2015**

	Total Export Value ($ million)	Halal Export Value ($ million)	Halal Export Share (%)
Total Exports	**194,339**	**9,860**	**5**
Export destinations			
Philippines	3,294	410	12.5
US	7,276	680	9.4
Netherlands, The	5,849	360	6.2
Australia	7,020	420	6.0
PRC	25,384	1,192	4.7
Thailand	**11,097**	**461**	**4.2**
Singapore	27,097	979	3.6
Indonesia	**18,171**	**613**	**3.4**
Japan	18,171	553	3.0
India	7,915	345	4.4

PRC = People's Republic of China, US = United States.
Source: Department of Statistics Malaysia. 2016. Economic Census 2016: Halal Statistic Malaysia. Putrajaya: DOS Malaysia.

The contribution of the production and trading of halal products is still small in Malaysia, but it has great potential at the regional and global levels. Under the IMT–GT Vision 2036 blueprint, halal products are one of the seven strategic pillars and key focus areas.[85] Accordingly, the Halal Corridor needs to be developed by creating a regional chain among halal parks in Malaysia, Indonesia, and Thailand.

Thailand

Thailand's comparative advantage in food production and exports is driven by the abundance of raw food materials and technological advances in food production which is recognized in the world market. Thailand is the world's leading exporter of several agricultural products that include fishery (shrimps and fish), chicken, rice, and canned pineapples. Thailand is the world's largest exporter of shrimps and the third largest exporter of fish and seafood, following the PRC and Norway.

Halal industry. The halal industry is being promoted in the southern border provinces of Pattani, Yala, Narathiwat, Satun, and Songkhla situated in EC1, EC2, and EC6. The population in these provinces, especially those living near the borders, are converts to Islam and adhere to strict Islamic practices that are different from other areas in the country. These states have a combined population of approximately 3.6 million, of which 62% are Muslims. The ranking of provinces according to the size of their Muslim populations is: Narathiwat, 86%; Pattani, 81%; Yala, 77%; Satun, 74%; and Songkhla 33% of the total population of the province.[86] The government has adopted a policy to develop these areas as the center of production and export of halal food in Thailand. At present, it is in the process of establishing the Halal Food Industrial Estate in Pattani. Many provinces in the south are already engaged in raw materials production for halal food such as marine animals and seafood, and agricultural products including livestock such as goat, sheep, cow, and buffalo.

---

[85]   CIMT. 2017. IMT-GT Vision 2036. CIMT: Putrajaya

[86]   The Halal Science Center. 2019. Chulalongkorn University.

Around 370 halal food business establishments in the southern border provinces and 813 products are registered for the certification of halal standards at the Halal Affairs, Provincial Islamic Council.[87]

As Thailand is not a Muslim country, the reliability of Thailand's halal food certification standards affects the perception of Muslim consumers compared to Muslim halal food exporters such as Malaysia and Indonesia. As a result, Malaysia's halal food certification labels receive more confidence and recognition than Thailand's halal product certification labels. Confidence in the integrity of halal food is a very important consideration in the trading of halal food. It is important for non-Muslim farm operators to understand this relationship and adopt good practices that will instill confidence and trust on the part of their Muslim trade partners.[88]

Certification standards. The standards for certifying the quality of halal food in terms of production, inspection procedures, transportation, and logistics are important areas of focus in further developing the industry. These standards are especially important for halal food exports to acquire a quality brand aligned with international standards that will create confidence and recognition of Thailand's halal food certification labels in the world market. In 2017, there were 4,683 halal-certified companies by the Central Islamic Council of Thailand, representing an increase of 114% compared to 2,188 companies in 1999. Ninety percent of these companies were involved in food production, restaurants, slaughterhouses, and imports of raw materials and halal finished products. Halal certification and labels create consumer confidence in product quality and integrity. This is particularly important for upstream livestock products that must also comply with Good Agricultural Practice for Farm Animals.

Export markets. Thailand's export of halal food is still small (less than 1%) compared to the total value of its food export. The major export markets include members of the Association of Southeast Asian Nations (ASEAN) and the Middle East. The ASEAN member states with large Muslim populations are Indonesia, Malaysia, Singapore, and Brunei Darussalam. Indonesia, the country with the largest Muslim population in the world (200 million or 84% of total population), is the largest halal consumer and has a growing middle class of 20 million with increasing purchasing power. However, Indonesia does not produce sufficient food to meet domestic demand and has resorted to importing meat, livestock, and milk. Thailand's halal food exports are projected to rise as exporters avail themselves of the tax and tariff incentives under the ASEAN Free Trade Area. The development and diversification of Thailand's halal industry to respond to changing market demand and consumer preferences can expand export markets, ramp up export income, and realize its strategy of becoming the Kitchen of the World.

Thailand's main export products are natural halal food (upstream products) such as rice, sugar, tapioca flour, processed seafood, canned fruits and vegetables, fresh and processed chicken, etc. Thailand is ranked the 10th largest halal food exporter to Muslim countries with exports valued at approximately $6,000 million or 3.7% of the total value of food trade to Muslim countries, and growing at 8% over the past 5 years. Other leading halal food exported to Muslim markets are India, with the global share of 9.4%, followed by Brazil (8.3%), the US (6.7%), the Russia Federation (5.5%), and the PRC (4.8%). All these major exporters are non-Muslim countries.

---

[87]   I. Darakai, A. Yusoh, K. Botlum, and Y. Dorlee. 2013. *The Halal Food Business Investment in Southern Border Province of Thailand A Case Study: Pattani, Yala, and Narathiwat Provinces*. Phatthalung.

[88]   Chaiwat Wattanachan. 2012. Halal Production and Processing Process.

Findings and Recommendations

Indonesia

The Government of Indonesia has been vigorously developing halal industries, especially in the last 2 years. In support of this effort, some measures that can be considered in relation to economic corridor development are as follows:

(i)   Some prominent ports along the IMT-GT economic corridors could be appointed as halal product gateways, both for export and import. This involves customizing some facilities to fulfill the Halal Logistics Standards for warehouses, distribution–transportation, and terminals.

(ii) North Sumatera, West Sumatera, and Aceh are the main producers of fish, vegetables, and fruits in Sumatera, while the designated halal industrial zones are in Bintan and Batam in Riau Islands. Port-to-port connections between these areas should be developed and strengthened to facilitate the movement of goods between ports of origin and destination ports. Designated ports should be equipped to comply with the Halal Logistics Standard.

(iii) EC6 has the potential to become a center for the downstream halal industry since there will be two designated halal industrial zones in Riau Islands. This potential could be strengthened by combining various subsectors of the halal industry such as food, modest fashion, and Muslim-friendly travel, which are the leading sectors along the proposed EC6 routes. Riau Islands has the third biggest tourist arrivals in Indonesia, after Bali and Jakarta.

Malaysia

ECs 1, 2, 4, and 6 have a comparative advantage in the halal food industry, with the state of Selangor having the highest number of halal establishments in the peninsula. All states in the ECs have halal parks developed mostly by state governments or federal-owned agencies. Manufacturers involved in the halal food industry or halal services require a certificate from the Department of Islamic Development Malaysia (JAKIM) to operate in the halal parks or industrial estates.

Malaysia has a relatively developed Halal ecosystem and a strong halal brand. Nevertheless, there is weak integrated halal supply chain between businesses from input suppliers, manufacturers, logistics providers, wholesalers, and retailers. This is reflected by the low number of participating halal establishments in the food value chain.

Apart from halal parks, the government should provide fiscal and nonfiscal incentives to firms to increase the number of halal establishments at various levels of the value chain. The halal industry has the potential to improve supply chain integration from upstream to downstream activities.

As with the palm oil and rubber value chains, transport links that enhance the efficiency of logistics services are important. These include last mile connectivity to both hinterlands and gateways, connectivity from industrial estates to seaports, and railway spur lines that link ports to economic centers. Inland ports also need to be enhanced to allow many value chain functions to take place further inland to benefit both producers and consumers.

The states of Kelantan, Terengganu, and Pahang are among the major producers of halal food products. The ECRL route from Kota Bharu to Port Klang and the East Coast Highway from Tumpat to Kuala Lumpur will develop a road–rail–ports intermodal link particularly to Kemaman Port and Kuantan Port. Manufacturers in the EC6 can also use this overland route as a land bridge to export their products by using ports on the west coast, such as Port Klang and Tanjung Bruas Port.

One of the concerns raised in the IMT-GT IB 2017–2021 is the gap in halal certification practices between the IMT-GT countries. Fully aware of this problem, the responsible agencies—JAKIM, the Central Islamic Council of Thailand, and the Indonesian Council of Ulama (MUI)—are currently coordinating the certification practices through the IMT-GT Working Group on Halal Products for the IMT's Halal Logo to be recognized and well-accepted globally. This will help the IMT expand its regional and global trade of halal products.

Thailand

Thailand has a great opportunity to become a supplier and producer of halal products. With the new EC6, it will be possible to have a more integrated halal food cross-border value chain between Thailand and Malaysia. To support further integration of the value chain in Thailand and Malaysia, the following spatial connectivity improvements would be needed:

(i)   Construction of the bridge over Kolok River at Tak Bai–Pengkalan Kubur connecting Tak Bai and cities in Kelantan State; the bridge will facilitate the movement of Malaysian visitors to Pattani, Narathiwat, and Songkhla to purchase halal food, and will also establish an alternative export channel to Malaysia and Indonesia;

(ii) Establishing the Narathiwat SEZ can help promote and attract investments in processed halal food industries and create a better link between raw materials supply and processing facilities; and

(iii) Supporting the Southern Border Provinces Administrative Center's development of the halal logistics system in the southern border provinces can help them prepare to cope with economic expansion of the Deep South.

At the subregional level, Indonesia, Malaysia, and Thailand are collaborating to harmonize halal standards to come up with a unified IMT-GT halal brand that will be recognized globally. This is one of the priority initiatives under IMT-GT IB 2017–2021 under the IMT-GT Working Group on halal products and services.

ADDRESSING GAPS IN INSTITUTIONAL MECHANISMS FOR ECONOMIC CORRIDOR DEVELOPMENT

National Level Mechanisms

There is no formal coordination mechanism for economic corridor development in IMT-GT at the subregional level. However, the existing IMT-GT institutional framework includes mechanisms for national and provincial or state level coordination where the locational aspects of sectoral interventions are considered. These mechanisms vary in each country, influenced by such factors as political structures and processes, degree of centralization and decentralization, interorganizational relationships, and availability of resources, among others.

At the national level, the national secretariats serve as the focal agency and and intermediary between ministers and senior officials at the policy level, and line agencies and provinces and states at the operational level. They serve as a conduit of information for all stakeholders on IMT-GT meeting outcomes at various levels, the status of programs and projects, program and project level concerns, and the schedule of meetings and events. More importantly, they perform a crucial advisory role to the senior officials and ministers on matters of strategy for the IMT-GT. The national secretariats are based in the ministries responsible for development planning at the capitals. At the subregional level, they work closely with the Centre for IMT-GT Subregional Cooperation (CIMT) as the subregional secretariat.

Compared to sectoral coordination involving line ministries, which is relatively well-established, coordination of provinces and states presents additional challenges on account of policy domains at different spatial levels (national vs. local) interfacing with sectoral policies. There are also specialized bodies responsible for area development programs such as the Northern Corridor Implementing Agency (NCIA) and ECERDC in Malaysia and the Southern Border Provinces Administrative Center in Thailand. Physical distance can also affect the effectiveness of coordination when provincial officials have to travel to the capitals for meetings organized by the national secretariats although this has been largely mitigated now with the more prevalent use of information and communication technology (ICT).

Indonesia

In Indonesia, the coordination among the leaders/officials of the 10 provinces in Sumatera is through the Sumatera Governors' Forum held annually. The forum provides the venue for the provincial leaders to articulate their views, concerns, and project proposals to the national secretariat based at the Coordinating Ministry for Economic Affairs. The forum meetings are usually held in preparation for meetings of the IMT-GT ministers and the Chief Ministers and Governors Forum (CMGF). At times, the forum's meetings are held in conjunction with other meetings organized by the national secretariat or working groups to maximize the time and minimize the cost of travel to Jakarta.

Consistent with IMT-GT's private sector-led approach, the Joint Business Council (JBC)–Indonesia has been actively involved in providing inputs to the IMT-GT priority sectors and areas. In terms of economic corridor development, it helps to identify key commodities with growth potentials, the strategic location for economic centers, and opportunities for business cooperation. The JBC has taken the view that IMT-GT's focus on infrastructure should be accompanied by special privileges for businesses operating in the IMT-GT area to encourage more investments. The IMT-GT has agreed to take measures to provide JBC with a legal status to strengthen the organization as a regional coordinating body, enhance its policy advocacy role, and enable it to raise funds independently and enter into formal contracts.

There is no special forum for discussing IMT-GT economic corridors as a separate subject, although economic corridors as a topic could be touched upon in regular meetings organized by the national secretariat. There are only four provinces in Sumatera that are part of existing economic corridors—Aceh, North Sumatera, Riau, and South Sumatera—and each one is participating in a different corridor. This has limited the scope of discussions that are usually focused on specific projects rather than on the wider perspective of cross-border spatial strategies. The reconfiguration of the five existing ECs, and the proposed route for EC6 include all the provinces in Sumatera. Thus, it is envisaged that more strategic and holistic discussions can take place, that could bring about better coordinated economic corridor initiatives within Sumatera.

Bilateral meetings of local governments with counterpart provinces in other countries have been found to be practical and productive although this does not take place regularly and is initiated by the local governments on a case-by-case basis. For instance, the Provincial Governor of Songkhla visited Medan in September 2019 to discuss the possibility of direct flights from Medan to Hat Yai as an initiative under EC1. To improve coordination at the provincial level, the CMGF has planned the establishment of its own secretariat in Indonesia. Among others, the secretariat would ensure that provincial and national programs and projects are aligned and that a budget allocation can be secured to have them implemented.

Malaysia

Malaysia's approach to national economic corridor development is guided by the National Physical Plan (NPP) as the overarching spatial framework for the country. Plan Malaysia provides an important link which ensures that development planning at the state level is in line with the NPP. There are specialized regional bodies responsible for spatial planning of national economic corridors in the northern, eastern, and southern states. These agencies are the NCIA, ECERDC, and the Iskandar Regional Development Authority. The NPP and the specialized regional bodies ensure that the approach to national economic corridor development is coherent and aligned at both the federal and state levels.

The specialized bodies take into account the relevant developments in neighboring countries, including in the IMT-GT, in planning and implementing their strategies, programs, and projects. This notwithstanding, an occasional forum can be organized to promote greater awareness of developments in IMT-GT economic corridors. This forum can be held once a year before the CMGF to sensitize the chief ministers on the developments in the IMT-GT. Apart from the chief ministers, representatives from specialized bodies, as well as JBC representatives should be invited to this forum to be organized by the national secretariat.

The IMT-GT national secretariat based at the Economic Planning Unit, Regional Development Division, performs the role of coordinating all stakeholders involved in IMT-GT initiatives at the federal and state levels as well as with line ministries specialized regional development bodies[89] and the private sector. The existing mechanism follows both a bottom–up and top–down approach between the federal, state, and line ministries. Relevant agencies and private stakeholders are invited to provide inputs on IMT-GT initiatives and projects that include those related to economic corridor development. The communications flow is a two-way process between the different stakeholders and the national secretariat. The national secretariat serves as the main intermediary among these various stakeholders in terms of providing information on programs and projects as well as on the outcomes of IMT-GT meetings.

---

[89] These are (i) the NCIA, (ii) ECERDC, and (iii) the Iskandar Regional Development Authority.

The national secretariat's capacity for coordinating regional cooperation programs could be further enhanced. At present, the national secretariat's staff is limited considering its wide portfolio of subregional programs, namely, the IMT-GT, Brunei Darussalam–Indonesia–Malaysia–Philippines East ASEAN Growth Area, Malaysia–Thailand Joint Development Strategy for Border Areas, and the Malaysia–Singapore Joint Ministerial Committee for Iskandar Malaysia. Additional resources are required for the national secretariat to efficiently and effectively manage the various regional cooperation programs in their portfolio.

Thailand

In Thailand, the coordination at the provincial level for IMT-GT activities is led by CMGF Thailand, utilizing staff from Prince Songkla University, which is funded by the Ministry of Interior (MOI). The agencies involved in this mechanism include the NESDC (as national secretariat), the IMT-GT JBC, and the members of the working groups on transport and ICT, trade and investment, and tourism. The provinces are made aware of economic corridor strategies, programs, and projects endorsed by IMT-GT senior officials and ministers, as well as IMT-GT meeting outcomes.

A Cabinet resolution has authorized the NESDC, which functions as the national secretariat, to monitor the progress of cooperation in JBC, the CMGF, and the working groups. As national secretariat, the NESDC organizes coordination meetings with relevant stakeholders to solicit their inputs that could guide Thailand's participation in IMT-GT. The line of communications is from the provinces to NESDC, the MOI, and CMGF Thailand, which disseminates the information to all 14 participating IMT-GT provinces. Local governments are involved in the planning and implementation of IMT-GT economic corridor projects, which CMGF Thailand coordinates and monitors.

The spatial development strategy in Thailand draws from regional development strategies. The present development strategy for Southern Thailand emphasizes the role of economic corridor development focusing on the establishment of SEZs such as that being developed in Ranong–Chumphon–Surat Thani. The SEC has recently been designated as a new area for SEZ development to complement SEZs in Sadao and Narathiwat. The SEC strategy guides Thailand's participation in IMT-GT economic corridor development initiatives.

Currently, Thailand is using Motorway-Rail Map to guide development planning for the entire country. Prior to this, only regional development plans have been utilized. The MOI has divided the southern provinces into three clusters, namely (i) Andaman provinces cluster from Ranong to Satun; (ii) Gulf of Thailand cluster from Chumphon to Songkhla; and (iii) the three southernmost provinces cluster of Pattani, Yala, and Narathiwat. Each cluster is headed by the most senior governor with provincial committees chaired by other governors. The head or chair of business organizations are invited to attend the cluster meetings which are frequently arranged. Line ministries adhere to plans by the MOI since their provincial units are attached to the provincial governor's office.

Subregional Mechanisms

Within the IMT-GT subregional institutional framework (Figure 17), the CMGF is the platform for representing the interests of the provinces and states. It reports directly to the IMT-GT ministers and, working closely with the senior officials, provides policy inputs at the local government level for the effective implementation of the 5-year implementation blueprints to realize Vision 2036. It creates awareness among local governments about the opportunities generated from cooperation among the IMT-GT provinces and states and facilitates project implementation at the local level. CMGF's meetings are held in conjunction with the annual meeting of the IMT-GT ministers where updates on provincial developments and projects, as well as business opportunities are presented. While the CMGF has been a useful venue for presenting development opportunities in IMT-GT provinces, it has not functioned as a mechanism for coordinating the strategies for economic corridor development at the IMT-GT level.

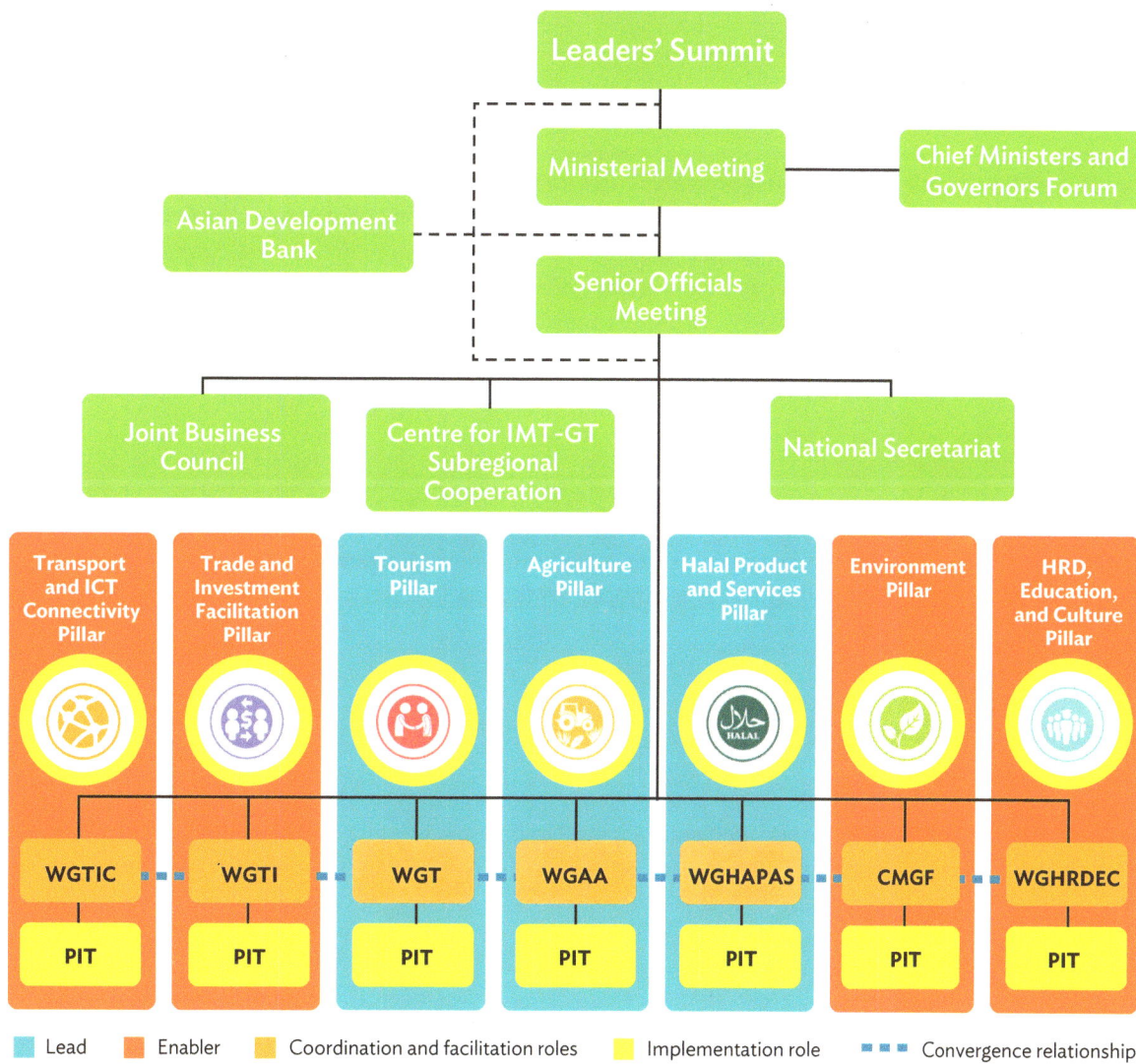

Figure 17: IMT-GT Institutional Coordination Mechanism Structure

CIMT = Centre for IMT-GT Subregional Cooperation; CMGF = Chief Ministers and Governors Forum; HRD = human resource development; ICT = information and communication technology; IMT-GT = Indonesia–Malaysia–Thailand Growth Triangle; PIT = Project Implementation Team; WGAA = Working Group on Agriculture and Agrobased Industry; WGHAPAS = Working Group on Halal Products and Services; WGHRDEC = Working Group on Human Resource Development, Education, and Culture; WGT = Working Group on Tourism; WGTI = Working Group on Trade and Investment; WGTIC = Working Group on Transport and Information and Communication Technology Connectivity.
Source: CIMT (2016). IMT-GT IB 2017-2021. Putrajaya: CIMT.

The CIMT, as subregional secretariat, provides overall support to the IMT-GT activities including those involving economic corridors. CIMT's roles include (i) facilitating the consultation processes among IMT-GT institutions and providing institutional support to various initiatives; (ii) facilitating the planning, development, and implementation of priority projects; (iii) enhancing and establishing external relations with development partners; and (iv) developing databases on IMT-GT activities and disseminating information. CIMT's functions are basically project-focused and support all stages of the project cycle.

Sector working groups develop strategies, programs, and projects to operationalize the strategic thrusts of the IMT-GT. These include priority connectivity projects in the economic corridors as well as sector initiatives to promote economic growth in IMT-GT areas. Working group membership includes representatives and relevant stakeholders in the line ministries, provinces and states, and the private sector as appropriate. The working groups are involved in the different stages of the project cycle, working closely with the CIMT.

The JBC is the official voice of the private sector in the IMT-GT subregion. Its role includes (i) fostering closer relationships among business and business organizations in IMT-GT subregion; (ii) advocating policies, programs, and projects supportive of increasing private sector participation in the development of the region; (iii) identifying IMT-GT commercial projects and key IMT-GT infrastructure requirements; and (iv) promoting linkages with the private sector bodies outside the subregion. The council is invited to participate in meetings of working groups, senior officials, ministers, and the national secretariats to give their views and perspectives on various initiatives. They can also propose, and participate in, IMT-GT projects.

The IMT-GT Ministerial Meeting is the oversight body responsible for developing the strategic thrusts of the program as well as the implementation of various initiatives. As the highest policy making body below the Leaders' Summit, the Ministerial Meetings deliberate on policy issues that need to be elevated for the leader's decision and guidance. The senior officials support the ministers in the performance of their functions. They are responsible for coordinating the overall implementation of programs and projects under the Implementation Blueprints.

Addressing Institutional Gaps for Economic Corridor Development

Although national coordination mechanisms are in place to engage provinces and states in IMT-GT initiatives, there is no explicit and well-developed mechanism for coordinating economic corridor development in IMT-GT. This gap may be due to a limited appreciation of the concept of economic corridors at the regional level. Some misconceptions are: (i) that an economic corridor is mainly a transport corridor connecting points in a linear fashion, (ii) that spatial planning is the same as economic corridor planning, and (iii) that juxtaposed national economic corridors constitute a regional corridor (Figure 18).

As explained in Chapter 5, economic corridors involve a highly complex interrelationship of economic units or nodes. While these nodal linkages can develop randomly as a result of market forces, there is scope for also influencing the development of these nodes through a combination of policy interventions and public investments in infrastructure. The coordination of policy and public investments become more complex for cross-border economic corridors that involve multiple jurisdictions at the central government and local levels.

Figure 18: Coordination Mechanisms for Economic Corridor Development

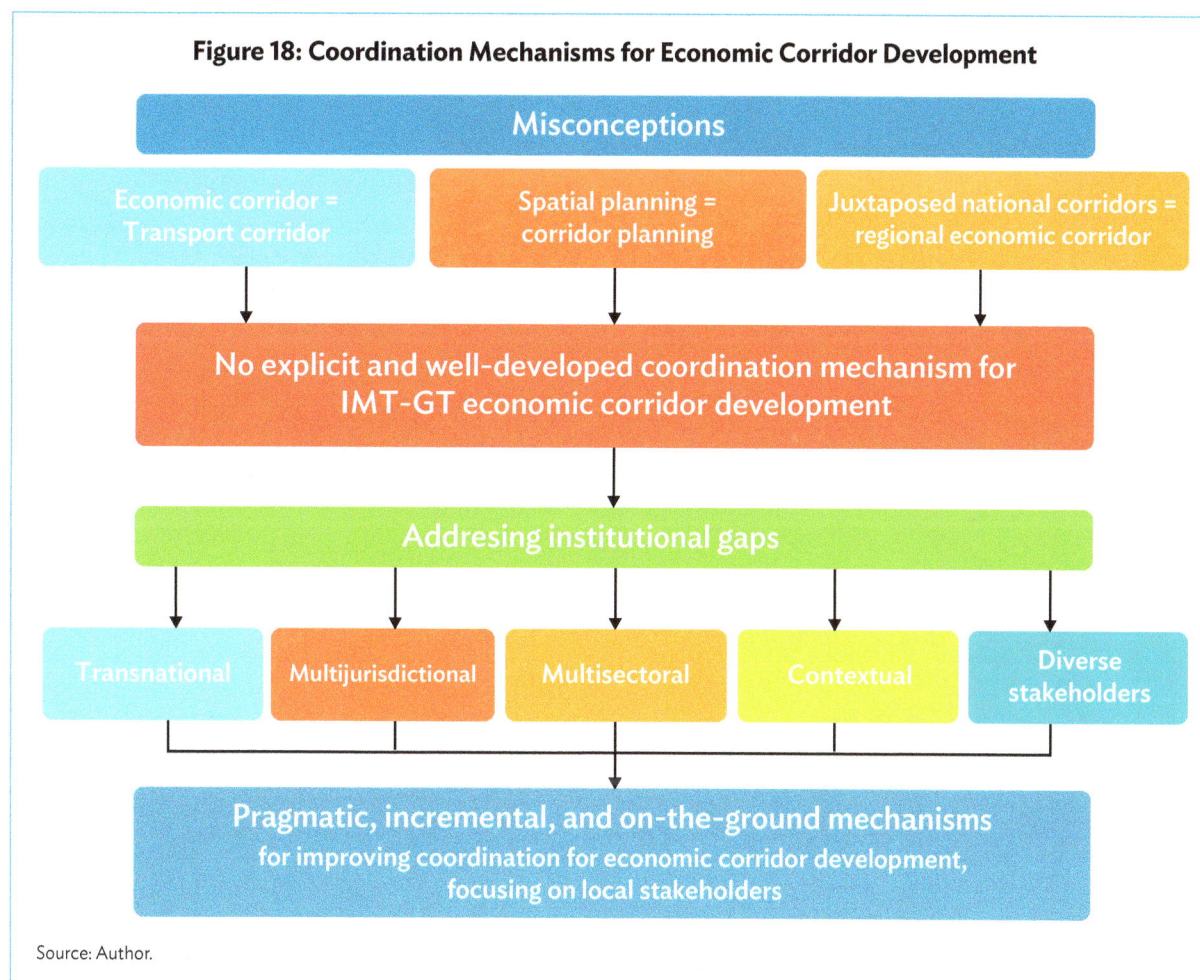

Source: Author.

The multijurisdictional nature of regional or cross-border economic corridors would require coordination mechanisms that involve regional planning and oversight bodies. The existing IMT-GT institutional mechanism can serve as a good starting point for developing such regional mechanisms, although this will have to evolve gradually over the medium term. Recognizing the potential challenges of establishing formal structures, a set of pragmatic and incremental activities could be initiated or piloted in the near-term. These activities may include, but not limited to, the following:

- At the provincial and state level involving two or three countries:
  - Promote a better understanding and appreciation of the concept of economic corridors at the provincial and state levels; these could be done through a series of learning events for different stakeholder groups;
  - Provide a forum for provinces or states to meet before the CMGF to apprise them of the latest developments in the IMT-GT corridors;
  - Encourage regular meetings of clusters of provinces and states in a given corridor to plan for cross-border initiatives; these initiatives need not necessarily be in the form of large projects, but can focus on improvements in administrative process (trade facilitation) at the border or gateway ports;

- Support dialogues of private sector groups on business opportunities focused on value chain products and services (e.g., logistics) as well as on infrastructure gaps that need to be addressed in the economic corridors.

- At the national level:

  - Support the establishment of a CMGF secretariat; Thailand's approach of using a provincial university as secretariat may be a good model to follow since a secretariat should be able to provide analytical and technical support beyond day-to-day coordination of activities; the secretariat should be based in a province or state to signify local government ownership and facilitate the conduct of activities at the local level such as those earlier mentioned;

  - Strengthen the capacity of the national secretariats through additional human resources to enable it to effectively manage the coordination of subregional cooperation programs, including subregional economic corridor development.

- At the subregional level:

  - Organize working groups focused on economic corridor development (along the lines of convergence groups). These economic corridor working groups should be issue- or projects-focused and have flexible membership determined by the issue(s) or projects on its agenda.

  - Organize occasional forums where special bodies such as the Southern Border Province Administrative Centre, Northern Corridor Implementation Agency, ECERDC, Iskandar Regional Development Authority, and the relevant body in Sumatera, could exchange views and updates on IMT-GT economic corridor development.

  - Expand CIMT's database by organizing an economic corridor projects database to include all projects (national and regional) in a given corridor; and

  - Establish an IMT-GT economic corridors portal linked to national portals that would contain information on business opportunities, development projects, and news and events happening in the corridors; this could be a joint project of the JBC and CIMT.

General Findings and Recommendations

Physical connectivity in the economic corridors has made noteworthy progress. The review of the five existing economic corridors indicated that physical connectivity has made noteworthy progress since 2007 when the IMT-GT decided to adopt economic corridor development as a priority thrust. With few exceptions, roads along the transport backbones are in good condition, efficient, and safe, supported largely by public investments. BCPs are accessible from the main transport routes, and some could be reached by alternative routes.

This second generation of roads can extend to the hinterlands, spurring growth in much wider areas of poverty—where balanced, inclusive development is needed. Such roads could widen national ECs, creating links to arterial trade and transport routes, as well as secondary borders—which would become more important as local value chains develop.

Rail connectivity is generally lagging behind roads because of the massive capital outlays required, affecting its economic viability. Trains are more cost-effective, especially when transporting high volumes of freight, providing shippers with access to larger cargo capacity; and burning less fuel, trains are more environment-friendly. However, to be viable, railways need sufficient demand for the transport of goods and passengers—which present conditions in the IMT-GT do not seem to warrant.

Some maritime links envisaged for the existing corridors have not materialized. The IMT-GT's economic activities tend to use ports, taking advantage of the subregion's strategic location along the Strait of Malacca. However, some of the maritime links intended for the corridors have not materialized. There is no maritime connectivity between Penang and Belawan (EC1), the maritime link between Dumai and Melaka is mainly for passenger ferry services (EC4), and there are no commercial shipping routes for cargo from Malahayati Port to Ranong and Phuket (EC5).

While roads are supply-driven, maritime links are demand-driven. Port choices are made by shippers, transport carriers, and port service providers. They consider factors including the suitability of port infrastructure, berth availability, handling equipment, storage facilities, port charges, and its operating efficiency. Thus, although some of the intended sea-links in corridors did not materialize, several other maritime connections have developed between Malaysian and Sumateran ports along the Strait of Malacca.

The subregion's location along the Strait gives it a unique advantage, which must be optimized. To achieve this, **greater focus must be given to enhancing multimodal connectivity along the Strait, involving road–rail connections to ports**. Nationally, this would include:

- Using trains to move freight to and from seaports, especially containers on high-volume routes. Reducing port and inland transit costs, this also accelerates clearance. Additional facilities such as ICDs and freight wagons are also needed to meet demand for intermodal links.

- Effective inland transit systems that would involve the use of ICDs and bonded logistics facilities that can enhance the efficiency of supply chains by minimizing clearance formalities. Given the increase in the demand for inland terminals with the establishment of industrial parks and SEZs near the ports, the development of inland transit systems can avoid the concentration of dry ports near the border and further expedite the movement of goods.

At the subregional level, trade facilitation will need to focus on both land- and sea-based transport given the multimodal approach in most of the corridors. The current focus on land-based facilitation will need to be balanced with initiatives on port-based facilitation, especially with plans to develop international hub ports in the subregion to handle bulk and container cargoes. There are several ways for countries' ports to cooperate, which could include removing nontariff barriers to reduce delays, enhancing facilities, improving compliance with international conventions, and setting standards for ports' operating efficiency

Land bridge services currently operating between Malaysia and Thailand are a cost-effective alternative to transporting goods entirely by sea and the possible expansion of this service should be promoted. The land bridge service permits the cross-border movement of containers between Malaysia and Thailand by railways; the containers are sealed once for the entire trip and cargo clears both Malaysian and Thai Customs at the port of origin. Land bridges provide continuity between maritime and long-distance inland transport networks. This mode lends itself to cooperation between the public and the private sectors and should be part of the larger effort to develop multimodality in the economic corridors.

Cross-border trade, although active, constitutes a relatively small share of the countries' trade and has not increased significantly through the years. This could imply that land connectivity per se may not have had a transformative impact on trade. Most of the trade in IMT-GT, especially of major commodities, goes through the ports, with land routes primarily serving as means of transit for goods to be shipped to international destinations, rather than linking economic units within the corridor.

The trajectory of the IMT-GT countries toward trade outside the subregion, rather than within the subregion, can be explained by the fact that the three countries produce the same or similar basic commodities, in particular, palm oil, rubber, seafoods, and agricultural food products. The countries' national development strategies have laid out ambitious plans and programs to locate industrial zones closer to gateways, ports, BCPs, and agglomeration areas. These indicate that the interrelationship between trade and investment is being fostered to shift from simple border trade to investment-creating trade that promotes processing activities within the value chain.

The IMT-GT has started a major initiative to develop the value chain for rubber through the Rubber Cities Project. Still at its early stage, the project is developing value chain ecosystems at the national level in specifically designated locations or cities. It is anticipated that over the medium- to long-term, this will evolve into regional value chain ecosystems that would involve regionwide incentives, tariff preferences, and joint research and development for product innovation, among others.

The IMT-GT has recognized the importance of value chain mapping and is taking steps to move forward on this activity. **Value chain mapping should incorporate aspects of transport geography, logistics, and network effects, in addition to the study of trade patterns in the supply and demand for intermediate and final goods**. To underscore the relationship between economic corridors and value chains, the study has identified the provinces or states and nodes that dominate the production, processing and distribution process in three major value chains—palm oil, rubber, and halal foods.

The reconfiguration of economic corridors presented in the study was based on the role of the designated nodes and the relationship between them and additional nodes to form a network of IMT-GT corridors. The reconfiguration of the corridors has generated interlink corridors, which is the route between two or more economic corridors that enable them to function as a network. The effective functioning of networks would have to be supported by economic openness (i.e., providing access and mobility to a region), investing in infrastructure, or reinforcing a specific trade or transport corridor. However, the emergence of networks is rarely planned—but rather the consequence of continuous improvements, as opportunities arise.

The expanded concept of economic corridors as networks rather than as point-to-point connections makes it imperative for spatial development to be coordinated under an IMT-GT-wide approach. At present, there is no clear, deliberate approach to economic corridor development in IMT-GT. Economic corridor projects are typically national projects located in a corridor; and the mere collation of these projects would be considered as the development approach to the corridor. With a network perspective, this piecemeal approach should be replaced by more comprehensive spatial planning aimed at reducing economic distances between nodes—to promote complementary production and trade, and upscale economies for better competitiveness.

Interlink corridors should be the focus of better coordinated economic corridor planning. The interlink corridors (Chapter 5) as part of the network of corridors in IMT-GT can open up new possibilities for cooperation (e.g., a palm oil belt or an integrated tourism corridor). When considering ECs as networks, there are no longer strict physical borders defining them: their boundaries are porous, so markets—responding to policies—will determine the location and pattern of economic activities.

A network analysis is ideal to serve the purposes of corridor planning; but a more practical and immediate step would be to initiate and institutionalize dialogue at operational levels among provinces and states. While policy interventions could still be needed, as most bottlenecks are corridor-specific, they may require customized inputs to enable smoother flows between producers and consumers. Local dialogues or stakeholder meetings could be good initiatives to identify location-specific bottlenecks, then remove administrative and procedural barriers, to increase the flow between nodes. Practical measures resulting from such local meetings considering their value chain links can then be reported to the CMGF and working groups.

While recognizing the IMT-GT has implemented noteworthy national projects in the corridors, a truly regional approach to EC development has yet to fully materialize. Coordinated planning at all levels—district, regency, provincial, and central—is important, and should be part of a national planning process as well as the IMT-GT's institutional framework. The current IMT-GT platform could serve as a foundation for building a system that takes into account the multitiered, multijurisdictional aspects of corridor development—although these will have to evolve gradually over the medium-term. Recognizing the potential challenges of establishing formal structures, pragmatic and incremental activities could be initiated or piloted in the near-term. These measures could include:

- At the provincial and state level (involving two or three countries):

    - Promote a better appreciation of ECs at the provincial and state levels, through a series of learning events for stakeholders.

    - Encourage regular meetings of clusters of provinces and states in a given corridor to plan for cross-border initiatives; these initiatives need not necessarily be in the form of large projects, but can focus on improvements in administrative process (trade facilitation) at the border or gateway ports.

    - Support dialogues of private sector groups on business opportunities focused on value chain products or processes (e.g., logistics services).

- At the national level:

  - Support the establishment of a CMGF secretariat; Thailand's approach of using a provincial university as secretariat may be a good model to follow since a secretariat should be able to provide analytical and technical support beyond day-to-day coordination of activities; the secretariat should be based in a province or state to signify local government ownership and facilitate the conduct of activities at the local level.

- At the subregional level:

  - Organize working groups focused on economic corridor development (along the lines of convergence groups); these economic corridor working groups should be issue- or project-focused and have flexible membership determined by the issue(s) or projects on its agenda.

  - Expand CIMT's database by organizing an economic corridor project database to include all projects (national as well as regional) in a given corridor.

  - Establish an IMT-GT economic corridors portal linked to national portals that would contain information on development projects and news and events happening in the corridors, and information on business opportunities. This could be a joint project of the CIMT and JBC.

The recommended route for the sixth economic corridor (EC6) involves 17 provinces and states, covering almost the entire span of the IMT-GT subregion. It covers three provinces in Southern Thailand, eight states in Malaysia in two alternative routes, and six provinces in Sumatera—four provinces in mainland Sumatera, and two archipelagic provinces in the southeastern part. The provinces in Thailand include Pattani, Yala, and Narathiwat. The states in Malaysia include Kelantan, Terengganu, Pahang, Perak, Selangor, Melaka, Negeri Sembilan, and Johor. In Indonesia, the provinces included are South Sumatera, Bengkulu, Jambi, Lampung, Riau Islands, and Bangka Belitung Islands. Two alternative routes are proposed in Malaysia: a route along the eastern coast passing through Tok Bali, Kuala Terengganu, Kemaman Port, Kuantan Port connecting to Port Klang up to Tanjung Bruas Port in Melaka. The other route has a westward orientation passing through Perak (Gerik, Ipoh City, Lumut Port), Port Klang, and up to Tanjung Bruas Port in Melaka.

Our review of physical connectivity in the proposed route indicates that road and rail connections between Malaysia and Thailand are adequate, although gaps in certain segments must be addressed. Maritime and air connectivity, however, need further development. While major ports in Malaysia have maritime trade links with ports in Sumatera and Southern Thailand, links with ports in Riau Islands and Bangka Belitung Islands are limited to ferry services. The configuration of EC6 is designed to mesh with other IMT-GT corridors, creating a network of transport links supporting the regional allocation and distribution of resources and benefits across the growth triangle.

Corridor-Specific Findings and Recommendations

This report suggests new names for the six corridors (Table 51), to reflect the wider region of subnational areas covered by a corridor, rather than specific provinces or states (Map 26). This revised nomenclature suggests that ECs are nonlinear—not just connecting points—but also cover wider areas influenced by transport routes, including industrial parks, SEZs, ports, inland waterways, and agglomerations. These new designations also allow flexibility to add nodes in the corridor, based on the evolving economic landscape, opportunities and challenges.

Map 26: Six Indonesia–Malaysia–Thailand Growth Triangle Economic Corridors

Source: Asian Development Bank.

Table 51: Corridor-Specific Findings and Recommendations

Economic Corridor 1. Extended Songkhla–Penang–Medan Economic Corridor	
New Name: Southern Thailand–Northern Malaysia–North Sumatera Economic Corridor	
Area	**Findings and Recommendations**
Road connectivity	Roads connecting existing corridor nodes are in good condition.
Rail connectivity	Rail services between Su-ngai Kolok and Pasir Mas will need to be revived. There is a critical missing rail link which must be reestablished between Su-ngai Kolok in Narathiwat (2 km) and Pasir Mas in Kelantan (18 km) as part of the proposed route for EC6. There are no cross-border trains between Malaysia and Thailand. Currently, there are no trains going across to the Malaysia–Thailand border. SRT's international express is no longer serving the route up to Butterworth. Malaysia's KTM trains are also no longer servicing the route to Hat Yai.
Maritime connectivity	There is no maritime connectivity between Penang and Belawan at present. Belawan Port currently functions only as a feeder port due to its inadequate water depth and lack of vessel channels. Kuala Tanjung Port is being developed as an alternative port hub and will eventually replace the role of Belawan Port which will be an interisland domestic port in 2027.
Air linkages	Air connectivity within provinces and states in EC1 is limited. There are several flights between Penang and Medan, but there are no direct flights from Penang to Songkhla. Air connectivity within the corridor is mostly indirect and goes through the capitals—Bangkok, Kuala Lumpur, and Jakarta.
Cross-border infrastructure	Cross-border infrastructure is in good condition and BCP facilities are generally adequate. BCPs in EC1 are connected by good roads from the capital and with each other.
Cross-border trade	Cross-border trade at Thailand's BCPs with Malaysia has increased only moderately, while cross-border trade at Malaysia's BCPs with Thailand has increased only minimally during the period 2015–2018. North Sumatera's declining trade with Malaysia suggests the need for diversification of traded products aligned with the planned development of new ports in Sumatera.
Reconfiguration	The following nodes were included in North Sumatera: • Kuala Tanjung Port • Sibolga • Lake Toba An additional node was added for Malaysia, i.e., Kangar, the capital of Perlis. The following additional provinces and nodes in Thailand were included: • Chumphon Province and Chumphon City • Surat Thani Province, Surat Thani City, and Ko Samui • Phatthalung Province and Phatthalung City

Economic Corridor 2. Strait of Malacca Economic Corridor	
New Name: Andaman Sea–Strait of Malacca Economic Corridor	
Area	**Findings and Recommendations**
Road connectivity	Roads connecting Thailand and Malaysia ports along the Strait of Malacca are adequate and in good condition.
	The construction of a new bridge at Satun and Perlis along the Andaman Sea coast is an important project that should be expedited. The bridge will support land connectivity along the Andaman Sea coast along the coasts of Tammalang in Satun to Ko Puyu and then to Perlis in Malaysia.
	Although the land routes between major nodes are adequate, there is a need to look into a second generation of road links within the corridor as industrial parks and new economic centers expand the catchment areas of the ports and open potential new trade routes.
Rail links	Road connectivity is complemented by rail links between Port Klang, Perak, and Songkhla as well as a land bridge from Port Klang extending all the way to Hat Yai.
Maritime connectivity	Given that several Malaysia ports are already part of existing IMT-GT corridors, expanding connectivity of EC2 to Sumatera Island can further increase trade along the Straits. Most of the growth centers in Indonesia's National Medium-Term Development Plan 2020–2024 are in Sumatera's eastern coast along the Strait of Malacca and can benefit from enhanced connectivity with Malaysia ports. Port-to-port collaboration can be considered as a modality for cooperation.
Multimodal connectivity	Land bridge services provide an efficient third alternative to road and sea transport between Malaysia and Thailand and should be promoted under public–private partnership arrangements.
	Multimodal connectivity along the Strai of Malacca should be enhanced. Except for Port Klang and Penang Port (which are supported by land bridges), other ports in Malaysia (e.g., Lumut Port and Tanjung Bruas Port) lack connectivity with other modes of transport (e.g., rail and aviation).
	Multimodal transport systems will require developing effective inland transit systems. This would involve among others, the use of inland container depots and bonded logistics facilities, which can enhance the efficiency of the supply chain without undergoing clearance formalities and duty payment at the borders. Given the potential increase in the demand for inland terminals with the establishment of industrial parks and special economic zones near the ports, the development of inland transit systems can avoid the concentration of dry ports near the border and further expedite border movement of goods.
	Given the multimodal approach to EC2, transport and trade facilitation will need to focus on both land- and sea-based transport. The current focus on land-based trade facilitation will need to be balanced with initiatives for port-based trade facilitation, especially with the expansion in port capacities to handle bulk and container cargoes.
Air linkages	Air connectivity is limited. There are no direct flights connecting the provinces and states in Malaysia and Southern Thailand, but these can be accessed through other destinations in the two countries.
Cross-border infrastructure	Access to the BCPs by road and rail is adequate. Roads leading to Thailand BCPs at Wang Prachan and Padang Besa are in good condition. The border infrastructure in Malaysia BCPs—Wang Kelian, Padang Besar, and Pengkalan Hulu are also adequate and in good condition.
	The building and facilities at BCPs are well-maintained and adequate space is available for inspection and other formalities. Operating hours are generally the same for the BCPs.

continued on next page

Table 51 (continued)

Economic Corridor 1. Extended Songkhla–Penang–Medan Economic Corridor	
New Name: Southern Thailand–Northern Malaysia–North Sumatera Economic Corridor	
Area	**Findings and Recommendations**
Cross-border trade	One-stop services should be made a regular feature of BCP operations, and the required facilities should be made part of CIQS expansion and improvements. Presently, the Wang Prachan–Wang Kelian joint development project will establish a Customs checkpoint that provides a one-stop service.
	Malaysia's border trade with Thailand is concentrated in Padang Besar/Padang Besa BCPs. There has been an increasing use of rail transport for exports to Thailand.
	Thailand's border trade with Malaysia is driven mostly by imports, which have grown faster than exports on average over the period 2015–2018.
Reconfiguration	In Malaysia, the following additional nodes were included in existing states: • Chuping Valley and Kuala Perlis (Perlis) • Kamunting and Lumut (Perak) • Batu Kawan (Penang) • Kuah (Kedah) • Tanjung Bruas Port (Melaka) • Port Dickson and Seremban (Negeri Sembilan) In Thailand, the following additional provinces and nodes were included: • Krabi Province and Krabi City • Phangnga and Phangnga City • Tammalang Port and Tarutao Island (Satun)

Economic Corridor 3. Banda Aceh–Medan–Pekanbaru–Palembang Economic Corridor	
New name: Trans-Sumatera Economic Corridor	
Area	**Findings and Recommendations**
Road connectivity	Connectivity among the four EC3 provinces (Aceh, Riau, North Sumatera, and South Sumatera) is adequate, but the quality of roads is uneven. The road surface is smooth but travel in some segments can be slow due to congestion and occasional potholes resulting from poor maintenance.
	The development of EC3 should focus not only on land connectivity between provinces in Sumatera, but also in developing transportation systems and links between industrial zones and ports. Investments in land-based infrastructure (both road and rail) should be leveraged with improvements in the services and performance of ports to make them competitive with other Asian ports, notably Port Klang and the ports in Singapore.
Rail connectivity	There is no single railway line that connects the provinces in Sumatera Islands although there is a plan to construct a Trans-Sumatera Railway. There are only partial railway links that facilitate transport of goods from production centers to the ports.
	As external trade expands and value chains develop in Sumatera, railways as an alternative and more efficient mode of transport will become increasingly important and should be given priority.
Air connectivity	Domestic flights are well-served by the airports in the four provinces.
	Good air connectivity with Malaysia has resulted in Malaysians dominating foreign visitor composition in all four EC3 provinces.
Trade	As the four provinces produce similar products, mainly palm oil and rubber, commodities are largely directed to the ports rather than to the domestic market for consumption or further processing.

continued on next page

Table 51 (continued)

Economic Corridor 3. Banda Aceh–Medan–Pekanbaru–Palembang Economic Corridor	
New name: Trans-Sumatera Economic Corridor	
Area	**Findings and Recommendations**
Reconfiguration	The following additional nodes were included in the existing four provinces: • Arun Lhokseumawe (Aceh) • Sei Mangkei (North Sumatera) • Kuala Tanjung (North Sumatera) • Tanjung Buton (Riau) • Tanjung Api-Api (South Sumatera) The following additional provinces and nodes were included: • West Sumatera Province, Padang City, and Bukittingi • Jambi Province and Jambi City • Bengkulu Province and Bengkulu City • Lampung Province, Bandar Lampung, and Bakauheni Port

Economic Corridor 4. Melaka–Dumai Economic Corridor	
New Name: Central Sumatera–Southern Malaysia Economic Corridor	
Area	**Findings and Recommendations**
Road connectivity	Road connectivity between Dumai and Pekanbaru is adequate. The toll road between the two cities has recently been completed (September 2020). Most of the road segments in the Trans-Sumatera Highway are paved but some sections are in poor condition due to the large number of trucks transporting palm oil. Tanjung Bruas Port is accessible by good roads from Melaka City. There is no train connection from Tanjung Bruas to Pulau Sebang/Tampin (at the border of Melaka and Negeri Sembilan).
Rail connectivity	There is currently no active railway line in Riau but there are railway projects in the pipeline that would connect Pekanbaru to Padang (West Sumatera), Rantau Prapat (North Sumatera), and Jambi.
Maritime connectivity	There is no direct link between Dumai Port and Tanjung Bruas Port but there are maritime trade and passenger ferry links between Dumai and Malaysia ports such as Port Klang, Port of Port Dickson, Melaka International Ferry Terminal (MIFT), and Muar Port. The Ro-Ro Ferry Services Project between Sri Junjungan Port and Tanjung Bruas Port (the designated ports for the project) needs to be expedited to provide a low-cost and faster mode of transporting goods that could benefit small and medium enterprises.
Supply Chains	Riau Province should develop palm oil processing industries to produce higher value-added exports for CPO. Although Dumai is the largest port of loading for CPO, there is no SEZ in the province dedicated to the processing of palm oil. The establishment of an SEZ for this purpose is being planned by the government. This will be a catalyst to boost Riau Province's declining export levels, compared to rapidly rising imports from Malaysia.
Air connectivity	Air connectivity is adequate. There are direct flights from Dumai to Melaka; and from Melaka to Pekanbaru. Other routes must go through the capital cities.
Maritime Trade	The value of trade between Riau and Melaka has been increasing by an average of 3% from 2014–2018 with exports consistently topping imports resulting in a trade balance in favor of Riau. Imports however are growing faster than exports. Trade with Thailand is less than 1%.

continued on next page

Table 51 (continued)

Economic Corridor 4. Melaka–Dumai Economic Corridor	
New Name: Central Sumatera–Southern Malaysia Economic Corridor	
Area	**Findings and Recommendations**
Potential new linkages	Riau Province can effectively play its role as a growth corridor by mainstreaming outer islands (i.e., Rupat Island) into its economy for a more balanced distribution of the benefits of growth. A tourism special economic zone is being planned in Rupat Island, which would link with tourism opportunities in Melaka. As a part of Sumatera's growth corridor, Riau could also enhance its linkages with West Sumatera along the western coast. This will enable West Sumatera, which belongs to the equalization corridor, to expand its trade and value chain opportunities.
Reconfiguration	The inclusion of Johor in EC4 will open important links to Riau Islands (in particular, Batam) and Bangka Belitung Islands, which are part of the proposed route for EC6. Melaka's role can leverage on the rapid and accelerated urban and commercial developments taking place in Johor. Extending EC4 to Johor can have a significant impact on the corridors' influence area including the proposed routes for EC6. The following additional nodes were included in the existing provinces: • Sri Junjungan Port and Rupat Island (Riau Province) • MIFT and Melaka City (Melaka) The following provinces and nodes were added: • West Sumatera, Padang • State of Johor, Johor Bahru, Tanjung Pelepas Port (Gelang Patah), Johor Port (Pasir Gudang)

Economic Corridor 5. Ranong–Phuket–Aceh Economic Corridor	
New Name: Southwestern Thailand–Northern Sumatera–Northwestern Malaysia Economic Corridor	
Areas	**Findings and Recommendations**
Road connectivity	The road from Ranong to Phuket is in good condition, efficient, and safe. At present, the entire route from Ranong to Phuket is being upgraded to four lanes.
Maritime connectivity	Maritime links between Aceh, Ranong, and Phuket have not developed as intended. There are no commercial shipping routes from Malahayati Port to ports in Ranong and Phuket, although Malahayati Port services routes to other international destinations such as Dubai and India. It also serves domestic containers from provinces in Sumatera.
Air linkages	Air connectivity is limited. There are no direct flights from Banda Aceh to Ranong and Phuket. Flights from Phuket are directed to the capitals (e.g., Kuala Lumpur) but none to Aceh.
Tourism	The potential for Aceh and Sabang to tap into Phuket's burgeoning tourism market has not been realized, with no demand generated for ferry services. Collaboration should be pursued to develop cruise tourism between Sabang–Phuket–Langkawi (SAPULA), to increase demand for maritime services in the corridor and stimulate ancillary economic activities in these provinces. The inclusion of Phangnga and Krabi will support Thailand's strategy to develop an inland tourism network between the Gulf of Thailand and the Andaman Sea. This inland network can eventually link with SAPULA as well as other tourism belts emerging from the expansion of EC4.

continued on next page

Table 51 (continued)

Economic Corridor 5. Ranong–Phuket–Aceh Economic Corridor	
New Name: Southwestern Thailand–Northern Sumatera–Northwestern Malaysia Economic Corridor	
Areas	**Findings and Recommendations**
Reconfiguration	The concept of an integrated tourism corridor should be explored across several corridors (EC2, EC4, and EC5) to leverage on the subregion's comparative advantage in tourism and optimize its investments in tourism infrastructure. The following nodes were included in Kedah, Malaysia: • Langkawi • Teluk Ewa Port The following additional provinces and nodes in Thailand were included: • Krabi Province and Krabi City • Phangnga Province and Phangnga City

Economic Corridor 6. Southeastern Thailand–Eastern Malaysia–Southern Sumatera Economic Corridor	
Areas	**Findings and Recommendations**
Proposed route	The proposed route for EC6 will traverse the following provinces and states • Indonesia: South Sumatera, Jambi, Bengkulu, Lampung, Riau Islands, Bangka Belitung Islands • Malaysia: Kelantan, Terengganu, Pahang, Perak, Selangor, Melaka, Johor, Negeri Sembilan • Thailand: Pattani, Yala, Narathiwat
Status of physical connectivity	Roads connecting Pattani, Yala, and Narathiwat in Thailand are adequate, safe, and in good condition as they are part of national road systems. The road conditions from Kelantan in Malaysia are also adequate, safe, and in good condition in the two alternative routes. Road connectivity is complemented by rail links and land bridges. Access roads to BCPs at Narathiwat and Kelantan are adequate.
Connectivity gaps at Thailand–Malaysia border	Developing connectivity between Narathiwat and Kelantan would be crucial in enabling Thailand to connect with the East Coast Rail Link. Three connectivity projects to make this happen are: • Improvement of the railway route between Su-ngai Kolok–Rantau Panjang–Tumpat; • Construction of the second bridge over Kolok River at Su-ngai Kolok–Rantau Panjang; and • Construction of a new bridge over Kolok River at Tak Bai District.
Intermodal links	Road, rail, and port interfaces will be a dominant feature of connectivity in EC6. Intermodal facilitation will be crucial and should be the focus of a second generation of trade facilitation initiatives in IMT-GT by way of moving forward from the present focus on land-based CIQ facilitation.
Road–rail connectivity	Road–rail connectivity infrastructure should be given more emphasis in economic corridor planning for EC6. Road–rail connectivity that links the core to the periphery areas has an externality that can boost economic activity in the economic corridor.
Maritime links	Maritime trade links between Riau Islands and Bangka Belitung Islands with Malaysia are limited and should be developed further.

BCP = border crossing point; CIQ = customs, immigration, and quarantine; CPO = crude palm oil; EC = economic corridor; IMT-GT = Indonesia–Malaysia–Thailand Growth Triangle; km = kilometer; KTM = Keretapi Tanah Melayu; MIFT = Melaka International Ferry Terminal; SEZ = special economic zone; SRT = State Railway of Thailand.
Source: Author.